2001
A BRAND-NEW YEAR—
A PROMISING NEW START

Enter Sydney Omarr's star-studded world of accurate day-by-day predictions for every aspect of your life. With expert readings and forecasts, you can chart a course to romance, adventure, good health, or career opportunities while gaining valuable insight into yourself and others. Offering a daily outlook for 18 full months, this fascinating guide shows you:

- The important dates in your life
- What to expect from an astrological reading
- How the stars can help you stay healthy and fit
- Your lucky lottery numbers
  And more!

Let this expert's sound advice guide you through a year of heavenly possibilities—for today and for every day of 2001!

SYDNEY OMARR'S DAY-BY-DAY
ASTROLOGICAL GUIDE FOR

ARIES—March 21–April 19
TAURUS—April 20–May 20
GEMINI—May 21–June 20
CANCER—June 21–July 22
LEO—July 23–August 22
VIRGO—August 23–September 22
LIBRA—September 23–October 22
SCORPIO—October 23–November 21
SAGITTARIUS—November 22–December 21
CAPRICORN—December 22–January 19
AQUARIUS—January 20–February 18
PISCES—February 19–March 20

IN 2001

WIN A PERSONALIZED HOROSCOPE FOR A FULL YEAR!

Enter the Sydney Omarr Horoscope Sweepstakes!

No purchase necessary. Details below.

Name _____

Address_____

City_____ State_____ Zip_____

Mail to:
Sydney Omarr Horoscope Sweepstakes
c/o Penguin Putnam Inc.
375 Hudson St., 5th floor
New York, NY 10014

All entries must be postmarked by August 31, 2000 and received by September 8, 2000.

1. NO PURCHASE NECESSARY TO ENTER OR WIN A PRIZE. To enter the Sydney Omarr Horoscope Sweepstakes, complete this official entry form or, on 3" x 5" piece of paper, write your name and complete address. Mail your entry to: Sydney Omarr Horoscope Sweepstakes; c/o Penguin Putnam Inc.; 375 Hudson St., 5th floor; New York, NY 10014. Enter as often as you wish, but mail each entry in a separate envelope. No mechanically reproduced or computer generated entries allowed. All entries must be postmarked by 8/31/2000 and received by 9/8/2000 to be eligible. Not responsible for late, lost, damaged, incomplete, illegible, postage due or misdirected mail entries.

2. Winners will be selected from all eligible entries in a random drawing on or about 9/14/00, by Penguin Putnam Inc., whose decisions are final and binding. Odds of winning are dependent upon the number of entries received. Winners will be notified by mail and may be required to execute an affidavit of eligibility and release which must be returned within 14 days of notification or an alternate winner will be selected.

3. One (1) Grand Prize winner will receive a personalized one-year horoscope from an astrologer chosen by Sydney Omarr. One (1) Second Prize winner will receive a personalized one-month horoscope from an astrologer chosen by Sydney Omarr.. Estimated value of all prizes: $250.

4. Sweepstakes open to residents of the U.S. and Canada 18 years of age or older, except employees and the immediate families of Penguin Putnam Inc., its affiliated companies, advertising and promotion agencies. Void in Puerto Rico, the province of Quebec and wherever else prohibited by law. All Federal, State, Local, and Provincial laws apply. Taxes, if any, are the sole responsibility of the prize winners. Canadian winners will be required to answer an arithmetical skill testing question administered by mail. Winners consent to the use of their name and/or photos or likenesses for advertising purposes without additional compensation (except where prohibited).

5. For the names of the prize winners, send a self-addressed, stamped envelope after 9/28/00 to : SYDNEY OMARR HOROSCOPE SWEEPSTAKES WINNERS, Penguin Putnam Inc., 375 Hudson St., 5th floor, New York, NY 10014.

SYDNEY OMARR'S

DAY-BY-DAY ASTROLOGICAL GUIDE FOR

LEO

July 23–August 22

2001

A SIGNET BOOK

SIGNET
Published by New American Library, a division of
Penguin Putnam Inc., 375 Hudson Street,
New York, New York 10014, U.S.A.
Penguin Books Ltd, 27 Wrights Lane,
London W8 5TZ, England
Penguin Books Australia Ltd, Ringwood,
Victoria, Australia
Penguin Books Canada Ltd, 10 Alcorn Avenue,
Toronto, Ontario, Canada M4V 3B2
Penguin Books (N.Z.) Ltd, 182–190 Wairau Road,
Auckland 10, New Zealand

Penguin Books Ltd, Registered Offices:
Harmondsworth, Middlesex, England

First published by Signet, an imprint of New American Library,
a division of Penguin Putnam Inc.

First Printing, June 2000
10 9 8 7 6 5 4 3 2 1

 REGISTERED TRADEMARK—MARCA REGISTRADA

Printed in the United States of America

CONTENTS

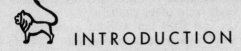

INTRODUCTION

Changing Times— Going Global After Y2K

The year 2001 will find more and more of us going global via home computers. And as we travel the expanding cyberworld, we find astrology very much a part of the on-line scenery. Astrology areas are among the most visited on big commercial Web sites. With a more serious educational purpose, there are interactive sites that present new techniques and rediscovered ancient ones as well as offer courses to students of all levels. For the astrologer, computer technology has been a godsend, eliminating long hours of calculation and research, and enabling them to exchange ideas across the planet and access knowledge that is difficult to obtain in many third world cultures.

On the other hand, the year 2001 conjures up vivid memories of the star of Stanley Kubrick's classic sci-fi film, *2001: A Space Odyssey,* an almost-human computer called "Hal," which caused the downfall of the film's space voyage. The film was an eerie premonition of the Y2K alarm that many of the systems we rely on might shut down suddenly at the change of a date. While there's no doubt that the ubiquitous computer will be an important signature of the twenty-first century, we are reminded that, as the original "Hal" forewarned, the computer has a potential fallible dark side manifested in malfunctions and high-tech crimes. Though it has caused our personal universe to expand with unimagined possibilities of global communication, the computer also has presented us with many personal challenges, such as acquiring new skills, protecting our privacy, filtering content from impressionable children, and communicating with cyberfriends from other cultures.

But what of the astrology fan without a computer? There are many valid ways to put astrology into your life that are as relevant now as they have been for millennia past. The basic information hasn't changed, nor have the easy techniques in this book that have been tested over decades.

In addition to daily forecasts that help you make the most of each day, this book tells you what you need to know about your sun sign, your potential for success, your family life, how to create the perfect environment, and how to get along with everyone else under the sun. A chapter on the unique visual language of astrology will help you read the symbols on your horoscope chart. Easy basic information gives you an inside look at how astrology works. Then you can look up the other planets in your horoscope to find out how each contributes to your unique personality.

If you're intrigued by the variety of personal readings advertised, there is guidance on finding a qualified astrologer.

Many readers are fascinated by astrology's insights into the upsides and downsides of relationships. This year, you'll find out who you're likely to click with most and what sun sign combos are more challenging. There's a quiz to rate your relationships that will give you clues about the important people in your life.

For surfers on the Internet, there's our pick of the best of thousands of sites, where you can download a copy of your chart, network with other astrology fans, order books and programs, or enjoy some interactive fun and games. Plus Sydney Omarr's updated "Yellow Pages" of the best astrology resources for books, tapes, and further astrological studies.

As we go on our personal odysseys through cyberspace or relax in our cozy armchair with a good book, we are still searching for the same things that always have made life worth living: love, meaningful work, fulfilling relationships. With Sydney Omarr's astonishingly accurate day-by-day forecasts, you can chart your way to a starlit future and reap happiness, success, and good fortune the whole year through.

CHAPTER 1

What's Hot for 2001!

This year's picks and predictions . . .
worldwide trends that can change your life.

We're entering a decisive decade, when many problems are coming to the forefront simultaneously: global expansion, territorial disputes, overpopulation, dangers of nuclear warfare, environmental crises. After last year, a time when one of the most powerful lineups of planets in history occurred in the sign of Taurus, this year will be a time of processing the changes that have happened. It looks like a slower, more thoughtful year, when we'll be formulating our strategies and philosophies for the future. Here are key planets calling the shots and the trends to watch.

Masters of the Universe Recognize a Higher Power

The slow-moving planet Pluto is our guide to the hottest trends. With this planet, there is no going back. Pluto brings about a heightened consciousness and transformation of matters related to the sign it is traveling through. Now in Sagittarius, Pluto's task is to eliminate outworn belief systems to prepare us philosophically and spiritually for the future.

All that is associated with Sagittarius is sure to be emphasized—religion, advertising, banking, higher education, the travel industry, the legal professions, publishing, gambling, outdoor sports, pets.

At this writing, churches are filling up again and spiritual advisers are making office calls in New York's canyons of power. Pluto in Sagittarius brings a new emphasis on spirituality, which began in 1995 and will continue in a crescendo until 2008, when it finally moves on to Capricorn. Expect the emphasis to shift from the materialistic and power-hungry nineties to a quest for the meaning of it all, as upward strivers discover that money and power are not enough.

Global environmental crisis and charismatic spiritual leaders are likely to prompt more serious thought and spiritual quests. Extreme forms of religion, a new emphasis on saints, such as Joan of Arc, and other metaphysical beings are other manifestations. Home altars and private sanctuaries are becoming a part of our personal environment. The oriental art of *feng shui* is moving westward, helping to create a more harmonious, spiritual atmosphere in offices and homes, which also promotes luck and prosperity.

In this pet-happy nation, look for extremes related to animal welfare, the life and death of animals. Vegetarianism becomes a more popular alternative lifestyle. The care, feeding, and control of animals becomes an even larger issue as their habitats are destroyed.

The Sagittarian love of the outdoors has already become manifest in the popularity of the extreme sports, especially those that require strong legs like rock climbing or snowboarding. Rugged sporty all-terrain vehicles continue to be popular. Expect the trend toward more adventurous travel and fitness or sports-oriented vacations to continue to be popular: exotic trips to unexplored territories, difficult hikes and mountain-climbing expeditions, spa vacations, sports-associated resorts.

Publishing has been transformed by the new electronic media, with an enormous variety of books available in print. The on-line bookstore will continue to prosper under Pluto in Sagittarius. It is fascinating that the phenomenally popular Amazon.com, the on-line bookstore, took the Sagittarius-influenced name of the fierce female archer-warriors who went to the extreme of removing their right breast to better shoot their arrows.

Mars, the planet of action, triggers things off this year. After racing through all the signs at a breakneck pace last year, it grinds to a slow halt spending almost seven months in Sagittarius, from mid-February to early September. There, it will join Pluto in mid-March, igniting powerful Sagittarius-oriented events. This long stay gives us plenty of time to think about the consequences of our actions, where we're going, and the meaning of it all. We may see a recurrence of events from September 1999, the last meeting of these two power planets.

We can't leave out globalization in all its forms, which has become a main theme of the past few years. We are reforming boundaries, creating new forms of travel that will definitely include space travel. We'll be thinking about more energy efficient ways to get around, especially in the area of mass transit.

Who's Lucky? Make Hay, Gemini and Cancer!

Good fortune, expansion, and big money opportunities are associated with the movement of Jupiter, the planet that embodies the principle of expansion. Jupiter has a twelve-year cycle, staying in each sign for approximately one year.

When Jupiter enters a sign, the fields associated with that sign usually provide excellent opportunities. Areas of speculation associated with the sign Jupiter is passing through will have the hottest market potential—the ones that currently arouse excitement and enthusiasm.

The flip side of Jupiter is that there are no limits . . . you can expand off the planet under a Jupiter transit, which is why the planet is often called the "Gateway to Heaven." If something is going to burst—such as an artery—or over-extend or go over the top in some way, it could happen under a supposedly "lucky" Jupiter transit . . . so be aware.

This year, Jupiter won't finish its journey through Gemini until mid-July, when it moves into Cancer. So sun sign Geminis and Cancers or those with strong Gemini or Cancer influence in their horoscopes should have abundant growth opportunities. On the other hand, those born under Sagittarius and Capricorn will need to make adjustments, because this particular expansive tendency is opposed to their natural tendencies. With Saturn coming up more slowly, right behind Jupiter, this is a year to guard against overexpansion, overoptimism, and overextending yourself, without the appropriate organization and structure to back up your ventures. In other words, cover your bases!

Jupiter in Gemini should bring opportunities in all forms of communications, sales, cell phones, E-commerce, talk shows, voice mail, etc. In mid-July, opportunities open up in Cancer-related areas, which include home-related industries, child care, shelter industries, cruises, maternal issues, shipping and boating, water sports.

Saturn Puts on the Brakes in Taurus and Gemini

Saturn key words are focus, time, commitment, accomplishment, discipline, restriction. If Jupiter gives you a handout, then Saturn hands you the bill. With Saturn, nothing's free; you work for what you get, so it's always a good idea to find the areas (or houses) of your horoscope where Saturn is passing, to show where you must focus your energy on what is of lasting value. With Saturn, you must be sure to finish what you start, be responsible, put in the hard work and stick with it.

This year, Saturn finishes up making many demands on Taureans, as well as the other fixed signs (Leo, Scorpio, Aquarius). Saturn is quite powerful in the fixed signs, which are more focused and methodical by nature. In these signs, however, it facilitates more stubborn, tyrannical forces, demanding much wisdom and maturity to handle. Since Taurus is associated with financial matters, the earning and spending of money, possessions of all kinds, and our attitude toward them, expect the forces of limitation

6

to operate here. It will be imperative to curb spending, operate on a budget. When it moves into Gemini on April 21, Taureans should be able to feel the weight lifting.

On the other hand, the normally light-spirited Geminis, who also have Jupiter bringing them many new opportunities until the summer, will have to deal with a serious, sobering influence of Saturn, just when they were enjoying an expansive period. There will be a price to pay, so the Jupiter transit will not be all fun and games. Geminis will have to back up the risks they take and be sure they can deliver on promises. However, learning to balance these two forces can bring lasting rewards. It'll be a powerful challenge for changeable Geminis who will be the ones to pay the piper for the next two years.

Uranus and Neptune in Aquarius— The High-Tech Signs

Uranus and Neptune are pushing us in the future as they continue their long stays in Aquarius. Where there is Neptune, look for imagination and creativity, and since this is the planet of deception and illusion, here comes criminal activity, such as cyber-crime. Uranus overthrows the worn-out status quo and points us toward the future.

Since these planets influence fashion trends, look for clothes of techno-fibers that won't wear out! Fashion will be futuristic, yet also have an elusive, dreamy quality, thanks to Neptune. The hands and breast area are the focus of special attention this year. Perhaps there will be pockets for mini-computers and telephones, since high-tech gadgets are meant to travel with us, creating our own portable command control centers. The inspiration of the futuristic designs of the 1950s and 1970s and of sci-fi films should continue as we redesign our lives.

Our lust for techno-toys should make this a gadget-crazed time. Interactive forms of amusement and communication will rival television for our leisure. In fact,

7

television may be on its way out as we opt for more exciting forms of entertainment.

As these two planets blend with the others, unique trends are formed, such as the high-tech auctions and E-commerce that marked Jupiter/Saturn in Taurus. As they favorably influence Saturn/Jupiter in Gemini, expect an explosion of innovative forms of communication to happen this year. We'll be talking a blue streak across the planet, perhaps by individual satellite lines. Wires disappear as products work by "waves." As Jupiter moves into Cancer, look for news in high-tech home products, innovative ways to become a mother, futuristic cruise ships, new concepts in living quarters, and superfoods that optimize our health.

CHAPTER 2

Easy Astrology

You don't have to be an expert in astrology to understand how it works. This chapter is designed to walk you through the basic concepts, to pique your interest and satisfy your curiosity, so you'll know a sign from a house and what the planets mean. But don't expect to stop at this chapter! What makes astrology great is that, like your new PC, you can start using it right away. However, the more you use it, the more you'll crave the extra bells and whistles. Perhaps from here, you'll upgrade your knowledge with a computer program that calculates charts for everyone you know in a nanosecond, or you'll join an astrology class in your city, or you'll want to explore different techniques of astrology, go on to the asteroids and the fixed stars. The sky's the limit, literally. So let's take off!

The Basics—Signs, Houses, Constellations, and the Zodiac

Everyone knows what a sign is . . . or do they? A *sign* is literally a piece of territory marked off on a circle in the sky called the zodiac. Things happen within a sign, but a sign does not DO anything—that's the job of the planets. Signs have certain characteristics that are unique to them and are described by their element (earth, air, fire, water), by their quality or mode (cardinal [active], fixed, mutable), by their polarity (masculine/feminine, yin/yang), and finally by their position in the zodiac.

Now back to celestial real estate. *Signs* are equal 30-

degree portions of the *zodiac,* an imaginary 360-degree belt circling Earth. They're named after *constellations,* patterns of stars that originally marked the twelve divisions, like billboards. However, over the centuries, the constellations have shifted from our point of view here on Earth. So the constellation that once marked a particular sign may now be in the place "owned" by another sign. (Most Western astrologers use the twelve-equal-part division of the zodiac, however there are some methods of astrology that still do use the constellations instead of the signs.) However, the names of the signs remain the same as their original place-markers.

Most people think of themselves in terms of their *sun sign,* which refers to the sign the sun seems to be passing through at a given moment, from our point of view here on Earth. (In reality, we are the ones that are traveling around the sun.) For instance, "I'm an Aries" means that the sun was passing through Aries at my birth. However, there are nine other planets (plus asteroids, fixed stars, and sensitive points) that also form our total astrological personality, and some or many of these will be located in other signs. No one is completely "Aries," with all their astrological components in one sign! (Please note that in astrology the sun and moon are usually referred to as "planets," though of course they're not.)

How to Define a Sign

What makes Aries the sign of go-getters and Taureans savvy with money? And Geminis talk a blue streak and Sagittarians are footloose. Descriptions of the signs are not accidental; they are characterized by different combinations of four concepts: a sign's element, quality, polarity, and place on the zodiac.

Take the element of fire: it's associated with passion, heat. Then have it work in an active energetic way. Give it a jolt of positive energy and place it first in line. And doesn't that sound like the active, me-first, driving, hotheaded, energetic Aries?

Then take the element of earth: it's practical, sensual, where things grow. Add the fixed, stable mode. Give it energy that reacts to its surroundings, that settles in. Make it the consolidating force after the passion of Aries. Now you've got a good idea of how sensual, earthy Taurus operates.

Another way to grasp the idea is to pretend you're doing a magical puzzle based on the numbers that can divide into 12 (the number of signs): 4, 3, and 2. There are four "building blocks" or elements, three ways a sign operates (qualities or modes), and two polarities. These alternate in turn around the zodiac, with a different combination coming up for each sign.

THE FOUR ELEMENTS

Here's how they add up. The *four elements* describe the physical concept of the sign. Is it fiery (dynamic), earthy (practical), airy (mental), watery (emotional)? Divide the twelve signs by the four elements and you get three zodiac signs of each element: fire (Aries, Leo, Sagittarius), earth (Taurus, Virgo, Capricorn), air (Gemini, Libra, Aquarius), water (Cancer, Scorpio, Pisces). These are the same elements that make up our planet: earth, air, fire, and water. But astrology uses the elements as *symbols* that link our body and psyche to the rhythms of the cosmos. If major planets in a horoscope are passing through fire signs, the person will likely have a warm, enthusiastic personality, able to fire up or motivate others. These are people who make ideas catch fire, spring into existence, but they also have hot tempers. Those with major planets in earth signs are the builders of the zodiac who follow through after the initiative of fire signs to make things happen. These people are solid, practical realists who enjoy material things and sensual pleasures. They are interested in ideas that can be used to achieve concrete results. With major planets in air signs, a person will be more mental, a good communicator. Following the consolidating earth signs, air sign people reach out to inspire others through the use of words, social contacts, discussion, and debate. Water sign people complete each

11

four-element series, adding the ingredients of emotion, compassion, and imagination. These people are nonverbal communicators who attune themselves to their surroundings and react through the medium of feelings.

THE THREE QUALITIES

The second consideration when defining a sign is how it will operate. Will it take the initiative, or move slowly and deliberately, or adapt easily? It's *quality* (or modality) will tell. There are three qualities and four signs of each quality: cardinal, fixed, and mutable.

Cardinal signs begin each session (Aries, Cancer, Libra, Capricorn). People with major planets in cardinal signs tend to be active, involved in projects. They are usually on the fast track to success, impatient to get things under way. Those with major planets in *fixed signs* (Taurus, Leo, Scorpio, Aquarius) move steadily, always in control. Since these signs happen in the middle of a season, after the initial character of the season is established, it follows that people with major planets in fixed signs would tend to be more centered; they move more deliberately, do things more slowly, but thoroughly. The fixed signs fall in parts of your horoscope when you take root and integrate your experiences. *Mutable signs* (Gemini, Virgo, Sagittarius, Pisces) embody the principle of distribution. Planets in these signs will break up the cycle, prepare the way for a change by distributing the energy to the next group. People with predominantly mutable planets are likely to be flexible, adaptable, communicative. They can move in many directions easily, darting around obstacles.

THE TWO POLARITIES

In addition to an element and a quality, each sign has a *polarity,* either a positive or negative electrical charge that generates energy around the zodiac, like a giant battery. Polarity refers to opposites, which you could also define as masculine/feminine, yin/yang, active/reactive. Alternating around the zodiac, the six fire and air signs are positive, active, masculine, and yang in polarity. Therefore, planets in these signs are open, expanding outward. The six earth and water signs are negative, reactive, feminine, and yin— in other words, nurturing and receptive in polarity, which allows the energy to develop and take shape.

All positive energy would be like a car without brakes. All negative energy would be like a stalled vehicle, going nowhere. Both polarities are needed in balanced proportion.

THE ORDER OF THE SIGNS

The specific order of the signs is vital to the balance of the zodiac and the transmission of energy around the cycle. Though each sign is quite different from its neighbors on either side, each seems to grow out of its predecessor like links in a chain, transmitting a synthesis of energy accumulated along the chain to the following sign, beginning with the fire-powered, active, positive, cardinal sign of Aries and ending with watery, mutable, reactive Pisces.

Houses of the Horoscope— Where the Action Is

We come to the concept of *houses* once we set up a horoscope, which is a map of the heavens at a given moment in time. The horoscope chart looks somewhat like a wheel divided with twelve spokes. In between each of the "spokes" is a section called a "house." Each house covers a different area of life and is influenced by a particular sign and a planet. In addition, the house is colored by the sign that is passing over the spoke (or cusp) at the moment when the horoscope chart is cast.

Numerically, the house order begins at the left center spoke (or the 9 position if you were reading a clock) and is read counter-clockwise around the chart.

The First House—Home of Aries and Mars

This is the house of "firsts"—the first impression you make, how you initiate matters, the image you choose to project. This is where you advertise yourself, where you project your personality. Planets that fall here will intensify the way you come across to others. Often the first house will project an entirely different type of energy than the sun sign. For instance, a Capricorn with Leo in the first house will come across as much more flamboyant than the average Capricorn. The sign on the cusp of this house is known as your ascendant or rising sign.

The Second House—Home of Taurus and Venus

Here is your contact with the material world. In this house are your attitudes about money, possessions, finances, whatever belongs to you, and what you own, as well as your earning and spending capacity. On a deeper level, this house reveals your sense of self-worth, the inner values that draw wealth in various forms.

The Third House—Home of Gemini and Mercury

This house describes how you communicate with others—are you understood? Here you reach out to others nearby and interact with the immediate environment. This is how your thinking process works, the way you express your thoughts. In relationships, here are your first experiences with brothers and sisters, how you handle people close to you, such as your neighbors or pals. It's also where you take short trips, write letters, or use the telephone. It shows how your mind works in terms of left-brain logical and analytical functions.

The Fourth House—Home of Cancer and the Moon

This shows how you are nurtured and made to feel secure—your roots! Located at the bottom of the chart, the fourth house, like the home, shows the foundation of life, your deepest psychological underpinnings. Here is where you have the deepest confrontation with who you are, and how you make yourself feel secure. It shows your early home environment and the circumstances at the end of your life—your final "home"—as well as the place you call home now. Astrologers look here for information about the primary nurturers in your life.

The Fifth House—Home of Leo and the Sun

This is how you express yourself creatively—your idea of play. The Leo house is where the creative potential develops. Here you show off your talents and also where you procreate, in the sense that children are outgrowths of your creative ability. It most represents your inner childlike self, the part of you that finds joy in play. If inner security has been established by the time you reach this house, you are now free to have fun, romance, love affairs—to give of yourself. This is also the place astrologers look for the playful kind of love affairs, flirtations, and brief romantic encounters (rather than long-term commitments).

The Sixth House—Home of Virgo and Mercury

Here is your "repair and maintenance" department. It shows how you function in daily life, where you get things done, and where you determine how you look after others and fulfill service duties, such as taking care of pets. Here is your daily survival, your "job" (as opposed to your career, which is the domain of the tenth house), your diet, and your health and fitness regimens. Here is where you take care of your body and organize yourself so you can perform efficiently in the world.

The Seventh House—Home of Libra and Venus

This house shows your attitude toward partners and those with whom you enter commitments, contracts, or agree-

ments. This house has to do with your relationships, your close, intimate, one-on-one relationships (even your open enemies—those you "face off" with). Open hostilities, lawsuits, divorces, and marriages happen here. If the first house is the "I," the seventh or opposite house is the "not-I"—the complementary partner you attract by the way you come across. If you are having trouble with partnerships, consider what you are attracting by the interaction of your first and seventh houses.

The Eighth House—Home of Scorpio and Pluto (also Mars)

This refers to how you merge with something or someone, and how you handle power and control. This is one of the most mysterious and powerful houses, where your energy transforms itself from "I" to "we." As you give up your personal power and control by uniting with something or someone, two kinds of energies merge and become something greater, leading to a regeneration of the self on a higher level. Here are your attitudes toward sex, shared resources, taxes (what you share with the government). Because this house involves what belongs to others, you face issues of control and power struggles, or undergo a deep psychological transformation as you bond with another. Here you transcend yourself with the occult, dreams, drugs, or psychic experiences that reflect the collective unconscious.

The Ninth House—Home of Sagittarius and Jupiter

Where you search for wisdom and higher knowledge—your belief system. While the third house represents the "lower mind," its opposite on the wheel, the ninth house, is the "higher mind"—the abstract, intuitive, spiritual mind that asks "big" questions such as "Why are we here?" The ninth house shows what you believe in. After the third house explored what was close at hand, the ninth stretches out to explore more exotic territory, either by traveling, broadening yourself mentally with higher education, or stretching spiritually with religious activity. You take risks in your ninth house, you break rules and boundaries, since you are concerned with how everything is related. Here is where you write a book or extensive thesis, where you pontificate, philosophize, or preach.

The Tenth House—Home of Capricorn and Saturn

Here is your public image and how you handle authority. Located directly overhead at the "high noon" position on the horoscope wheel, this house is associated with high-profile activities, where the world sees you. It deals with your career (but not your routine "job"), and your reputation. Here is where you go public, take on responsibilities (as opposed to the fourth house, where you stay home). This will affect the career you choose and your "public relations." This house is also associated with your father or the main authority figure in your life.

The Eleventh House—Home of Aquarius and Uranus

Here is your support system, how you relate to society and your goals. In this house, you extend your identity to belong to a group, a team, a club, a goal, or a belief system. You worry about being popular, winning the election, or making the team; you define what you really want, the kinds of friends you have, your political affiliations, and the kind of groups you'll belong to. Here is "what other people think." Here is where you could become a socially conscious humanitarian—or a party-going social butterfly. It's where you look to others to stimulate you and discover your kinship to the rest of humanity. The sign on the cusp of this house can help you understand what you gain and lose from friendships.

The Twelfth House—Home of Pisces and Neptune

Here is where the boundaries between yourself and others become blurred, where you become selfless. In your trip around the zodiac, you've gone from the "I" of self-assertion in the first house to the final house symbolizing the dissolution that happens before rebirth. It's where accumulated experiences are processed in the unconscious. Spiritually oriented astrologers look to this house for evidence of past lives and karma. Places where we go for solitude or to do spiritual or reparative work belong here, such as retreats, religious institutions, hospitals. Here are also institutions such as prisons where we withdraw from society or are forced to withdraw because of antisocial behavior. Selfless giving through charitable acts is part of this house as is helpless dependence on charity. In your daily life, the twelfth house reveals your deepest intimacies, your best-kept secrets, especially those you hide from yourself, repressed deep in the unconscious. It is where we surrender a sense of a separate self to a deep feeling of wholeness, such as selfless service in religion or any activity that involves merging with the greater whole. Many sports stars have important planets in the twelfth house that enable them to play in the "zone," find an inner, almost mystical strength that transcends their limits.

The Planets Power Up Your Houses

Houses are stronger or weaker depending on how many planets are inhabiting them. If there are many planets occupying a given house, it follows that the activities of that house will be emphasized in your life. If the planet that rules the house naturally is also located there, this too adds power to the house.

CHAPTER 3

Look Up Your Planets

The Doers in Your Chart— the Planets

The ten planets in your chart will play starring or supporting roles, depending on their position in your horoscope. A planet in the first house, particularly one that's close to your rising sign, is sure to be a featured player. Planets that are grouped together usually operate together like a team, playing off each other, rather than expressing their energy singularly. A planet that stands alone, away from the others, is usually outstanding and sometimes calls the shots.

Each planet has two signs where it is especially at home. These are called its *dignities*. The most favorable place for a planet is in the sign or signs it rules; the next best place is in a sign where it is *exalted*, or especially harmonious. On the other hand, there are places in the horoscope where a planet has to work harder to play its role. These places are called the planets *detriment* and *fall*. The sign opposite a planet's rulership, which embodies the opposite area of life, is its *detriment*. The sign opposite its exaltation is its *fall*. Though these terms may suggest unfortunate circumstances for the planet, that is not always true. In fact, a planet that is debilitated can actually be more complete, because it must stretch itself to meet the challenges of living in a more difficult sign. Like world leaders who've had to struggle for greatness, this planet may actually develop great strength and character.

Here's a list of the best places for each planet to be. Note that as new planets were discovered in this century, they replaced the traditional rulers of signs that best complemented their energies.

ARIES—Mars
TAURUS—Venus, in its most sensual form
GEMINI—Mercury, in its communicative role
CANCER—the moon
LEO—the sun
VIRGO—Mercury, this time in its more critical capacity
LIBRA—Venus, in its more aesthetic, judgmental form
SCORPIO—Pluto, replacing the sign's original ruler, Mars
SAGITTARIUS—Jupiter
CAPRICORN—Saturn
AQUARIUS—Uranus, replacing Saturn, its original ruler
PISCES—Neptune, replacing Jupiter, its original ruler

A person who has many planets in exalted signs is lucky indeed, for here is where the planet can accomplish the most, be its most influential and creative.

The SUN—exalted in Aries, where its energy creates action
The MOON—exalted in Taurus, where instincts and reactions operate on a highly creative level
MERCURY—exalted in Aquarius, where it can reach analytical heights
VENUS—exalted in Pisces, a sign whose sensitivity encourages love and creativity
MARS—exalted in Capricorn, a sign that puts energy to work productively
JUPITER—exalted in Cancer, where it encourages nurturing and growth
SATURN—at home in Libra, where it steadies the scales of justice and promotes balanced, responsible judgment
URANUS—powerful in Scorpio, where it promotes transformation

NEPTUNE—especially favored in Cancer, where it gains
  the security to transcend to a higher state
PLUTO—exalted in Pisces, where it dissolves the old
  cycle, to make way for transition to the new

The Sun Is Always Top of the List

Your sun sign is the part of you that shines brightest.
Then other planets add special coloration that sets you
apart from other members of your sign. If you know a
person's sun sign, you will already know some useful
generic qualities, but when you know all the planets, you
have a much more accurate profile and can predict more
accurately how that individual will act. The sun's just one
card in your hand—when you know the other planets,
you can really play to win!

Since the sun is always the first consideration, it is
important to treat it as the star of the show. It is your
conscious ego and it is always center stage, even when
sharing a house or a sign with several other planets. This
is why sun sign astrology works for so many people. In
chart interpretations, the sun can also play the parental
role.

The sun rules the sign of Leo, gaining strength through
the pride, dignity, and confidence of the fixed-fire personality. It is exalted in the "me-first" Aries. In its detriment, Aquarius, the sun-ego is strengthened through
group participation and social consciousness, rather than
through self-centeredness (note how many Aquarius people are involved in politics, social work, public life . . .
follow the demands of their sun sign to be spokesperson
for a group). In its fall, Libra, the sun needs the strength
of a partner—an "other"—to enhance balance and self-
expression.

Like your sun sign, each of the other nine planet per-
sonalities is colored by the sign it is passing through at
the time. For example, Mercury, the planet that rules the
way you communicate, will express itself in a dynamic,
headstrong Aries way if it is passing through the sign of

Aries when you were born. You will communicate in a much different way if it is passing through the slower, more patient sign of Taurus. And so on through the list. Here's a rundown of the planets and how they behave in every sign.

The Moon Expresses
Your Inner Feelings

The moon can teach you about the inner side of yourself, your needs and secrets, as well as those of others. It is your most personal planet, the receptive, reflective, female, nurturing side of you. And it reflects who you were nurtured by—the "Mother" or mother figure in your chart. In a man's chart, the moon position also describes his female, receptive, emotional side, and the woman in his life who will have the deepest effect. (Venus reveals the kind of woman who attracts him physically).

The sign the moon was passing through at your birth reflects your instinctive emotional nature, what appeals to you subconsciously. Since accurate moon tables are too extensive for this book, check through these descriptions to find the moon sign that feels most familiar, or better yet, have your chart calculated by a computer service to get your accurate moon placement.

The moon rules maternal Cancer and is exalted in Taurus—both comforting, home-loving signs where the natural emotional energies of the moon are easily and productively expressed. But when the moon is in the opposite signs—in its Capricorn detriment and its Scorpio fall—it leaves the comfortable nest and deals with emotional issues of power and achievement in the outside world. Those of you with the moon in these signs will find your emotional role more challenging in life.

Moon in Aries

You are an idealistic, impetuous person who falls in and out of love easily. This placement makes you both independent and ardent. You love a challenge, but could cool once your quarry is captured. You should cultivate patience and tolerance—or you might tend to gravitate toward those who treat you roughly, just for the sake of challenge and excitement.

Moon in Taurus

You are a sentimental soul who is very fond of the good life and gravitates toward solid, secure relationships. You like displays of affection and creature comforts—all the tangible trappings of a cozy, safe, calm atmosphere. You are sensual and steady emotionally, but very stubborn and determined. You can't be pushed and tend to dislike changes. You should make an effort to broaden your horizons and to take a risk sometimes.

Moon in Gemini

You crave mental stimulation and variety in life, which you usually get through either an ever-varied social life, the excitement of flirtation, and/or multiple professional involvements. You may marry more than once and have a rather chaotic emotional life due to your difficulty with commitment and settling down. Be sure to find a partner who is as outgoing as you are. You will have to learn at some point to focus your energies because you tend to be somewhat fragmented—to do two things at once, to have two homes or even two lovers. If you can find a creative way to express your many-faceted nature, you'll be ahead of the game.

Moon in Cancer

This is the most powerful lunar position, which is sure to make a deep imprint on your character. Your needs are very much associated with your reaction to the needs of others. You are very sensitive and self-protective, though some of you may mask this with a hard shell. This placement also gives you an excellent memory, keen intuition, and an uncanny ability to perceive the needs of others. All of the lunar phases will affect you, especially full moons and eclipses, so you would do well to mark them on your calendar. Because you're happiest at home, you may work at home or turn your office into a second home, where you can nurture and comfort people. (You may tend to "mother the world.") With natural psychic, intuitive ability, you might be drawn to occult work in some way. Or you may get professionally involved with providing food and shelter to others.

Moon in Leo

This warm, passionate moon takes everything to heart. You are attracted to all that is noble, generous, and aristocratic in life (and may be a bit of a snob). You have an innate ability to take command emotionally, but you do need strong support, loyalty, and loud applause from those you love. You are possessive of your loved ones and your turf and will roar if anyone threatens to take over your territory.

Moon in Virgo

You are rather cool until you decide if others measure up. But once someone or something meets your ideal standards, you hold up your end of the arrangement perfectly. You may, in fact, drive yourself too hard to attain some notion of perfection. Try to be a bit easier on yourself and others. Don't always act the censor! You love to be the teacher and are drawn to situations where you can change others for the better, but sometimes you must learn to accept others for what they are—enjoy what you have!

Moon in Libra

A partnership-oriented moon—you may find it difficult to be alone or to do things alone. After you have learned emotional balance by leaning on yourself first, you can have excellent relationships. It is best for you to avoid extremes, however, which set your scales swinging and can make your love life precarious. You thrive in a rather conservative, traditional, romantic relationship, where you receive attention and flattery—but not possessiveness—from your partner. You'll be your most charming in an elegant, harmonious atmosphere.

Moon in Scorpio

This is a moon that enjoys and responds to intense, passionate feelings. You may go to extremes and have a very dramatic emotional life, full of ardor, suspicion, jealousy, and obsession. It would be much healthier to channel your need for power and control into meaningful work. This is a good position for anyone in the fields of medicine, police work, research, the occult, psychoanalysis, or intuitive work, because life-and-death situations don't faze you. However, you do take personal disappointments very hard.

Moon in Sagittarius

You take life's ups and downs with good humor and the proverbial grain of salt. You'll love 'em and leave 'em, take off on a great adventure at a moment's notice. "Born free" could be your slogan. Attracted by the exotic, you have wanderlust mentally and physically. You may be too much in search of new mental and spiritual stimulation to ever settle down.

Moon in Capricorn

Are you ever accused of being too cool and calculating? You have an earthy side, but you take prestige and position very seriously. Your strong drive to succeed extends to your romantic life, where you will be devoted to improving your lifestyle, rising to the top. A structured situation where you can advance methodically makes you feel wonderfully secure. You may be attracted to someone older or very much younger or from a different social world. It may be difficult to look at the lighter side of emotional relationships; however, the "up" side of this moon in the sign of its detriment is that you tend to be very dutiful and responsible to those you care for.

Moon in Aquarius

You are a people collector with many friends of all backgrounds. You are happiest surrounded by people and may feel uneasy when left alone. Though you usually stay friends with lovers, intense emotions and demanding one-on-one relationships turn you off. You don't like anything to be too rigid or scheduled. Though tolerant and understanding, you can be emotionally unpredictable and may opt for an unconventional love life. With plenty of space, you will be able to sustain relationships with liberal, freedom-loving types.

Moon in Pisces

You are very responsive and empathetic to others, especially if they have problems or are the underdog. (Be on guard against attracting too many people with sob stories.) You'll be happiest if you can express your creative imagination in the arts or in the spiritual or healing professions. Because you may tend to escape in fantasies or overreact to the moods of others, you need an emotional anchor to help you keep a firm foothold in reality. Steer clear of too much escapism (especially in alcohol) or reclusiveness. Places near water soothe your moods. Working in a field that gives you emotional variety will also help you be productive.

Close Neighbors—Mercury, Venus, and Mars

These planets work in your immediate personal life.
    Mercury affects how you communicate and how your

mental processes work. Are you a quick study who grasps information rapidly, or do you learn more slowly and thoroughly? How is your concentration? Can you express yourself easily? Are you a good writer? All these questions can be answered by your Mercury placement.

Venus shows what you react to. What turns you on? What appeals to you aesthetically? Are you charming to others? Are you attractive to look at? Your taste, your refinement, and your sense of balance and proportion are all Venus-ruled.

Mars is your outgoing energy, your drive and ambition. Do you reach out for new adventures? Are you assertive? Are you motivated? Self-confident? Hot-tempered? How you channel your energy and drive is revealed by your Mars placement.

Mercury Says It All

Since Mercury never travels far from the sun, read Mercury in your sun sign, then the sign preceding and following it. Then decide which reflects the way your mind works.

Mercury in Aries

Your mind is very active and assertive. You never hesitate to say what you think or shy away from a battle. In fact, you may relish a verbal confrontation. Tact is not your strong point, so you may have to learn not to trip over your tongue.

Mercury in Taurus

Though you may be a slow learner, you have good concentration and mental stamina. You want to make your ideas really happen. You'll attack a problem methodically and consider every angle thoroughly, never jumping to conclusions. You'll stick with a subject until you master it.

Mercury in Gemini

You are a wonderful communicator with great facility for expressing yourself both verbally and in writing. You talk and talk, love gathering all kinds of information. You probably finish other people's sentences, talk with hand gestures. You can talk to anybody anytime . . . and probably have phone bills to prove it. You read anything from sci fi to Shakespeare and might need an extra room just for your book collection. Though you learn fast, you may lack focus and discipline. Watch a tendency to jump from subject to subject.

Mercury in Cancer

You rely on intuition more than logic. Your mental processes are usually colored by your emotions, so you may seem shy or hesitant to voice your opinions. However, this placement gives you the advantage of great imagination and empathy in the way you communicate with others.

Mercury in Leo

You are enthusiastic and very dramatic in the way you express yourself. You like to hold the attention of groups and could be a great public speaker. Your mind thinks big, so you'd prefer to deal with the overall picture rather than with the details.

Mercury in Virgo

This is one of the best places for Mercury. It should give you critical ability, attention to details, and thorough analysis. Your mind focuses on the practical side of things. This type of thinking is very well suited to being a teacher or editor.

Mercury in Libra

You're either a born diplomat who smoothes over ruffled feathers or a talented debater. However, since you're forever weighing the pros and cons of a situation, you may vacillate when making decisions.

Mercury in Scorpio

This is an investigative mind that stops at nothing to get the answers. You may have a sarcastic, stinging wit, a gift for the cutting remark. There's always a grain of truth to your verbal sallies, thanks to your penetrating insight.

Mercury in Sagittarius

You are a super-salesman with a tendency to expound. Though you are very broad-minded, you can be dogmatic when it comes to telling others what's good for them. You won't hesitate to tell the truth as you see it, so watch a tendency toward tactlessness. On the plus side, you have a great sense of humor. This position of Mercury is often considered by astrologers to be at a disadvantage because Sagittarius opposes Gemini, the sign Mercury rules, and squares off with Virgo, another Mercury-ruled sign. What often happens is that Mercury in Sagittarius oversteps its bounds and loses sight of the facts in a situation. Do a reality check before making promises that you may not be able to deliver.

Mercury in Capricorn

This placement endows good mental discipline. You have a love of learning and a very orderly approach to your subjects. You will patiently plod through the facts and figures until you have mastered the tasks. You grasp structured situations easily, but may be short on creativity.

Mercury in Aquarius

With Uranus and Neptune in Aquarius now energizing your Mercury, you're sure to be on the cutting edge of new ideas. An independent, original thinker, you'll have more far-out ideas than the average person and be quick to check out any unusual opportunities. Your opinions are so well researched and grounded in fact that once your mind is made up, it is difficult to change.

Mercury in Pisces

You have the psychic intuitive mind of a natural poet. Learn to make use of your creative imagination. You may think in terms of helping others, but check a tendency to be vague and forgetful of details.

Venus Relates

Venus tells how you relate to others and to your environment. It shows where you receive pleasure, what you love to do. Find your Venus placement on the chart in this book by looking for the year of your birth in the left-hand column. Then follow the line of that year across the page until you reach the time period of your birthday. The sign heading that column will be your Venus. If you were born on a day when Venus was changing signs, check the signs preceding or following that day to determine if that feels more like your Venus nature.

Venus in Aries

You can't stand to be bored, confined, or ordered around. But a good challenge, maybe even a rousing row, turns you on. Confess—don't you pick a fight now and then just to get someone stirred up? You're attracted by the chase, not the catch, which could cause some problems in your love life, if the object of your affection becomes too attainable. You like to wear red and be first with the latest fashion. You'll spot a trend before anyone else.

Venus in Taurus

All your senses work in high gear. You love to be surrounded by glorious tastes, smells, textures, sounds, and visuals—austerity is not for you. Neither is being rushed. You like time to enjoy your pleasures. Soothing surroundings with plenty of creature comforts are your cup of tea. You like to feel secure in your nest, with no sudden jolts or surprises. You like familiar objects—in fact, you may hate to let anything or anyone go.

Venus in Gemini

You are a lively, sparkling personality who thrives in a situation that affords a constant variety and a frequent change of scenery. A varied social life is important to you, with plenty of stimulation and a chance to engage in some light flirtation. Commitment may be difficult, because playing the field is so much fun.

Venus in Cancer

An atmosphere where you feel protected, coddled, and mothered is best for you. You love to be surrounded by children in a cozy, homelike situation. You are attracted to those who are tender and nurturing, who make you feel secure and well provided for. You may be quite secretive about your emotional life or attracted to clandestine relationships.

Venus in Leo

First-class attention in large doses turns you on, and so does the glitter of real gold and the flash of mirrors. You like to feel like a star at all times, surrounded by your admiring audience. The side effect is that you may be attracted to flatterers and tinsel, while the real gold requires some digging.

Venus in Virgo

Everything neatly in its place? On the surface, you are attracted to an atmosphere where everything is in perfect order, but underneath are some basic, earthy urges. You are attracted to those who appeal to your need to teach, be of service, or play out a *Pygmalion* fantasy. You are at your best when you are busy doing something useful.

Venus in Libra

Elegance and harmony are your key words. You can't abide an atmosphere of contention. Your taste tends toward the classic, with light harmonies of color—nothing clashing, trendy, or outrageous. You love doing things with a partner and should be careful to pick one who is decisive, but patient enough to let you weigh the pros and cons. And steer clear of argumentative types.

Venus in Scorpio

Hidden mysteries intrigue you—in fact, anything that is too open and aboveboard is a bit of a bore. You surely have a stack of whodunits by the bed, along with an erotic magazine or two. You like to solve puzzles, may also be fascinated with the occult, crime, or scientific research. Intense, all-or-nothing situations add spice to your life, and you love to ferret out the secrets of others. But you could get burned by your flair for living dangerously. The color black, spicy food, dark wood furniture, and heady perfume all get you in the right mood.

Venus in Sagittarius

If you are not actually a world traveler, your surroundings are sure to reflect your love of faraway places. You like a casual outdoor atmosphere and a dog or two to pet. There should be plenty of room for athletic equipment and suitcases. You're attracted to kindred souls who love to travel and who share your freedom-loving philosophy of life. Athletics and spiritual or New Age pursuits could be other interests.

Venus in Capricorn

No fly-by-night relationships for you! You want substance in life and you are attracted to whatever will help you get where you are going. Status objects turn you on. And so do those who have a serious responsible, businesslike approach, or who remind you of a beloved parent. It is characteristic of this placement to be attracted to someone of a different generation. Antiques, traditional clothing, and dignified behavior favor you.

Venus in Aquarius

This Venus wants to make friends more than to make love. You like to be in a group, particularly one pushing a worthy cause. You feel quite at home surrounded by people, remaining detached from any intense commitment. Original ideas and unpredictable people fascinate you. You don't like everything to be planned out in advance, preferring spontaneity and delightful surprises.

Venus in Pisces

This Venus loves to give of yourself, and you find plenty of takers. Stray animals and people appeal to your heart and your pocketbook, but be careful to look at their motives realistically once in a while. You are extremely vulnerable to sob stories of all kinds. Fantasy, theater, and psychic or spiritual activities also speak to you.

Mars Moves and Shakes

Mars is the mover and shaker in your life. It shows how you pursue your goals and whether you have energy to

33

burn or proceed at a slow, steady pace. Or are you nervous, restless, and unable to sit still? It will also show how you get angry: Do you explode, or do a slow burn, or hold everything inside, then get revenge later?

To find your Mars, turn to the chart on page 68. There you will find an abbreviation of your Mars sign. If the description of your Mars sign doesn't ring true, read the description of the sign preceding and following it. You may have been born on a day when Mars was changing signs, and your Mars would then be in the adjacent sign.

Mars in Aries

In the sign it rules, Mars shows its brilliant fiery nature. You have an explosive temper and can be quite impatient, but on the other hand, you have tremendous courage, energy, and drive. You'll let nothing stand in your way as you race to be first! Obstacles are met head-on and broken through by force. However, those that require patience and persistence can have you exploding in rage. You're a great starter, but not necessarily around for the finish.

Mars in Taurus

Slow, steady, concentrated energy gives you the power. You've great stamina and you never give up. Your tactic is to wear away obstacles with your persistence. Often you come out a winner because you've had the patience to hang in there. When angered, you do a slow burn.

Mars in Gemini

You can't sit still for long. This Mars craves variety. You often have two or more things going on at once—it's all an amusing game to you. Your life can get very complicated, but that only adds spice and stimulation. What drives you into a nervous, hyper state? Boredom, sameness, routine, and confinement. You can do wonderful things with your hands and you have a way with words.

Mars in Cancer

You rarely attack head-on—instead, you'll keep things to yourself, make plans in secret, and always cover your actions. This might be interpreted by some as manipulative, but you are only being self-protective. You get furious when anyone knows too much about you. But you do like to know all about others. Your mothering and feeding instincts can be put to good use, if you work in the food, hotel, or child-care business. You may have to overcome your fragile sense of security, which prompts you not to take risks and get physically upset when criticized. Don't take things so personally!

Mars in Leo

You have a very dominant personality that takes center stage—modesty is not one of your traits, nor is taking a backseat. You prefer giving the orders and have been known to make a dramatic scene if they are not obeyed. Properly used, this Mars confers leadership ability, endurance, and courage.

Mars in Virgo

You are the fault-finder of the zodiac, who notices every detail. Mistakes of any kind make you very nervous. You may worry, even if everything is going smoothly. You may not express your anger directly, but you sure can nag. You have definite likes and dislikes, and you are sure you can do the job better than anyone else. You are certainly more industrious and detail-oriented than other signs. Your Mars energy is often most positively expressed in some kind of teaching role.

Mars in Libra

This Mars will have a passion for beauty, justice, and art. Generally, you will avoid confrontations at all costs. You prefer to spend your energy finding diplomatic solutions or weighing pros and cons. Your other techniques are passive aggression or exercising your well-known charm to get people to do what you want.

Mars in Scorpio

This is a powerful placement, so intense that it demands careful channeling into worthwhile activities. Otherwise, you could become obsessed with your sexuality or might use your need for power and control to manipulate others. You are strong-willed, shrewd, and very private about your affairs, and you'll usually have a secret agenda behind your actions. Your great stamina, focus, and discipline would be excellent assets for careers in the military or medical fields, especially research or surgery. When angry, you don't get mad—you get even!

Mars in Sagittarius

This expansive Mars often propels people into sales, travel, athletics, or philosophy. Your energies function well when you are on the move. You have a hot temper and are inclined to say what you think before you consider the consequences. You shoot for high goals—and talk endlessly about them—but you may be weak on groundwork. This Mars needs a solid foundation. Watch a tendency to take unnecessary risks.

Mars in Capricorn

This is an ambitious Mars with an excellent sense of timing. You have an eye for those who can be of use to you, and you may dismiss people ruthlessly when you're angry. But you drive yourself hard and deliver full value. This is a good placement for an executive. You'll aim for status and a high material position in life, and keep climbing despite the odds. A great Mars to have!

Mars in Aquarius

This is the most rebellious Mars. You seem to have a drive to assert yourself against the status quo. You may enjoy provoking people, shocking them out of traditional views. Or this placement could express itself in an offbeat sex life. Somehow you often find yourself in unconventional situations. You enjoy being a leader of an active group, which pursues forward-looking studies, politics, or goals.

Mars in Pisces

This Mars is a good actor who knows just how to appeal to the sympathies of others. You create and project wonderful fantasies or use your sensitive antennae to crusade for those less fortunate. You get what you want through creating a veil of illusion and glamour. This is a good Mars for someone in the creative fields, a dancer, performer, or photographer, or for someone in motion pictures. Many famous film stars have this placement. Watch a tendency to manipulate by making others feel sorry for you.

Jupiter Gives You the Breaks

Jupiter is the planet in your horoscope that makes you want MORE. This big, bright, swirling mass of gases is associated with abundance, prosperity, and the kind of windfall you get without too much hard work. You're optimistic under Jupiter's influence, when anything seems possible. You'll travel, expand your mind with higher education, and publish to share your knowledge widely. But a strong Jupiter has its downside, too, because Jupiter's influence is neither discriminating nor disciplined. It represents the principle of growth without judgment, and could result in extravagance, weight gain, laziness, and carelessness, if not kept in check.

Be sure to look up your Jupiter in the tables in this book. When the current position of Jupiter is favorable, you may get that lucky break. This is a great time to try new things, take risks, travel, or get more education. Opportunities seem to open up easily, so take advantage of them.

Once a year, Jupiter changes signs. That means you are due for an expansive time every twelve years, when Jupiter travels through your sun sign. You'll also have "up" periods every four years, when Jupiter is in the same element as your sun sign.

Jupiter in Aries

You are the soul of enthusiasm and optimism. Your luckiest times are when you are getting started on an exciting project or selling an idea that you really believe in. You may have to watch a tendency to be arrogant with those who do not share your enthusiasm. You follow your impulses, often ignoring budget or other commonsense limitations. To produce real, solid benefits, you'll need patience and follow-through wherever this Jupiter falls in your horoscope.

Jupiter in Taurus

You'll spend on beautiful material things, especially those that come from nature—items made of rare woods, natural fabrics, or precious gems, for instance. You can't have too much comfort or too many sensual pleasures. Watch a tendency to overindulge in good food, or to overpamper yourself with nothing but the best. Spartan living is not for you! You may be especially lucky in matters of real estate.

Jupiter in Gemini

You are the great talker of the zodiac, and you may be a great writer, too. But restlessness could be your weak point. You jump around, talk too much, and could be a jack of all trades. Keeping a secret is especially difficult, so you'll also have to watch a tendency to spill the beans. Since you love to be at the center of a beehive of activity, you'll have a vibrant social life. Your best opportunities will come through your talent for language—speaking, writing, communicating, and selling.

Jupiter in Cancer

You are luckiest in situations where you can find emotional closeness or deal with basic security needs, such as food, nurturing, or shelter. You may be a great collector and you may simply love to accumulate things—you are the one who stashes things away for a rainy day. You probably have a very good memory and love children—in fact, you may have many children to care for. The food, hotel, child-care, or shipping business holds good opportunities for you.

Jupiter in Leo

You are a natural showman who loves to live in a larger-than-life way. Yours is a personality full of color that always finds its way into the limelight. You can't have too much attention or applause. Showbiz is a natural place for you, and so is any area where you can play to a crowd. Exercising your flair for drama, your natural playfulness, and your romantic nature brings you good fortune. But watch a tendency to be overly extravagant or to monopolize center stage.

Jupiter in Virgo

You actually love those minute details others find boring. To you, they make all the difference between the perfect and the ordinary. You are the fine craftsman who spots every flaw. You expand your awareness by finding the most efficient methods and by being of service to others. Many will be drawn to medical or teaching fields. You'll also have luck in publishing, crafts, nutrition, and service professions. Watch out for a tendency to overwork.

Jupiter in Libra

This is an other-directed Jupiter that develops best with a partner, for the stimulation of others helps you grow. You are also most comfortable in harmonious, beautiful situations, and you work well with artistic people. You have a great sense of fair play and an ability to evaluate the pros and cons of a situation. You usually prefer to play the role of diplomat rather than adversary.

Jupiter in Scorpio

You love the feeling of power and control, of taking things to their limit. You can't resist a mystery, and your shrewd, penetrating mind sees right through to the heart of most situations and people. You have luck in work that provides for solutions to matters of life and death. You may be drawn to undercover work, behind-the-scenes intrigue, psychotherapy, the occult, and sex-related ventures. Your challenge will be to develop a sense of moderation and tolerance for other beliefs. This Jupiter can be fanatical. You may have luck in handling other people's money—insurance, taxes, and inheritance can bring you a windfall.

Jupiter in Sagittarius

Independent, outgoing, and idealistic, you'll shoot for the stars. This Jupiter compels you to travel far and wide, both physically and mentally, via higher education. You may have luck while traveling in an exotic place. You also have luck with outdoor ventures, exercise, and animals, particularly horses. Since you tend to be very open about your opinions, watch a tendency to be tactless and to exaggerate. Instead, use your wonderful sense of humor to make your point.

Jupiter in Capricorn

Jupiter is much more restrained in Capricorn, the sign of rules and authority. Here, Jupiter can make you overwork and heighten any ambition or sense of duty you may have. You'll expand in areas that advance your position, putting you farther up the social or corporate ladder. You are lucky working within the establishment in a very structured situation, where you can show off your ability to organize and reap rewards for your hard work.

Jupiter in Aquarius

This is another freedom-loving Jupiter, with great tolerance and originality. You are at your best when you are working for a humanitarian cause and in the company of many supporters. This is a good Jupiter for a political career. You'll relate to all kinds of people on all social levels. You have an abundance of original ideas, but you are best off away from routine and any situation that imposes rigid rules. You need mental stimulation!

Jupiter in Pisces

You are a giver whose feelings and pocketbook are easily touched by others, so choose your companions with care. You could be the original sucker for a hard-luck story. Better find a worthy hospital or charity to appreciate your selfless support. You have a great creative imagination and may attract good fortune in fields related to oil, perfume, pharmaceuticals, petroleum, dance, footwear,

and alcohol. But beware of overindulgence in alcohol—
focus on a creative outlet instead.

Saturn Puts on the Brakes

Jupiter speeds you up with *lucky breaks,* then along
comes Saturn to slow you down with the *disciplinary
brakes.* Saturn has unfairly been called a malefic planet,
one of the bad guys of the zodiac. On the contrary, Saturn is one of our best friends, the kind who tells you
what you need to hear, even if it's not good news. Under
a Saturn transit, we grow up, take responsibility for our
lives, and emerge from whatever test this planet has in
store, far wiser, more capable, and mature.

When Saturn hits a critical point in your horoscope,
you can count on an experience that will make you slow
up, pull back, and reexamine your life. It is a call to
eliminate what is not working and to shape up. By the
end of its twenty-eight-year trip around the zodiac, Saturn will have tested you in all areas of your life. The
major tests happen in seven-year cycles, when Saturn
passes over the *angles* of your chart—your rising sign,
midheaven, descendant, and nadir. This is when the real
life-changing experiences happen. But you are also in for
a testing period whenever Saturn passes a *planet* in your
chart or stresses that planet from a distance. Therefore,
it is useful to check your planetary positions with the
timetable of Saturn to prepare in advance, or at least to
brace yourself.

When Saturn returns to its location at the time of your
birth, at approximately age twenty-eight, you'll have your
first Saturn return. At this time, a person usually takes
stock or settles down to find his mission in life and assumes full adult duties and responsibilities.

Another way Saturn helps us is to reveal the karmic
lessons from previous lives and gives us the chance to
overcome them. So look at Saturn's challenges as much-
needed opportunities for self-improvement. Under a Jupi-

ter influence, you'll have more fun, but Saturn gives you solid, long-lasting results.

Look up your natal Saturn in the tables in this book for clues on where you need work.

Saturn in Aries

Saturn here puts the brakes on Aries' natural drive and enthusiasm. You don't let anyone push you around and you know what's best for yourself. Following orders is not your strong point, and neither is diplomacy. You tend to be quick to go on the offensive in relationships, attacking first, before anyone attacks you. Because no one quite lives up to your standards, you often wind up doing everything yourself. You'll have to learn to cooperate, tone down self-centeredness.

Saturn in Taurus

A big issue is getting control of the cash flow. There will be lean periods that can be frightening, but you have the patience and endurance to stick them out and the methodical drive to prosper in the end. Learn to take a philosophical attitude like Ben Franklin, who also had this placement and who said, "A penny saved is a penny earned."

Saturn in Gemini

You are a serious student of life who may have difficulty communicating or sharing your knowledge. You may be shy, speak slowly, or have fears about communicating, like Eleanor Roosevelt. You dwell in the realms of science, theory, or abstract analysis, even when you are dealing with the emotions, like Sigmund Freud, who also had this placement.

Saturn in Cancer

Your tests come with establishing a secure emotional base. In doing so, you may have to deal with some very basic fears centering on your early home environment. Most of your Saturn tests will have emotional roots in those early childhood experiences. You may have difficulty remaining objective in terms of what you try to achieve, so it will be especially important for you to deal with negative feelings such as guilt, paranoia, jealousy, resentment, and suspicion. Galileo and Michelangelo also navigated these murky waters.

Saturn in Leo

This is an authoritarian Saturn, a strict, demanding parent who may deny the pleasure principle in your zeal to see that rules are followed. Though you may feel guilty about taking the spotlight, you are very ambitious and loyal. You have to watch a tendency toward rigidity, also toward overwork and holding back affection. Joseph Kennedy and Billy Graham share this placement.

Saturn in Virgo

This is a cautious, exacting Saturn, intensely hard on yourself. Most of all, you give yourself the roughest time with your constant worries about every little detail, often making yourself sick. You may have difficulties setting priorities and getting the job done. Your tests will come in learning tolerance and understanding of others. Charles de Gaulle, Mae West, and Nathaniel Hawthorne had this meticulous Saturn.

Saturn in Libra

Saturn is exalted here, which makes this planet an ally. You may choose very serious, older partners in life, perhaps stemming from a fear of dependency. You need to learn to stand solidly on your own before you commit to another. You are extremely cautious as you deliberate every involvement—with good reason. It is best that you find an occupation that makes good use of your sense of duty and honor. Steer clear of fly-by-night situations.

Both Khrushchev and Mao Tse-tung had this placement, too.

Saturn in Scorpio

You have great staying power. This Saturn tests you in situations involving the control of others. You may feel drawn to some kind of intrigue or undercover work, like J. Edgar Hoover. Or there may be an air of mystery surrounding your life and death, like Marilyn Monroe and Robert Kennedy, who had this placement. There are lessons to be learned from your sexual involvements—often sex is used for manipulation or is somehow out of the ordinary. The Roman emperor Caligula and the transvestite Christine Jorgensen are extreme cases.

Saturn in Sagittarius

Your challenges and lessons will come from tests of your spiritual and philosophical values, as happened to Martin Luther King and Gandhi. You are high-minded and sincere with this reflective, moral placement. Uncompromising in your ethical standards, you could become a benevolent despot.

Saturn in Capricorn

With the help of Saturn at maximum strength, your judgment will improve with age. And, like Spencer Tracy's screen image, you'll be the gray-haired hero with a strong sense of responsibility. You advance in life slowly but steadily, always with a strong hand at the helm and an eye for the advantageous situation. Like Pat Robertson, you're likely to stand for conservative values. Negatively, you may be a loner, prone to periods of melancholy.

Saturn in Aquarius

Your tests come from relationships with groups. Do you care too much about what others think? Do you feel like an outsider, like Greta Garbo? You may fear being different from others and therefore slight your own unique, forward-looking gifts, or, like Lord Byron and Howard Hughes, take the opposite tack and rebel in the extreme. You can apply discipline to accomplish great humanitarian goals, as Albert Schweitzer did.

Saturn in Pisces

Your fear of the unknown and the irrational may lead you to the safety and protection of an institution. You may go on the run like Jesse James, who had this placement, to avoid looking too deeply inside. Or you might go in the opposite, more positive direction and develop a disciplined psychoanalytic approach, which puts you more in control of your feelings. Some of you will take refuge in work with hospitals, charities, or religious institutions. Queen Victoria, who had this placement, symbolized an era when institutions of all kinds were sustained. Discipline applied to artistic work, especially poetry and dance, or spiritual work, such as yoga or meditation, might be helpful.

Uranus, Neptune, and Pluto Affect Your Whole Generation

These three planets remain in signs such a long time that a whole generation bears the imprint of the sign. Mass movements, great sweeping changes, fads that characterize a generation, and even the issues of the conflicts and wars of the time are influenced by the "outer three." When one of these distant planets changes signs, there is a definite shift in the atmosphere, the feeling of the end of an era.

Since these planets are so far away from the sun—too distant to be seen by the naked eye—they pick up signals from the universe at large. These planetary receivers literally link the sun with distant energies, and then perform a similar function in your horoscope by linking your central character with intuitive, spiritual, transformative forces from the cosmos. Each planet has a special domain and will reflect this in the area of your chart where it falls.

Uranus Wakes You Up

There is nothing ordinary about this quirky green planet that seems to be traveling on its side, surrounded by a swarm of moons. Is it any wonder that astrologers assigned it to Aquarius, the most eccentric and gregarious sign? Uranus seems to wend its way around the sun, marching to its own tune.

Uranus energy is electrical, happening in sudden flashes. It is not influenced by karma or past events, nor does it regard tradition, sex, or sentiment. The Uranian key words are surprise and awakening. Uranus wakes you up, jolts you out of your comfortable rut. Suddenly, there's that flash of inspiration, that bright idea, that totally new approach to revolutionize whatever scheme you were undertaking. A Uranus event takes you by surprise, happens from out of the blue, for better or for worse. The Uranus place in your life is where you awaken and become your own person, leaving the structures of Saturn behind. And it is probably the most unconventional place in your chart.

Look up the sign of Uranus at the time of your birth and see where you follow your own tune. If Uranus changed signs on your day of birth, this means you were born on the cusp—a very powerful placement.

Uranus in Aries

BIRTH DATES:
March 31, 1927–November 4, 1927
January 13, 1928–June 6, 1934
October 10, 1934–March 28, 1935
Your generation is original, creative, pioneering. It developed the computer, the airplane, and the cyclotron. You

let nothing hold you back from exploring the unknown and have a powerful mixture of fire and electricity behind you. Women of your generation were among the first to be liberated. You were the unforgettable style setters. You have a surprise in store for everyone. Like Yoko Ono, Grace Kelly, and Jacqueline Onassis, your life may be jolted by sudden and violent changes.

Uranus in Taurus

BIRTH DATES:
June 6, 1934–October 10, 1934
March 28, 1935–August 7, 1941
October 5, 1941–May 15, 1942

World War II began during your generation. You are probably self-employed or would like to be. You have original ideas about making money, and you brace yourself for sudden changes of fortune. This Uranus can cause shake-ups, particularly in finances, but it can also make you a born entrepreneur.

Uranus in Gemini

BIRTH DATES:
August 7, 1941–October 5, 1941
May 15, 1942–August 30, 1948
November 12, 1948–June 10, 1949

You were the first children to be influenced by television, and now in your adult years, your generation stocks up on answering machines, cordless phones, car phones, computers, and fax machines—any new way you can communicate. You have an inquiring mind, but your interests may be rather short-lived. This Uranus can be easily fragmented if there is no structure and focus.

Uranus in Cancer

BIRTH DATES:
August 30, 1948–November 12, 1948
June 10, 1949–August 24, 1955

January 28–June 10, 1956
This generation came at a time when divorce was becoming commonplace, so your home image is unconventional. You may have an unusual relationship with your parents; you may have come from a broken home or an unconventional one. You'll have unorthodox ideas about parenting, intimacy, food, and shelter. You may also be interested in dreams, psychic phenomena, and memory work.

Uranus in Leo

BIRTH DATES:
August 24, 1955–January 28, 1956
June 10, 1956–November 1, 1961
January 10, 1962–August 10, 1962

This generation understood how to use electronic media. Many of your group are now leaders in the high-tech industries, and you also understand how to use the new media to promote yourself. Like Isadora Duncan, you may have a very eccentric kind of charisma and a life that is sparked by unusual love affairs. Your children, too, may have traits that are out of the ordinary. Where this planet falls in your chart, you'll have a love of freedom, be a bit of an egomaniac, and show the full force of your personality in a unique way, like tennis great Martina Navratilova.

Uranus in Virgo

BIRTH DATES:
November 1, 1961–January 10, 1962
August 10, 1962–September 28, 1968
May 20, 1969–June 24, 1969

You'll have highly individual work methods, and many will be finding newer, more practical ways to use computers. Like Einstein, who had this placement, you'll break the rules brilliantly. Your generation came at a time of student rebellions, the civil rights movement, and the general acceptance of health foods. Chances are, you're concerned about pollution and cleaning up the environment. You may also be involved with nontraditional healing methods. Heavyweight champ Mike Tyson has this placement.

Uranus in Libra

BIRTH DATES:
September 28, 1968–May 20, 1969
June 24, 1969–November 21, 1974
May 1, 1975–September 8, 1975

Your generation will always be changing partners. Born during the era of women's liberation, you may have come from a broken home and have no clear image of what a marriage entails. There will be many sudden splits and experiments before you settle down. Your generation will be much involved in legal and political reforms and in changing artistic and fashion looks.

Uranus in Scorpio

BIRTH DATES:
November 21, 1974–May 1, 1975
September 8, 1975–February 17, 1981
March 20, 1981–November 16, 1981

Interest in transformation, meditation, and life after death signaled the beginning of New Age consciousness. Your generation recognizes no boundaries, no limits, and no external controls. You'll have new attitudes toward death and dying, psychic phenomena and the occult. Like Mae West and Casanova, you'll shock 'em sexually, too.

Uranus in Sagittarius

BIRTH DATES:
February 17, 1981–March 20, 1981
November 16, 1981–February 15, 1988
May 27, 1988–December 2, 1988

Could this generation be the first to travel in outer space? The last generation with this placement included Charles Lindbergh—at that time, the first zeppelins and the Wright Brothers were conquering the skies. Uranus here forecasts great discoveries, mind expansion, and long-distance travel. Like Galileo and Martin Luther, those born in these years will generate new theories about the cosmos and man's relation to it.

Uranus in Capricorn

BIRTH DATES:
December 20, 1904–January 30, 1912
September 4, 1912–November 12, 1912
February 15, 1988–May 27, 1988
December 2, 1988–April 1, 1995
June 9, 1995–January 12, 1996

This generation will challenge traditions with the help of electronic gadgets. In these years, we got organized with the help of technology put to practical use. Great leaders, who were movers and shakers of history, like Julius Caesar and Henry VIII, were born under this placement.

Uranus in Aquarius

BIRTH DATES:
January 30, 1912–September 4, 1912
November 12, 1912–April 1, 1919
August 16, 1919–January 22, 1920
April 1, 1995–June 9, 1995
January 12, 1996–March 11, 2003

The last generation with this placement produced great innovative minds such as Leonard Bernstein and Orson Welles. The next will become another radical breakthrough generation, much concerned with global issues that involve all humanity. Intuition, innovation, and sudden changes will surprise everyone when Uranus is in its home sign. This will be a time of experimentation on every level.

Uranus in Pisces

BIRTH DATES:
April 1, 1919–August 16, 1919

January 22, 1920–March 31, 1927
November 4, 1927–January 12, 1928
March 11, 2003–May 28, 2010

In this century, Uranus in Pisces focused attention on the rise of electronic entertainment—radio and the cinema—and the secretiveness of Prohibition. This produced a generation of idealists exemplified by Judy Garland's theme, "Somewhere Over the Rainbow."

Neptune Takes You Out of This World

Under Neptune's influence, you see what you want to see. But Neptune also encourages you to create, lets your fantasies and daydreams run free. Neptune is often maligned as the planet of illusions, drugs and alcohol, where you can't bear to face reality. But it also embodies the energy of glamour, subtlety, mystery, and mysticism, and governs anything that takes you beyond the mundane world, including out-of-body experiences.

Neptune acts to break through your ordinary perceptions and take you to another level of reality, where you experience either confusion or ecstasy. Neptune's force can pull you off course, just as this planet affects it neighbor, Uranus, but only if you allow this to happen. Those who use Neptune wisely can translate their daydreams into poetry, theater, design, or inspired moves in the business world, avoiding the tricky "con artist" side of this planet.

Find your Neptune listed here:

Neptune in Cancer

BIRTH DATES:
July 19, 1901–December 25, 1901
May 21, 1902–September 23, 1914
December 14, 1914–July 19, 1915
March 19, 1916–May 2, 1916

Dreams of the homeland, idealistic patriotism, and glamorization of the nurturing assets of women characterized this time. You who were born here have unusual psychic ability and deep insights into the basic needs of others.

Neptune in Leo

BIRTH DATES:
September 23, 1914–December 14, 1914
July 19, 1915–March 19, 1916
May 2, 1916–September 21, 1928
February 19, 1929–July 24, 1929

Neptune here brought us the glamour and high living of the 1920s and the big spenders of that time. Neptunian temptations of gambling, seduction, theater, and lavish entertaining distracted from the realities of the age. Those born in that generation also made great advances in the arts.

Neptune in Virgo

BIRTH DATES:
September 21, 1928–February 19, 1929
July 24, 1929–October 3, 1942
April 17, 1943–August 2, 1943

Neptune in Virgo encompassed the Great Depression and World War II, while those born at this time later spread the gospel of health and fitness. This generation's devotion to spending hours at the office inspired the term "workaholic."

Neptune in Libra

BIRTH DATES:
October 3, 1942–April 17, 1943
August 2, 1943–December 24, 1955
March 12, 1956–October 19, 1956
June 15, 1957–August 6, 1957

Neptune in Libra was the romantic generation who would later be concerned with relating. As this generation matured, there was a new trend toward marriage and commitment. Racial and sexual equality became important issues, as they redesigned traditional roles to suit modern times.

Neptune in Scorpio

BIRTH DATES:
December 24, 1955–March 12, 1956
October 19, 1956–June 15, 1957
August 6, 1957–January 4, 1970
May 3, 1970–November 6, 1970

Neptune in Scorpio brought in a generation that would become interested in transformative power. Born in an era that glamorized sex, drugs, rock and roll, and Eastern religion, they matured in a more sobering time of AIDS, cocaine abuse, and New Age spirituality. As they evolve, they will become active in healing the planet from the results of the abuse of power.

Neptune in Sagittarius

BIRTH DATES:
January 4, 1970–May 3, 1970
November 6, 1970–January 19, 1984
June 23, 1984–November 21, 1984

Neptune in Sagittarius was the time when space and astronaut travel became a reality. The Neptune influence glamorized new approaches to mysticism, religion, and mind expansion. This generation will take a new approach to spiritual life, with emphasis on visions, mysticism, and clairvoyance.

Neptune in Capricorn

BIRTH DATES:
January 19, 1984–June 23, 1984
November 21, 1984–January 29, 1998

Neptune in Capricorn brought a time when delusions about material power were first glamorized, then dashed on the rocks of reality. It was also a time when the psychic and occult worlds spawned a new category of business enterprise, and sold services on television.

Neptune in Aquarius

BIRTH DATES:
January 29, 1998–April 4, 2111
This should continue to be a time of breakthroughs, when the creative influence of Neptune reaches a universal audience. This is a time of dissolving barriers, of globalization, when we truly become one world.

Pluto Transforms You

Pluto is a mysterious little planet with a strange elliptical orbit that occasionally runs inside the orbit of its neighbor Neptune. Because of its eccentric path, the length of time Pluto stays in any given sign can vary from thirteen to thirty-two years. It has covered only seven signs in the last century. Though it is a tiny planet, its influence is great. When Pluto zaps a strategic point in your horoscope, your life changes dramatically.

This little planet is the power behind the scenes; it affects you at deep levels of consciousness, causing events to come to the surface that will transform you and your generation. Nothing escapes, or is sacred, with this probing planet. The Pluto place in your horoscope is where you have invisible power (Mars governs the visible power), where you can transform, heal, and affect the unconscious needs of the masses. Pluto tells lots about how your generation projects power, what makes it seem "cool" to others. And when Pluto changes signs, there's a whole new concept of what's cool.

Pluto in Gemini

BIRTH DATES:
Late 1800s–May 26, 1914
This was a time of mass suggestion and breakthroughs

in communications, when many brilliant writers, such as Ernest Hemingway and F. Scott Fitzgerald, were born. Henry Miller, D. H. Lawrence, and James Joyce scandalized society by using explicit sexual images and language in their literature. "Muckraking" journalists exposed corruption. Pluto-ruled Scorpio President Theodore Roosevelt said, "Speak softly, but carry a big stick." This generation had an intense need to communicate and made major breakthroughs in knowledge. A compulsive restlessness and a thirst for a variety of experiences characterizes many of this generation.

Pluto in Cancer

BIRTH DATES:
May 26, 1914–June 14, 1939

Dictators and mass media arose to wield emotional power over the masses. Women's rights was a popular issue. Deep sentimental feelings, acquisitiveness, and possessiveness characterized these times and people. Most of the great stars of the Hollywood era that embodied the American image were born during this period: Grace Kelly, Esther Williams, Frank Sinatra, Lana Turner, etc.

Pluto in Leo

BIRTH DATES:
June 14, 1939–August 19, 1957

The performing arts, under Leo's rule, never wielded more power over the masses than during this era. Pluto in Leo transforms via creative self-expression, exemplified by the almost shamanistic rock and roll stars such as Mick Jagger and John Lennon, who were born at this time. (So were Bill and Hillary Clinton.) People born with Pluto in Leo often tend to be self-centered and love to "do their own thing"—for better or for worse.

Pluto in Virgo

BIRTH DATES:
August 19, 1957–October 5, 1971
April 17, 1972–July 30, 1972

This became the "yuppie" generation that sparked a mass clean-up shape-up movement toward fitness, health, and obsessive careerism. It's a much more sober, serious, driven generation than the fun-loving Pluto in Leo. During this time, inventions took on a practical turn, as answering machines, fax machines, car phones, and home office equipment have all transformed the workplace.

Pluto in Libra

BIRTH DATES:
October 5, 1971–April 17, 1972
July 30, 1972–August 28, 1984

A mellower generation, people born at this time are concerned with partnerships, working together, and finding diplomatic solutions to problems. Marriage is important to this generation, who redefine it along more traditional, but equal-partnership lines. This was a time of women's liberation, gay rights, ERA, and legal battles over abortion, all of which transformed our ideas about relationships.

Pluto in Scorpio

BIRTH DATES:
August 28, 1984–January 17, 1995

Pluto was in its ruling sign for a comparatively short period of time. In 1989, it was at its perihelion, or the closest point to the sun and Earth. We have all felt this transforming power somewhere in our lives. This was a time of record achievements, destructive sexually transmitted diseases, nuclear power controversies, and explosive political issues. Pluto destroys in order to create new understanding—think of it as a phoenix rising from the ashes, which should be some consolation for those of you who have felt Pluto's force before 1995. Sexual shockers were par for the course during these intense years, when black clothing, transvestites, body piercing, tattoos, and sexually explicit advertising pushed the boundaries of good taste.

Pluto in Sagittarius

BIRTH DATES:
January 17, 1995–January 27, 2008

During our current Pluto transit through Sagittarius, we are being pushed to expand our horizons and find deeper meaning in life. For many of us, this will mean traveling the globe via our modems as we explore the vastness of the Internet. It signals a time of spiritual transformation and religion will exert much power in politics as well. Since Sagittarius is the sign that rules travel, there's a good possibility that Pluto, the planet of extremes, will make space travel a reality for some of us. Discovery of life on Mars, traveling here as minute life forms on meteors, could transform our ideas about where we came from. At this writing, a giant telescope in Puerto Rico has been reactivated to search the faraway galaxies for pulsing hints of life.

New dimensions in electronic publishing, concern with animal rights and the environment, and an increasing emphasis on extreme forms of religion are signs of Pluto in Sagittarius. Look for charismatic religious leaders to arise now. We'll also be developing far-reaching philosophies designed to elevate our lives with a new sense of purpose.

Look Up Your Planets

The following tables are provided so that you can look up the signs of the other major planets—Venus, Mars,

Saturn, and Jupiter. We do not have room for tables for the moon and Mercury, which change signs often.

How to Use the Venus Table

Find the year of your birth in the vertical column on the left, then follow across the page until you find the correct date. Your Venus sign is at the top of that column.

VENUS SIGNS 1901–2001

	Aries	Taurus	Gemini	Cancer	Leo	Virgo
1901	3/29–4/22	4/22–5/17	5/17–6/10	6/10–7/5	7/5–7/29	7/29–8/23
1902	5/7–6/3	6/3–6/30	6/30–7/25	7/25–8/19	8/19–9/13	9/13–10/7
1903	2/28–3/24	3/24–4/18	4/18–5/13	5/13–6/9	6/9–7/7	7/7–8/17
						9/6–11/8
1904	3/13–5/7	5/7–6/1	6/1–6/25	6/25–7/19	7/19–8/13	8/13–9/6
1905	2/3–3/6	3/6–4/9	7/8–8/6	8/6–9/1	9/1–9/27	9/27–10/21
	4/9–5/28	5/28–7/8				
1906	3/1–4/7	4/7–5/2	5/2–5/26	5/26–6/20	6/20–7/16	7/16–8/11
1907	4/27–5/22	5/22–6/16	6/16–7/11	7/11–8/4	8/4–8/29	8/29–9/22
1908	2/14–3/10	3/10–4/5	4/5–5/5	5/5–9/8	9/8–10/8	10/8–11/3
1909	3/29–4/22	4/22–5/16	5/16–6/10	6/10–7/4	7/4–7/29	7/29–8/23
1910	5/7–6/3	6/4–6/29	6/30–7/24	7/25–8/18	8/19–9/12	9/13–10/6
1911	2/28–3/23	3/24–4/17	4/18–5/12	5/13–6/8	6/9–7/7	7/8–11/8
1912	4/13–5/6	5/7–5/31	6/1–6/24	6/24–7/18	7/19–8/12	8/13–9/5
1913	2/3–3/6	3/7–5/1	7/8–8/5	8/6–8/31	9/1–9/26	9/27–10/20
	5/2–5/30	5/31–7/7				
1914	3/14–4/6	4/7–5/1	5/2–5/25	5/26–6/19	6/20–7/15	7/16–8/10
1915	4/27–5/21	5/22–6/15	6/16–7/10	7/11–8/3	8/4–8/28	8/29–9/21
1916	2/14–3/9	3/10–4/5	4/6–5/5	5/6–9/8	9/9–10/7	10/8–11/2
1917	3/29–4/21	4/22–5/15	5/16–6/9	6/10–7/3	7/4–7/28	7/29–8/21
1918	5/7–6/2	6/3–6/28	6/29–7/24	7/25–8/18	8/19–9/11	9/12–10/5
1919	2/27–3/22	3/23–4/16	4/17–5/12	5/13–6/7	6/8–7/7	7/8–11/8
1920	4/12–5/6	5/7–5/30	5/31–6/23	6/24–7/18	7/19–8/11	8/12–9/4
1921	2/3–3/6	3/7–4/25	7/8–8/5	8/6–8/31	9/1–9/25	9/26–10/20
	4/26–6/1	6/2–7/7				
1922	3/13–4/6	4/7–4/30	5/1–5/25	5/26–6/19	6/20–7/14	7/15–8/9
1923	4/27–5/21	5/22–6/14	6/15–7/9	7/10–8/3	8/4–8/27	8/28–9/20
1924	2/13–3/8	3/9–4/4	4/5–5/5	5/6–9/8	9/9–10/7	10/8–11/12
1925	3/28–4/20	4/21–5/15	5/16–6/8	6/9–7/3	7/4–7/27	7/28–8/21

60

Libra	Scorpio	Sagittarius	Capricorn	Aquarius	Pisces
8/23–9/17	9/17–10/12	10/12–1/16	1/16–2/9 11/7–12/5	2/9–3/5 12/5–1/11	3/5–3/29
10/7–10/31	10/31–11/24	11/24–12/18	12/18–1/11	2/6–4/4	1/11–2/6 4/4–5/7
8/17–9/6 11/8–12/9	12/9–1/5			1/11–2/4	2/4–2/28
9/6–9/30	9/30–10/25	1/5–1/30 10/25–11/18	1/30–2/24 11/18–12/13	2/24–3/19 12/13–1/7	3/19–4/13
10/21–11/14	11/14–12/8	12/8–1/1/06			1/7–2/3
8/11–9/7	9/7–10/9 12/15–12/25	10/9–12/15 12/25–2/6	1/1–1/25	1/25–2/18	2/18–3/14
9/22–10/16	10/16–11/9	11/9–12/3	2/6–3/6 12/3–12/27	3/6–4/2 12/27–1/20	4/2–4/27
11/3–11/28	11/28–12/22	12/22–1/15			1/20–2/4
8/23–9/17	9/17–10/12	10/12–11/17	1/15–2/9 11/17–12/5	2/9–3/5 12/5–1/15	3/5–3/29
10/7–10/30	10/31–11/23	11/24–12/17	12/18–12/31	1/1–1/15 1/29–4/4	1/16–1/28 4/5–5/6
11/19–12/8	12/9–12/31		1/1–1/10	1/11–2/2	2/3–2/27
9/6–9/30	1/1–1/4 10/1–10/24	1/5–1/29 10/25–11/17	1/30–2/23 11/18–12/12	2/24–3/18 12/13–12/31	3/19–4/12
10/21–11/13	11/14–12/7	12/8–12/31		1/1–1/6	1/7–2/2
8/11–9/6	9/7–10/9 12/6–12/30	10/10–12/5 12/31	1/1–1/24	1/25–2/17	2/18–3/13
9/22–10/15	10/16–11/8	1/1–2/6 11/9–12/2	2/7–3/6 12/3–12/26	3/7–4/1 12/27–12/31	4/2–4/26
11/3–11/27	11/28–12/21	12/22–12/31		1/1–1/19	1/20–2/13
8/22–9/16	9/17–10/11	1/1–1/14 10/12–11/6	1/15–2/7 11/7–12/5	2/8–3/4 12/6–12/31	3/5–3/28
10/6–10/29	10/30–11/22	11/23–12/16	12/17–12/31	1/1–4/5	4/6–5/6
11/9–12/8	12/9–12/31		1/1–1/9	1/10–2/2	2/3–2/26
9/5–9/30	1/1–1/3 9/31–10/23	1/4–1/28 10/24–11/17	1/29–2/22 11/18–12/11	2/23–3/18 12/12–12/31	3/19–4/11
10/21–11/13	11/14–12/7	12/8–12/31		1/1–1/6	1/7–2/2
8/10–9/6	9/7–10/10 11/29–12/31	10/11–11/28	1/1–1/24	1/25–2/16	2/17–3/12
9/21–10/14	1/1 10/15–11/7	1/2–2/6 11/8–12/1	2/7–3/5 12/2–12/25	3/6–3/31 12/26–12/31	4/1–4/26
11/13–11/26	11/27–12/21	12/22–12/31		1/1–1/19	1/20–2/12
8/22–9/15	9/16–10/11	1/1–1/14 10/12–11/6	1/15–2/7 11/7–12/5	2/8–3/3 12/6–12/31	3/4–3/27

VENUS SIGNS 1901–2001

	Aries	Taurus	Gemini	Cancer	Leo	Virgo
1926	5/7–6/2	6/3–6/28	6/29–7/23	7/24–8/17	8/18–9/11	9/12–10/5
1927	2/27–3/22	3/23–4/16	4/17–5/11	5/12–6/7	6/8–7/7	7/8–11/9
1928	4/12–5/5	5/6–5/29	5/30–6/23	6/24–7/17	7/18–8/11	8/12–9/4
1929	2/3–3/7 4/20–6/2	3/8–4/19 6/3–7/7	7/8–8/4	8/5–8/30	8/31–9/25	9/26–10/19
1930	3/13–4/5	4/6–4/30	5/1–5/24	5/25–6/18	6/19–7/14	7/15–8/9
1931	4/26–5/20	5/21–6/13	6/14–7/8	7/9–8/2	8/3–8/26	8/27–9/19
1932	2/12–3/8	3/9–4/3	4/4–5/5 7/13–7/27	5/6–7/12 7/28–9/8	9/9–10/6	10/7–11/1
1933	3/27–4/19	4/20–5/28	5/29–6/8	6/9–7/2	7/3–7/26	7/27–8/20
1934	5/6–6/1	6/2–6/27	6/28–7/22	7/23–8/16	8/17–9/10	9/11–10/4
1935	2/26–3/21	3/22–4/15	4/16–5/10	5/11–6/6	6/7–7/6	7/7–11/8
1936	4/11–5/4	5/5–5/28	5/29–6/22	6/23–7/16	7/17–8/10	8/11–9/4
1937	2/2–3/8 4/14–6/3	3/9–4/13 6/4–7/6	7/7–8/3	8/4–8/29	8/30–9/24	9/25–10/18
1938	3/12–4/4	4/5–4/28	4/29–5/23	5/24–6/18	6/19–7/13	7/14–8/8
1939	4/25–5/19	5/20–6/13	6/14–7/8	7/9–8/1	8/2–8/25	8/26–9/19
1940	2/12–3/7	3/8–4/3	4/4–5/5 7/5–7/31	5/6–7/4 8/1–9/8	9/9–10/5	10/6–10/31
1941	3/27–4/19	4/20–5/13	5/14–6/6	6/7–7/1	7/2–7/26	7/27–8/20
1942	5/6–6/1	6/2–6/26	6/27–7/22	7/23–8/16	8/17–9/9	9/10–10/3
1943	2/25–3/20	3/21–4/14	4/15–5/10	5/11–6/6	6/7–7/6	7/7–11/8
1944	4/10–5/3	5/4–5/28	5/29–6/21	6/22–7/16	7/17–8/9	8/10–9/2
1945	2/2–3/10 4/7–6/3	3/11–4/6 6/4–7/6	7/7–8/3	8/4–8/29	8/30–9/23	9/24–10/18
1946	3/11–4/4	4/5–4/28	4/29–5/23	5/24–6/17	6/18–7/12	7/13–8/8
1947	4/25–5/19	5/20–6/12	6/13–7/7	7/8–8/1	8/2–8/25	8/26–9/18
1948	2/11–3/7	3/8–4/3	4/4–5/6 6/29–8/2	5/7–6/28 8/3–9/7	9/8–10/5	10/6–10/31
1949	3/26–4/19	4/20–5/13	5/14–6/6	6/7–6/30	7/1–7/25	7/26–8/19
1950	5/5–5/31	6/1–6/26	6/27–7/21	7/22–8/15	8/16–9/9	9/10–10/3
1951	2/25–3/21	3/22–4/15	4/16–5/10	5/11–6/6	6/7–7/7	7/8–11/9

Libra	Scorpio	Sagittarius	Capricorn	Aquarius	Pisces
10/6–10/29	10/30–11/22	11/23–12/16	12/17–12/31	1/1–4/5	4/6–5/6
11/10–12/8	12/9–12/31	1/1–1/7	1/8	1/9–2/1	2/2–2/26
9/5–9/28	1/1–1/3	1/4–1/28	1/29–2/22	2/23–3/17	3/18–4/11
	9/29–10/23	10/24–11/16	11/17–12/11	12/12–12/31	
10/20–11/12	11/13–12/6	12/7–12/30	12/31	1/1–1/5	1/6–2/2
8/10–9/6	9/7–10/11	10/12–11/21	1/1–1/23	1/24–2/16	2/17–3/12
	11/22–12/31				
9/20–10/13	1/1–1/3	1/4–2/6	2/7–3/4	3/5–3/31	4/1–4/25
	10/14–11/6	11/7–11/30	12/1–12/24	12/25–12/31	
11/2–11/25	11/26–12/20	12/21–12/31		1/1–1/18	1/19–2/11
8/21–9/14	9/15–10/10	1/1–1/13	1/14–2/6	2/7–3/2	3/3–3/26
		10/11–11/5	11/6–12/4	12/5–12/31	
10/5–10/28	10/29–11/21	11/22–12/15	12/16–12/31	1/1–4/5	4/6–5/5
11/9–12/7	12/8–12/31		1/1–1/7	1/8–1/31	2/1–2/25
9/5–9/27	1/1–1/2	1/3–1/27	1/28–2/21	2/22–3/16	3/17–4/10
	9/28–10/22	10/23–11/15	11/16–12/10	12/11–12/31	
10/19–11/11	11/12–12/5	12/6–12/29	12/30–12/31	1/1–1/5	1/6–2/1
8/9–9/6	9/7–10/13	10/14–11/14	1/1–1/22	1/23–2/15	2/16–3/11
	11/15–12/31				
9/20–10/13	1/1–1/3	1/4–2/5	2/6–3/4	3/5–3/30	3/31–4/24
	10/14–11/6	11/7–11/30	12/1–12/24	12/25–12/31	
11/1–11/25	11/26–12/19	12/20–12/31		1/1–1/18	1/19–2/11
8/21–9/14	9/15–10/9	1/1–1/12	1/13–2/5	2/6–3/1	3/2–3/26
		10/10–11/5	11/6–12/4	12/5–12/31	
10/4–10/27	10/28–11/20	11/21–12/14	12/15–12/31	1/1–4/4	4/6–5/5
11/9–12/7	12/8–12/31		1/1–1/7	1/8–1/31	2/1–2/24
9/3–9/27	1/1–1/2	1/3–1/27	1/28–2/20	2/21–3/16	3/17–4/9
	9/28–10/21	10/22–11/15	11/16–12/10	12/11–12/31	
10/19–11/11	11/12–12/5	12/6–12/29	12/30–12/31	1/1–1/4	1/5–2/1
8/9–9/6	9/7–10/15	10/16–11/7	1/1–1/21	1/22–2/14	2/15–3/10
	11/8–12/31				
9/19–10/12	1/1–1/4	1/5–2/5	2/6–3/4	3/5–3/29	3/30–4/24
	10/13–11/5	11/6–11/29	11/30–12/23	12/24–12/31	
11/1–11/25	11/26–12/19	12/20–12/31		1/1–1/17	1/18–2/10
8/20–9/14	9/15–10/9	1/1–1/12	1/13–2/5	2/6–3/1	3/2–3/25
		10/10–11/5	11/6–12/5	12/6–12/31	
10/4–10/27	10/28–11/20	11/21–12/13	12/14–12/31	1/1–4/5	4/6–5/4
11/10–12/7	12/8–12/31		1/1–1/7	1/8–1/31	2/1–2/24

VENUS SIGNS 1901–2001

	Aries	Taurus	Gemini	Cancer	Leo	Virgo
1952	4/10–5/4	5/5–5/28	5/29–6/21	6/22–7/16	7/17–8/9	8/10–9/3
1953	2/2–3/3	3/4–3/31	7/8–8/3	8/4–8/29	8/30–9/24	9/25–10/18
	4/1–6/5	6/6–7/7				
1954	3/12–4/4	4/5–4/28	4/29–5/23	5/24–6/17	6/18–7/13	7/14–8/8
1955	4/25–5/19	5/20–6/13	6/14–7/7	7/8–8/1	8/2–8/25	8/26–9/18
1956	2/12–3/7	3/8–4/4	4/5–5/7	5/8–6/23	9/9–10/5	10/6–10/31
			6/24–8/4	8/5–9/8		
1957	3/26–4/19	4/20–5/13	5/14–6/6	6/7–7/1	7/2–7/26	7/27–8/19
1958	5/6–5/31	6/1–6/26	6/27–7/22	7/23–8/15	8/16–9/9	9/10–10/3
1959	2/25–3/20	3/21–4/14	4/15–5/10	5/11–6/6	6/7–7/8	7/9–9/20
					9/21–9/24	9/25–11/9
1960	4/10–5/3	5/4–5/28	5/29–6/21	6/22–7/15	7/16–8/9	8/10–9/2
1961	2/3–6/5	6/6–7/7	7/8–8/3	8/4–8/29	8/30–9/23	9/24–10/17
1962	3/11–4/3	4/4–4/28	4/29–5/22	5/23–6/17	6/18–7/12	7/13–8/8
1963	4/24–5/18	5/19–6/12	6/13–7/7	7/8–7/31	8/1–8/25	8/26–9/18
1964	2/11–3/7	3/8–4/4	4/5–5/9	5/10–6/17	9/9–10/5	10/6–10/31
			6/18–8/5	8/6–9/8		
1965	3/26–4/18	4/19–5/12	5/13–6/6	6/7–6/30	7/1–7/25	7/26–8/19
1966	5/6–6/31	6/1–6/26	6/27–7/21	7/22–8/15	8/16–9/8	9/9–10/2
1967	2/24–3/20	3/21–4/14	4/15–5/10	5/11–6/6	6/7–7/8	7/9–9/9
					9/10–10/1	10/2–11/9
1968	4/9–5/3	5/4–5/27	5/28–6/20	6/21–7/15	7/16–8/8	8/9–9/2
1969	2/3–6/6	6/7–7/6	7/7–8/3	8/4–8/28	8/29–9/22	9/23–10/17
1970	3/11–4/3	4/4–4/27	4/28–5/22	5/23–6/16	6/17–7/12	7/13–8/8
1971	4/24–5/18	5/19–6/12	6/13–7/6	7/7–7/31	8/1–8/24	8/25–9/17
1972	2/11–3/7	3/8–4/3	4/4–5/10	5/11–6/11		
			6/12–8/6	8/7–9/8	9/9–10/5	10/6–10/30
1973	3/25–4/18	4/18–5/12	5/13–6/5	6/6–6/29	7/1–7/25	7/26–8/19
1974						
	5/5–5/31	6/1–6/25	6/26–7/21	7/22–8/14	8/15–9/8	9/9–10/2
1975	2/24–3/20	3/21–4/13	4/14–5/9	5/10–6/6	6/7–7/9	7/10–9/2
					9/3–10/4	10/5–11/9

Libra	Scorpio	Sagittarius	Capricorn	Aquarius	Pisces
9/4–9/27	1/1–1/2	1/3–1/27	1/28–2/20	2/21–3/16	3/17–4/9
	9/28–10/21	10/22–11/15	11/16–12/10	12/11–12/31	
10/19–11/11	11/12–12/5	12/6–12/29	12/30–12/31	1/1–1/5	1/6–2/1
8/9–9/6	9/7–10/22	10/23–10/27	1/1–1/22	1/23–2/15	2/16–3/11
	10/28–12/31				
9/19–10/13	1/1–1/6	1/7–2/5	2/6–3/4	3/5–3/30	3/31–4/24
	10/14–11/5	11/6–11/30	12/1–12/24	12/25–12/31	
11/1–11/25	11/26–12/19	12/20–12/31		1/1–1/17	1/18–2/11
8/20–9/14	9/15–10/9	1/1–1/12	1/13–2/5	2/6–3/1	3/2–3/25
		10/10–11/5	11/6–12/6	12/7–12/31	
10/4–10/27	10/28–11/20	11/21–12/14	12/15–12/31	1/1–4/6	4/7–5/5
11/10–12/7	12/8–12/31		1/1–1/7	1/8–1/31	2/1–2/24
9/3–9/26	1/1–1/2	1/3–1/27	1/28–2/20	2/21–3/15	3/16–4/9
	9/27–10/21	10/22–11/15	11/16–12/10	12/11–12/31	
10/18–11/11	11/12–12/4	12/5–12/28	12/29–12/31	1/1–1/5	1/6–2/2
8/9–9/6	9/7–12/31		1/1–1/21	1/22–2/14	2/15–3/10
9/19–10/12	1/1–1/6	1/7–2/5	2/6–3/4	3/5–3/29	3/30–4/23
	10/13–11/5	11/6–11/29	11/30–12/23	12/24–12/31	
11/1–11/24	11/25–12/19	12/20–12/31		1/1–1/16	1/17–2/10
8/20–9/13	9/14–10/9	1/1–1/12	1/13–2/5	2/6–3/1	3/2–3/25
		10/10–11/5	11/6–12/7	12/8–12/31	
10/3–10/26	10/27–11/19	11/20–12/13	2/7–2/25	1/1–2/6	4/7–5/5
			12/14–12/31	2/26–4/6	
11/10–12/7	12/8–12/31		1/1–1/6	1/7–1/30	1/31–2/23
9/3–9/26	1/1	1/2–1/26	1/27–2/20	2/21–3/15	3/16–4/8
	9/27–10/21	10/22–11/14	11/15–12/9	12/10–12/31	
10/18–11/10	11/11–12/4	12/5–12/28	12/29–12/31	1/1–1/4	1/5–2/2
8/9–9/7	9/8–12/31		1/1–1/21	1/22–2/14	2/15–3/10
9/18–10/11	1/1–1/7	1/8–2/5	2/6–3/4	3/5–3/29	3/30–4/23
	10/12–11/5	11/6–11/29	11/30–12/23	12/24–12/31	
	11/25–12/18	12/19–12/31		1/1–1/16	1/17–2/10
10/31–11/24					
8/20–9/13	9/14–10/8	1/1–1/12	1/13–2/4	2/5–2/28	3/1–3/24
		10/9–11/5	11/6–12/7	12/8–12/31	
			1/30–2/28	1/1–1/29	
10/3–10/26	10/27–11/19	11/20–12/13	12/14–12/31	3/1–4/6	4/7–5/4
			1/1–1/6	1/7–1/30	1/31–2/23
11/10–12/7	12/8–12/31				

VENUS SIGNS 1901–2001

	Aries	Taurus	Gemini	Cancer	Leo	Virgo
1976	4/8–5/2	5/2–5/27	5/27—6/20	6/20–7/14	7/14–8/8	8/8–9/1
1977	2/2–6/6	6/6–7/6	7/6–8/2	8/2–8/28	8/28–9/22	9/22–10/17
1978	3/9–4/2	4/2–4/27	4/27–5/22	5/22–6/16	6/16–7/12	7/12–8/6
1979	4/23–5/18	5/18–6/11	6/11–7/6	7/6–7/30	7/30–8/24	8/24–9/17
1980	2/9–3/6	3/6–4/3	4/3–5/12	5/12–6/5	9/7–10/4	10/4–10/30
			6/5–8/6	8/6–9/7		
1981	3/24–4/17	4/17–5/11	5/11–6/5	6/5–6/29	6/29–7/24	7/24–8/18
1982	5/4–5/30	5/30–6/25	6/25–7/20	7/20–8/14	8/14–9/7	9/7–10/2
1983	2/22–3/19	3/19–4/13	4/13–5/9	5/9–6/6	6/6–7/10	7/10–8/27
					8/27–10/5	10/5–11/9
1984	4/7–5/2	5/2–5/26	5/26–6/20	6/20–7/14	7/14–8/7	8/7–9/1
1985	2/2–6/6	6/7–7/6	7/6–8/2	8/2–8/28	8/28–9/22	9/22–10/16
1986	3/9–4/2	4/2–4/26	4/26–5/21	5/21–6/15	6/15–7/11	7/11–8/7
1987	4/22–5/17	5/17–6/11	6/11–7/5	7/5–7/30	7/30–8/23	8/23–9/16
1988	2/9–3/6	3/6–4/3	4/3–5/17	5/17–5/27	9/7–10/4	10/4–10/29
			5/27–8/6	8/28–9/22	9/22–10/16	
1989	3/23–4/16	4/16–5/11	5/11–6/4	6/4–6/29	6/29–7/24	7/24–8/18
1990	5/4–5/30	5/30–6/25	6/25–7/20	7/20–8/13	8/13–9/7	9/7–10/1
1991	2/22–3/18	3/18–4/13	4/13–5/9	5/9–6/6	6/6–7/11	7/11–8/21
					8/21–10/6	10/6–11/9
1992	4/7–5/1	5/1–5/26	5/26–6/19	6/19–7/13	7/13–8/7	8/7–8/31
1993	2/2–6/6	6/6–7/6	7/6–8/1	8/1–8/27	8/27–9/21	9/21–10/16
1994	3/8–4/1	4/1–4/26	4/26–5/21	5/21–6/15	6/15–7/11	7/11–8/7
1995	4/22–5/16	5/16–6/10	6/10–7/5	7/5–7/29	7/29–8/23	8/23–9/16
1996	2/9–3/6	3/6–4/3	4/3–8/7	8/7–9/7	9/7–10/4	10/4–10/29
1997	3/23–4/16	4/16–5/10	5/10–6/4	6/4–6/28	6/28–7/23	7/23–8/17
1998	5/3–5/29	5/29–6/24	6/24–7/19	7/19–8/13	8/13–9/6	9/6–9/30
1999	2/21–3/18	3/18–4/12	4/12–5/8	5/8–6/5	6/5–7/12	7/12–8/15
					8/15–10/7	10/7–11/9
2000	4/6–5/1	5/1–5/25	5/25–6/13	6/13–7/13	7/13–8/6	8/6–8/31
2001	2/2–6/6	6/6–7/5	7/5–8/1	8/1–8/26	8/26–9/20	9/20–10/15

Libra	Scorpio	Sagittarius	Capricorn	Aquarius	Pisces
9/1–9/26	9/26–10/20	1/1–1/26	1/26–2/19	2/19–3/15	3/15–4/8
		10/20–11/14	11/14–12/8	12/9–1/4	
10/17–11/10	11/10–12/4	12/4–12/27	12/27–1/20/78		1/4–2/2
8/6–9/7	9/7–1/7			1/20–2/13	2/13–3/9
9/17–10/11	10/11–11/4	1/7–2/5	2/5–3/3	3/3–3/29	3/29–4/23
		11/4–11/28	11/28–12/22	12/22–1/16/80	
10/30–11/24	11/24–12/18	12/18–1/11/81			1/16–2/9
8/18–9/12	9/12–10/9	10/9–11/5	1/11–2/4	2/4–2/28	2/28–3/24
			11/5–12/8	12/8–1/23/82	
10/2–10/26	10/26–11/18	11/18–12/12	1/23–3/2	3/2–4/6	4/6–5/4
			12/12–1/5/83		
11/9–12/6	12/6–1/1/84			1/5–1/29	1/29–2/22
9/1–9/25	9/25–10/20	1/1–1/25	1/25–2/19	2/19–3/14	3/14–4/7
		10/20–11/13	11/13–12/9	12/10–1/4	
10/16–11/9	11/9–12/3	12/3–12/27	12/28–1/19		1/4–2/2
8/7–9/7	9/7–1/7			1/20–2/13	2/13–3/9
9/16–10/10	10/10–11/3	1/7–2/5	2/5–3/3	3/3–3/28	3/28–4/22
		11/3–11/28	11/28–12/22	12/22–1/15	
10/29–11/23	11/23–12/17	12/17–1/10			1/15–2/9
8/18–9/12	9/12–10/8	10/8–11/5	1/10–2/3	2/3–2/27	2/27–3/23
			11/5–12/10	12/10–1/16/90	
10/1–10/25	10/25–11/18	11/18–12/12	1/16–3/3	3/3–4/6	4/6–5/4
			12/12–1/5		
11/9–12/6	12/6–12/31	12/31–1/25/92		1/5–1/29	1/29–2/22
8/31–9/25	9/25–10/19	10/19–11/13	1/25–2/18	2/18–3/13	3/13–4/7
			11/13–12/8	12/8–1/3/93	
10/16–11/9	11/9–12/2	12/2–12/26	12/26–1/19		1/3–2/2
8/7–9/7	9/7–1/7			1/19–2/12	2/12–3/8
9/16–10/10	10/10–11/13	1/7–2/4	2/4–3/2	3/2–3/28	3/28–4/22
		11/3–11/27	11/27–12/21	12/21–1/15	
10/29–11/23	11/23–12/17	12/17–1/10/97			1/15–2/9
8/17–9/12	9/12–10/8	10/8–11/5	1/10–2/3	2/3–2/27	2/27–3/23
			11/5–12/12	12/12–1/9	
9/30–10/24	10/24–11/17	11/17–12/11	1/9–3/4	3/4–4/6	4/6–5/3
11/9–12/5	12/5–12/31	12/31–1/24		1/4–1/28	1/28–2/21
8/31–9/24	9/24–10/19	10/19–11/13	1/24–2/18	2/18–3/12	3/13–4/6
			11/13–12/8	12/8	
10/15–11/8	11/8–12/2	12/2–12/26	12/26/2001–1/19/2002	12/8/2000–1/3/2001	1/3–2/2

How to Use the Mars, Jupiter, and Saturn Tables

Find the year of your birth on the left side of each column. The dates when the planet entered each sign are listed on the right side of each column. (Signs are abbreviated to the first three letters.) Your birthday should fall on or between each date listed, and your planetary placement should correspond to the earlier sign of that period.

MARS SIGN 1901–2001

Year	Month	Day	Sign		Year	Month	Day	Sign
1901	MAR	1	Leo		1905	JAN	13	Scp
	MAY	11	Vir			AUG	21	Sag
	JUL	13	Lib			OCT	8	Cap
	AUG	31	Scp			NOV	18	Aqu
	OCT	14	Sag			DEC	27	Pic
	NOV	24	Cap		1906	FEB	4	Ari
1902	JAN	1	Aqu			MAR	17	Tau
	FEB	8	Pic			APR	28	Gem
	MAR	19	Ari			JUN	11	Can
	APR	27	Tau			JUL	27	Leo
	JUN	7	Gem			SEP	12	Vir
	JUL	20	Can			OCT	30	Lib
	SEP	4	Leo			DEC	17	Scp
	OCT	23	Vir		1907	FEB	5	Sag
	DEC	20	Lib			APR	1	Cap
1903	APR	19	Vir			OCT	13	Aqu
	MAY	30	Lib			NOV	29	Pic
	AUG	6	Scp		1908	JAN	11	Ari
	SEP	22	Sag			FEB	23	Tau
	NOV	3	Cap			APR	7	Gem
	DEC	12	Aqu			MAY	22	Can
1904	JAN	19	Pic			JUL	8	Leo
	FEB	27	Ari			AUG	24	Vir
	APR	6	Tau			OCT	10	Lib
	MAY	18	Gem			NOV	25	Scp
	JUN	30	Can		1909	JAN	10	Sag
	AUG	15	Leo			FEB	24	Cap
	OCT	1	Vir			APR	9	Aqu
	NOV	20	Lib			MAY	25	Pic

	JUL	21	Ari		AUG	19	Can
	SEP	26	Pic		OCT	7	Leo
	NOV	20	Ari	1916	MAY	28	Vir
1910	JAN	23	Tau		JUL	23	Lib
	MAR	14	Gem		SEP	8	Scp
	MAY	1	Can		OCT	22	Sag
	JUN	19	Leo		DEC	1	Cap
	AUG	6	Vir	1917	JAN	9	Aqu
	SEP	22	Lib		FEB	16	Pic
	NOV	6	Scp		MAR	26	Ari
	DEC	20	Sag		MAY	4	Tau
1911	JAN	31	Cap		JUN	14	Gem
	MAR	14	Aqu		JUL	28	Can
	APR	23	Pic		SEP	12	Leo
	JUN	2	Ari		NOV	2	Vir
	JUL	15	Tau	1918	JAN	11	Lib
	SEP	5	Gem		FEB	25	Vir
	NOV	30	Tau		JUN	23	Lib
1912	JAN	30	Gem		AUG	17	Scp
	APR	5	Can		OCT	1	Sag
	MAY	28	Leo		NOV	11	Cap
	JUL	17	Vir		DEC	20	Aqu
	SEP	2	Lib	1919	JAN	27	Pic
	OCT	18	Scp		MAR	6	Ari
	NOV	30	Sag		APR	15	Tau
1913	JAN	10	Cap		MAY	26	Gem
	FEB	19	Aqu		JUL	8	Can
	MAR	30	Pic		AUG	23	Leo
	MAY	8	Ari		OCT	10	Vir
	JUN	17	Tau		NOV	30	Lib
	JUL	29	Gem	1920	JAN	31	Scp
	SEP	15	Can		APR	23	Lib
1914	MAY	1	Leo		JUL	10	Scp
	JUN	26	Vir		SEP	4	Sag
	AUG	14	Lib		OCT	18	Cap
	SEP	29	Scp		NOV	27	Aqu
	NOV	11	Sag	1921	JAN	5	Pic
	DEC	22	Cap		FEB	13	Ari
1915	JAN	30	Aqu		MAR	25	Tau
	MAR	9	Pic		MAY	6	Gem
	APR	16	Ari		JUN	18	Can
	MAY	26	Tau		AUG	3	Leo
	JUL	6	Gem		SEP	19	Vir

	NOV	6	Lib		APR	7	Pic
	DEC	26	Scp		MAY	16	Ari
1922	FEB	18	Sag		JUN	26	Tau
	SEP	13	Cap		AUG	9	Gem
	OCT	30	Aqu		OCT	3	Can
	DEC	11	Pic		DEC	20	Gem
1923	JAN	21	Ari	1929	MAR	10	Can
	MAR	4	Tau		MAY	13	Leo
	APR	16	Gem		JUL	4	Vir
	MAY	30	Can		AUG	21	Lib
	JUL	16	Leo		OCT	6	Scp
	SEP	1	Vir		NOV	18	Sag
	OCT	18	Lib		DEC	29	Cap
	DEC	4	Scp	1930	FEB	6	Aqu
1924	JAN	19	Sag		MAR	17	Pic
	MAR	6	Cap		APR	24	Ari
	APR	24	Aqu		JUN	3	Tau
	JUN	24	Pic		JUL	14	Gem
	AUG	24	Aqu		AUG	28	Can
	OCT	19	Pic		OCT	20	Leo
	DEC	19	Ari	1931	FEB	16	Can
1925	FEB	5	Tau		MAR	30	Leo
	MAR	24	Gem		JUN	10	Vir
	MAY	9	Can		AUG	1	Lib
	JUN	26	Leo		SEP	17	Scp
	AUG	12	Vir		OCT	30	Sag
	SEP	28	Lib		DEC	10	Cap
	NOV	13	Scp	1932	JAN	18	Aqu
	DEC	28	Sag		FEB	25	Pic
1926	FEB	9	Cap		APR	3	Ari
	MAR	23	Aqu		MAY	12	Tau
	MAY	3	Pic		JUN	22	Gem
	JUN	15	Ari		AUG	4	Can
	AUG	1	Tau		SEP	20	Leo
1927	FEB	22	Gem		NOV	13	Vir
	APR	17	Can	1933	JUL	6	Lib
	JUN	6	Leo		AUG	26	Scp
	JUL	25	Vir		OCT	9	Sag
	SEP	10	Lib		NOV	19	Cap
	OCT	26	Scp		DEC	28	Aqu
	DEC	8	Sag	1934	FEB	4	Pic
1928	JAN	19	Cap		MAR	14	Ari
	FEB	28	Aqu		APR	22	Tau

	JUN	2	Gem		AUG	19	Vir
	JUL	15	Can		OCT	5	Lib
	AUG	30	Leo		NOV	20	Scp
	OCT	18	Vir	1941	JAN	4	Sag
	DEC	11	Lib		FEB	17	Cap
1935	JUL	29	Scp		APR	2	Aqu
	SEP	16	Sag		MAY	16	Pic
	OCT	28	Cap		JUL	2	Ari
	DEC	7	Aqu	1942	JAN	11	Tau
1936	JAN	14	Pic		MAR	7	Gem
	FEB	22	Ari		APR	26	Can
	APR	1	Tau		JUN	14	Leo
	MAY	13	Gem		AUG	1	Vir
	JUN	25	Can		SEP	17	Lib
	AUG	10	Leo		NOV	1	Scp
	SEP	26	Vir		DEC	15	Sag
	NOV	14	Lib	1943	JAN	26	Cap
1937	JAN	5	Scp		MAR	8	Aqu
	MAR	13	Sag		APR	17	Pic
	MAY	14	Scp		MAY	27	Ari
	AUG	8	Sag		JUL	7	Tau
	SEP	30	Cap		AUG	23	Gem
	NOV	11	Aqu	1944	MAR	28	Can
	DEC	21	Pic		MAY	22	Leo
1938	JAN	30	Ari		JUL	12	Vir
	MAR	12	Tau		AUG	29	Lib
	APR	23	Gem		OCT	13	Scp
	JUN	7	Can		NOV	25	Sag
	JUL	22	Leo	1945	JAN	5	Cap
	SEP	7	Vir		FEB	14	Aqu
	OCT	25	Lib		MAR	25	Pic
	DEC	11	Scp		MAY	2	Ari
1939	JAN	29	Sag		JUN	11	Tau
	MAR	21	Cap		JUL	23	Gem
	MAY	25	Aqu		SEP	7	Can
	JUL	21	Cap		NOV	11	Leo
	SEP	24	Aqu		DEC	26	Can
	NOV	19	Pic	1946	APR	22	Leo
1940	JAN	4	Ari		JUN	20	Vir
	FEB	17	Tau		AUG	9	Lib
	APR	1	Gem		SEP	24	Scp
	MAY	17	Can		NOV	6	Sag
	JUL	3	Leo		DEC	17	Cap

1947	JAN	25	Aqu		MAR	20	Tau
	MAR	4	Pic		MAY	1	Gem
	APR	11	Ari		JUN	14	Can
	MAY	21	Tau		JUL	29	Leo
	JUL	1	Gem		SEP	14	Vir
	AUG	13	Can		NOV	1	Lib
	OCT	1	Leo		DEC	20	Scp
	DEC	1	Vir	1954	FEB	9	Sag
1948	FEB	12	Leo		APR	12	Cap
	MAY	18	Vir		JUL	3	Sag
	JUL	17	Lib		AUG	24	Cap
	SEP	3	Scp		OCT	21	Aqu
	OCT	17	Sag		DEC	4	Pic
	NOV	26	Cap	1955	JAN	15	Ari
1949	JAN	4	Aqu		FEB	26	Tau
	FEB	11	Pic		APR	10	Gem
	MAR	21	Ari		MAY	26	Can
	APR	30	Tau		JUL	11	Leo
	JUN	10	Gem		AUG	27	Vir
	JUL	23	Can		OCT	13	Lib
	SEP	7	Leo		NOV	29	Scp
	OCT	27	Vir	1956	JAN	14	Sag
	DEC	26	Lib		FEB	28	Cap
1950	MAR	28	Vir		APR	14	Aqu
	JUN	11	Lib		JUN	3	Pic
	AUG	10	Scp		DEC	6	Ari
	SEP	25	Sag	1957	JAN	28	Tau
	NOV	6	Cap		MAR	17	Gem
	DEC	15	Aqu		MAY	4	Can
1951	JAN	22	Pic		JUN	21	Leo
	MAR	1	Ari		AUG	8	Vir
	APR	10	Tau		SEP	24	Lib
	MAY	21	Gem		NOV	8	Scp
	JUL	3	Can		DEC	23	Sag
	AUG	18	Leo	1958	FEB	3	Cap
	OCT	5	Vir		MAR	17	Aqu
	NOV	24	Lib		APR	27	Pic
1952	JAN	20	Scp		JUN	7	Ari
	AUG	27	Sag		JUL	21	Tau
	OCT	12	Cap		SEP	21	Gem
	NOV	21	Aqu		OCT	29	Tau
	DEC	30	Pic	1959	FEB	10	Gem
1953	FEB	8	Ari		APR	10	Can

	JUN	1	Leo		NOV	14	Cap
	JUL	20	Vir		DEC	23	Aqu
	SEP	5	Lib	1966	JAN	30	Pic
	OCT	21	Scp		MAR	9	Ari
	DEC	3	Sag		APR	17	Tau
1960	JAN	14	Cap		MAY	28	Gem
	FEB	23	Aqu		JUL	11	Can
	APR	2	Pic		AUG	25	Leo
	MAY	11	Ari		OCT	12	Vir
	JUN	20	Tau		DEC	4	Lib
	AUG	2	Gem	1967	FEB	12	Scp
	SEP	21	Can		MAR	31	Lib
1961	FEB	5	Gem		JUL	19	Scp
	FEB	7	Can		SEP	10	Sag
	MAY	6	Leo		OCT	23	Cap
	JUN	28	Vir		DEC	1	Aqu
	AUG	17	Lib	1968	JAN	9	Pic
	OCT	1	Scp		FEB	17	Ari
	NOV	13	Sag		MAR	27	Tau
	DEC	24	Cap		MAY	8	Gem
1962	FEB	1	Aqu		JUN	21	Can
	MAR	12	Pic		AUG	5	Leo
	APR	19	Ari		SEP	21	Vir
	MAY	28	Tau		NOV	9	Lib
	JUL	9	Gem		DEC	29	Scp
	AUG	22	Can	1969	FEB	25	Sag
	OCT	11	Leo		SEP	21	Cap
1963	JUN	3	Vir		NOV	4	Aqu
	JUL	27	Lib		DEC	15	Pic
	SEP	12	Scp	1970	JAN	24	Ari
	OCT	25	Sag		MAR	7	Tau
	DEC	5	Cap		APR	18	Gem
1964	JAN	13	Aqu		JUN	2	Can
	FEB	20	Pic		JUL	18	Leo
	MAR	29	Ari		SEP	3	Vir
	MAY	7	Tau		OCT	20	Lib
	JUN	17	Gem		DEC	6	Scp
	JUL	30	Can	1971	JAN	23	Sag
	SEP	15	Leo		MAR	12	Cap
	NOV	6	Vir		MAY	3	Aqu
1965	JUN	29	Lib		NOV	6	Pic
	AUG	20	Scp		DEC	26	Ari
	OCT	4	Sag	1972	FEB	10	Tau

Year	Month	Day	Sign	Year	Month	Day	Sign
	MAR	27	Gem	1978	JAN	26	Can
	MAY	12	Can		APR	10	Leo
	JUN	28	Leo		JUN	14	Vir
	AUG	15	Vir		AUG	4	Lib
	SEP	30	Lib		SEP	19	Scp
	NOV	15	Scp		NOV	2	Sag
	DEC	30	Sag		DEC	12	Cap
1973	FEB	12	Cap	1979	JAN	20	Aqu
	MAR	26	Aqu		FEB	27	Pic
	MAY	8	Pic		APR	7	Ari
	JUN	20	Ari		MAY	16	Tau
	AUG	12	Tau		JUN	26	Gem
	OCT	29	Ari		AUG	8	Can
	DEC	24	Tau		SEP	24	Leo
1974	FEB	27	Gem		NOV	19	Vir
	APR	20	Can	1980	MAR	11	Leo
	JUN	9	Leo		MAY	4	Vir
	JUL	27	Vir		JUL	10	Lib
	SEP	12	Lib		AUG	29	Scp
	OCT	28	Scp		OCT	12	Sag
	DEC	10	Sag		NOV	22	Cap
1975	JAN	21	Cap		DEC	30	Aqu
	MAR	3	Aqu	1981	FEB	6	Pic
	APR	11	Pic		MAR	17	Ari
	MAY	21	Ari		APR	25	Tau
	JUL	1	Tau		JUN	5	Gem
	AUG	14	Gem		JUL	18	Can
	OCT	17	Can		SEP	2	Leo
	NOV	25	Gem		OCT	21	Vir
1976	MAR	18	Can		DEC	16	Lib
	MAY	16	Leo	1982	AUG	3	Scp
	JUL	6	Vir		SEP	20	Sag
	AUG	24	Lib		OCT	31	Cap
	OCT	8	Scp		DEC	10	Aqu
	NOV	20	Sag	1983	JAN	17	Pic
1977	JAN	1	Cap		FEB	25	Ari
	FEB	9	Aqu		APR	5	Tau
	MAR	20	Pic		MAY	16	Gem
	APR	27	Ari		JUN	29	Can
	JUN	6	Tau		AUG	13	Leo
	JUL	17	Gem		SEP	30	Vir
	SEP	1	Can		NOV	18	Lib
	OCT	26	Leo	1984	JAN	11	Scp

	AUG	17	Sag		JUL	12	Tau
	OCT	5	Cap		AUG	31	Gem
	NOV	15	Aqu		DEC	14	Tau
	DEC	25	Pic	1991	JAN	21	Gem
1985	FEB	2	Ari		APR	3	Can
	MAR	15	Tau		MAY	26	Leo
	APR	26	Gem		JUL	15	Vir
	JUN	9	Can		SEP	1	Lib
	JUL	25	Leo		OCT	16	Scp
	SEP	10	Vir		NOV	29	Sag
	OCT	27	Lib	1992	JAN	9	Cap
	DEC	14	Scp		FEB	18	Aqu
1986	FEB	2	Sag		MAR	28	Pic
	MAR	28	Cap		MAY	5	Ari
	OCT	9	Aqu		JUN	14	Tau
	NOV	26	Pic		JUL	26	Gem
1987	JAN	8	Ari		SEP	12	Can
	FEB	20	Tau	1993	APR	27	Leo
	APR	5	Gem		JUN	23	Vir
	MAY	21	Can		AUG	12	Lib
	JUL	6	Leo		SEP	27	Scp
	AUG	22	Vir		NOV	9	Sag
	OCT	8	Lib		DEC	20	Cap
	NOV	24	Scp	1994	JAN	28	Aqu
1988	JAN	8	Sag		MAR	7	Pic
	FEB	22	Cap		APR	14	Ari
	APR	6	Aqu		MAY	23	Tau
	MAY	22	Pic		JUL	3	Gem
	JUL	13	Ari		AUG	16	Can
	OCT	23	Pic		OCT	4	Leo
	NOV	1	Ari		DEC	12	Vir
1989	JAN	19	Tau	1995	JAN	22	Leo
	MAR	11	Gem		MAY	25	Vir
	APR	29	Can		JUL	21	Lib
	JUN	16	Leo		SEP	7	Scp
	AUG	3	Vir		OCT	20	Sag
	SEP	19	Lib		NOV	30	Cap
	NOV	4	Scp	1996	JAN	8	Aqu
	DEC	18	Sag		FEB	15	Pic
1990	JAN	29	Cap		MAR	24	Ari
	MAR	11	Aqu		MAY	2	Tau
	APR	20	Pic		JUN	12	Gem
	MAY	31	Ari		JUL	25	Can

	SEP	9	Leo		MAY	5	Lib
	OCT	30	Vir		JUL	5	Scp
1997	JAN	3	Lib		SEP	2	Sag
	MAR	8	Vir		OCT	17	Cap
	JUN	19	Lib		NOV	26	Aqu
	AUG	14	Scp	2000	JAN	4	Pic
	SEP	28	Sag		FEB	12	Ari
	NOV	9	Cap		MAR	23	Tau
	DEC	18	Aqu		MAY	3	Gem
1998	JAN	25	Pic		JUN	16	Can
	MAR	4	Ari		AUG	1	Leo
	APR	13	Tau		SEP	17	Vir
	MAY	24	Gem		NOV	4	Lib
	JUL	6	Can		DEC	23	Scp
	AUG	20	Leo	2001	FEB	14	Sag
	OCT	7	Vir		SEP	8	Cap
	NOV	27	Lib		OCT	27	Aqu
1999	JAN	26	Scp		DEC	8	Pic

JUPITER SIGN 1901–2001

1901	JAN	19	Cap	1916	FEB	12	Ari
1902	FEB	6	Aqu		JUN	26	Tau
1903	FEB	20	Pic		OCT	26	Ari
1904	MAR	1	Ari	1917	FEB	12	Tau
	AUG	8	Tau		JUN	29	Gem
	AUG	31	Ari	1918	JUL	13	Can
1905	MAR	7	Tau	1919	AUG	2	Leo
	JUL	21	Gem	1920	AUG	27	Vir
	DEC	4	Tau	1921	SEP	25	Lib
1906	MAR	9	Gem	1922	OCT	26	Scp
	JUL	30	Can	1923	NOV	24	Sag
1907	AUG	18	Leo	1924	DEC	18	Cap
1908	SEP	12	Vir	1926	JAN	6	Aqu
1909	OCT	11	Lib	1927	JAN	18	Pic
1910	NOV	11	Scp		JUN	6	Ari
1911	DEC	10	Sag		SEP	11	Pic
1913	JAN	2	Cap	1928	JAN	23	Ari
1914	JAN	21	Aqu		JUN	4	Tau
1915	FEB	4	Pic	1929	JUN	12	Gem

1930	JUN	26	Can				
1931	JUL	17	Leo		MAR	20	Lib
1932	AUG	11	Vir		SEP	7	Scp
1933	SEP	10	Lib	1959	FEB	10	Sag
1934	OCT	11	Scp		APR	24	Scp
1935	NOV	9	Sag		OCT	5	Sag
1936	DEC	2	Cap	1960	MAR	1	Cap
1937	DEC	20	Aqu		JUN	10	Sag
1938	MAY	14	Pic		OCT	26	Cap
	JUL	30	Aqu	1961	MAR	15	Aqu
	DEC	29	Pic		AUG	12	Cap
1939	MAY	11	Ari		NOV	4	Aqu
	OCT	30	Pic	1962	MAR	25	Pic
	DEC	20	Ari	1963	APR	4	Ari
1940	MAY	16	Tau	1964	APR	12	Tau
1941	MAY	26	Gem	1965	APR	22	Gem
1942	JUN	10	Can		SEP	21	Can
1943	JUN	30	Leo		NOV	17	Gem
1944	JUL	26	Vir	1966	MAY	5	Can
1945	AUG	25	Lib		SEP	27	Leo
1946	SEP	25	Scp	1967	JAN	16	Can
1947	OCT	24	Sag		MAY	23	Leo
1948	NOV	15	Cap		OCT	19	Vir
1949	APR	12	Aqu	1968	FEB	27	Leo
	JUN	27	Cap		JUN	15	Vir
	NOV	30	Aqu		NOV	15	Lib
1950	APR	15	Pic	1969	MAR	30	Vir
	SEP	15	Aqu		JUL	15	Lib
	DEC	1	Pic		DEC	16	Scp
1951	APR	21	Ari	1970	APR	30	Lib
1952	APR	28	Tau		AUG	15	Scp
1953	MAY	9	Gem	1971	JAN	14	Sag
1954	MAY	24	Can		JUN	5	Sc
1955	JUN	13	Leo		SEP	11	Sag
	NOV	17	Vir	1972	FEB	6	Cap
1956	JAN	18	Leo		JUL	24	Sag
	JUL	7	Vir		SEP	25	Cap
	DEC	13	Lib	1973	FEB	23	Aqu
1957	FEB	19	Vir	1974	MAR	8	Pic
	AUG	7	Lib	1975	MAR	18	Ari
1958	JAN	13	Scp	1976	MAR	26	Tau
					AUG	23	Gem

	OCT	16	Tau
1977	APR	3	Gem
	AUG	20	Can
	DEC	30	Gem
1978	APR	12	Can
	SEP	5	Leo
1979	FEB	28	Can
	APR	20	Leo
	SEP	29	Vir
1980	OCT	27	Lib
1981	NOV	27	Scp
1982	DEC	26	Sag
1984	JAN	19	Cap
1985	FEB	6	Aqu
1986	FEB	20	Pic
1987	MAR	2	Ari
1988	MAR	8	Tau
	JUL	22	Gem
	NOV	30	Tau
1989	MAR	11	Gem
	JUL	30	Can
1990	AUG	18	Leo
1991	SEP	12	Vir
1992	OCT	10	Lib
1993	NOV	10	Scp
1994	DEC	9	Sag
1996	JAN	3	Cap
1997	JAN	21	Aqu
1998	FEB	4	Pic
1999	FEB	13	Ari
	JUN	28	Tau
	OCT	23	Ari
2000	FEB	14	Tau
	JUN	30	Gem
2001	JUL	14	Can

SATURN SIGN 1903–2001

1903	JAN	19	Aqu
1905	APR	13	Pic
	AUG	17	Aqu
1906	JAN	8	Pic
1908	MAR	19	Ari
1910	MAY	17	Tau
	DEC	14	Ari
1911	JAN	20	Tau
1912	JUL	7	Gem
	NOV	30	Tau
1913	MAR	26	Gem
1914	AUG	24	Can
	DEC	7	Gem
1915	MAY	11	Can
1916	OCT	17	Leo
	DEC	7	Can
1917	JUN	24	Leo
1919	AUG	12	Vir
1921	OCT	7	Lib
1923	DEC	20	Scp
1924	APR	6	Lib
	SEP	13	Scp
1926	DEC	2	Sag
1929	MAR	15	Cap
	MAY	5	Sag
	NOV	30	Cap
1932	FEB	24	Aqu
	AUG	13	Cap
	NOV	20	Aqu
1935	FEB	14	Pic
1937	APR	25	Ari
	OCT	18	Pic
1938	JAN	14	Ari
1939	JUL	6	Tau
	SEP	22	Ari
1940	MAR	20	Tau
1942	MAY	8	Gem
1944	JUN	20	Can
1946	AUG	2	Leo
1948	SEP	19	Vir

1949	APR	3	Leo		JUN	5	Leo
	MAY	29	Vir	1977	NOV	17	Vir
1950	NOV	20	Lib	1978	JAN	5	Leo
1951	MAR	7	Vir		JUL	26	Vir
	AUG	13	Lib	1980	SEP	21	Lib
1953	OCT	22	Scp	1982	NOV	29	Scp
1956	JAN	12	Sag	1983	MAY	6	Lib
	MAY	14	Scp		AUG	24	Scp
	OCT	10	Sag	1985	NOV	17	Sag
1959	JAN	5	Cap	1988	FEB	13	Cap
1962	JAN	3	Aqu		JUN	10	Sag
1964	MAR	24	Pic		NOV	12	Cap
	SEP	16	Aqu	1991	FEB	6	Aqu
	DEC	16	Pic	1993	MAY	21	Pic
1967	MAR	3	Ari		JUN	30	Aqu
1969	APR	29	Tau	1994	JAN	28	Pic
1971	JUN	18	Gem	1996	APR	7	Ari
1972	JAN	10	Tau	1998	JUN	9	Tau
	FEB	21	Gem		OCT	25	Ari
1973	AUG	1	Can	1999	MAR	1	Tau
1974	JAN	7	Gem	2000	AUG	10	Gem
	APR	18	Can		OCT	16	Tau
1975	SEP	17	Leo	2001	APR	21	Gem
1976	JAN	14	Can				

CHAPTER 4

The Astro-Visuals: What Those Mysterious Glyphs on Your Chart Mean

When you first try to decipher your horoscope chart, you may recognize the tiny moon and the symbol for your sign. Perhaps you'll also recognize Mars and Venus, since they are often used as male and female gender symbols outside of astrology. But the other marks could look as strange as Japanese to the uninitiated. Those little characters, called glyphs (or sigils), were created centuries ago so that any astrologer from Russia to Argentina could read your chart and know what it means. Since there are only twenty-two major glyphs, for the twelve signs and ten planets (not counting a few asteroids and other space creatures some astrologers use), it's a lot easier than learning to read Japanese!

There are several good reasons why you should learn the glyphs. First, they're interesting. The glyphs are much more than little drawings. They are magical codes that contain within them keys to the meanings of the planets. Cracking their codes teaches you immediately, in a visual way, much about the deeper meaning of a planet or sign.

Another good reason: if you ever get your horoscope chart done, either by an astrologer or by a computer, the chart will be written in glyphs! Though some charts have a list of the planets in plain English on the main page, others do not, leaving you mystified. You might pick out the symbol for the sun and the trident of Neptune. But then there's Jupiter, which looks something like the number 4, and Mercury, which looks like Venus wearing a hat.

Here's a code-cracker for the glyphs, beginning with the glyphs for the planets. To those who already *know* their glyphs, don't just skim over the chapter! There are hidden meanings to discover, so test your glyph-ese.

Think you know it all? Take the test at the end of the chapter to find out.

The Glyphs for the Planets

Almost all the glyphs of the planets are combinations of the most basic forms: the circle, the half circle or arc, and the cross. Artists and glyph designers have stylized these forms over the years, but the basic concept is always visible. Each component of the glyph has a special meaning in relation to the others, which combines to create the meaning of the completed symbol.

For instance, the circle, which has no beginning or end, is one of the oldest symbols of spirit or spiritual forces. The early diagrams of the heavens are shown in circular form. The semicircle or arc symbolizes the receptive, finite soul, which contains spiritual potential in the curving line. The vertical line symbolizes movement from heaven to Earth. The horizontal line describes temporal movement, here and now, within the confines of time and space. Superimposed together, the vertical and horizontal planes symbolize manifestation in the material world.

The Sun Glyph ☉

The sun is always shown by this powerful solar symbol, a circle with a point in the center. It is you, your spiritual center, your infinite personality incarnating the point into the finite cycles of birth and death.

This symbol was brought into common use in the sixteenth century, after a German occultist and scholar, Cornelius Agrippa (1486–1535), wrote a book called *Die Occulta Philosophia*, which became accepted as the standard work in its field. Agrippa collected many medieval astrological and magical symbols in this book, which were used by astrologers thereafter, copied from those found in Agrippa's book.

The Moon Glyph ☽

This is surely the easiest symbol to spot on a chart. The moon glyph is a left-facing arc stylized into the crescent moon, which perfectly captures the reactive, receptive, emotional nature of the moon. As part of a circle, the arc symbolizes the potential fulfillment of the entire circle. It is the life force that is still incomplete.

The Mercury Glyph ☿

This is the "Venus with a hat" glyph. With another stretch of the imagination, can't you see the winged cap of Mercury the messenger? The upturned crescent could be antennae that tune in and transmit messages from the sun, signifying that Mercury is the way you communicate, the way your mind works. The upturned arc is receiving energy into the spirit or solar circle, which will later be translated into action on the material plane, symbolized by the cross. All the elements are equally sized because Mercury is neutral . . . it doesn't play favorites! This planet symbolizes objective, detached, unemotional thinking.

The Venus Glyph ♀

Here the relationship is between two elements—the circle or spirit above the cross of matter. Spirit is elevated over matter, pulling it upward. Venus asks, "What is beautiful? What do you like best, what do you love to have done to you?" Venus determines both your ideal of beauty and what feels good sensually. It governs your own allure and power to attract, as well as what attracts and pleases you.

The Mars Glyph ♂

In this glyph, the cross of matter is stylized into an arrow-head pointed up and outward, propelled by the circle of spirit. You can deduce that Mars embodies your spiritual energy projected into the outer world. It's your assert-iveness, your initiative, your aggressive drive, what you like to do to others, your temper. If you know someone's Mars, you know whether they'll blow up when angry or do a slow burn. Your task is to use your outgoing Mars energy wisely and well.

The Jupiter Glyph ♃

Jupiter is the basic cross of matter, with a large stylized crescent perched on the left side of the horizontal, tem-poral plane. You might think of the crescent as an open hand—one meaning of Jupiter is "luck," what's handed to you. You don't work for what you get from Jupiter—it comes to you, if you're open to it.

The Jupiter glyph might also remind you of a jumbo jet plane with a huge tail fin, about to take off. This is the planet of travel, mental and spiritual, of expanding your horizons via new ideas, new spiritual dimensions, and new places. Jupiter embodies the optimism and en-thusiasm of the traveler about to embark on an excit-ing adventure.

The Saturn Glyph ♄

Flip Jupiter over and you've got Saturn. (This might not be immediately apparent, because Saturn is usually styl-ized in an "h" form like the one shown here.) But the principle it expresses is the opposite of Jupiter's expan-sive tendencies. Saturn pulls you back to Earth—the re-ceptive arc is pushed down underneath the cross of matter. Before there are any rewards or expansion, the duties and obligations of the material world must be con-sidered. Saturn says, "Stop, wait, finish your chores be-fore you take off!"

Saturn's glyph also resembles the sickle of old Father Time. Saturn was first known as Chronos, the Greek god of time, for time brings all matter to an end. When it was thought to be the most distant planet (before the discovery of Uranus), Saturn was believed to be the place that time stopped. After the soul, having departed from Earth, journeyed back to the outer reaches of the universe, it finally stopped at Saturn, or at "the end of time."

The Uranus Glyph ♅

The glyph for Uranus is often stylized to form a capital "H" after Sir William Herschel, the name of the planet's discoverer. But the more esoteric version curves the two pillars of the H into crescent antennae, or "ears," or like satellite discs receiving signals from space. These are perched on the horizontal material line of the cross (matter) and pushed from below by the circle of the spirit. To many sci-fi fans, Uranus looks like an orbiting satellite.

Uranus channels the highest energy of all, the white electrical light of the universal spiritual sun, the force that holds the cosmos together. This pure electrical energy is gathered from all over the universe. Because it doesn't follow an ordinary celestial drumbeat, it can't be controlled or predicted, which is also true of those who are strongly influenced by this eccentric planet. In the symbol, this energy is manifested through the balance of polarities (the two opposite arms of the glyph) like the two polarized wires of a lightbulb.

The Neptune Glyph ♆

Neptune's glyph is usually stylized to look like a trident, the weapon of the Roman god Neptune. However, on a more esoteric level, it shows the large upturned crescent of the soul pierced through by the cross of matter. Neptune nails down, or materializes, soul energy, bringing impulses from the soul level into manifestation. That is why Neptune is associated with imagination or "imagining in," making an image of the soul. Neptune works through feeling, sensitivity, and mystical capacity to bring the divine into the earthly realm.

The Pluto Glyph ♀

Pluto is written two ways. One is a composite of the letters PL, the first two letters of the word Pluto and coincidentally the initials of Percival Lowell, one of the planet's discoverers. The other, more esoteric symbol is a small circle, above a large open crescent that surmounts the cross of matter. This depicts Pluto's power to regenerate—you might imagine from this glyph a new little spirit emerging from the sheltering cup of the soul. Pluto rules the forces of life and death—after a Pluto experience, you are transformed, reborn in some way.

Sci-fi fans might visualize this glyph as a small satellite (the circle) being launched. It was shortly after Pluto's discovery that we learned how to harness the nuclear forces that made space exploration possible. Pluto rules the transformative power of atomic energy, which totally changed our lives and from which there was no turning back.

The Glyphs for the Signs

On an astrological chart, the glyph for the sign will appear after that of the planet. When you see the moon glyph followed by a number and the glyph for the sign, this means that the moon was passing over a certain degree of an astrological sign at the time of the chart. On the dividing points between the segments or "houses" on your chart, you'll find the symbol for the sign that rules the house.

Since sun sign symbols do not always bring together the same basic components of the planetary glyphs, where do their meanings come from? Many have been passed down from ancient Egyptian and Chaldean civilizations with few modifications. Others have been adapted over the centuries. In deciphering many of the glyphs, you'll often find that many symbols reveal a dual nature of the sign, which is not always apparent in sun sign descriptions. For instance, the Gemini glyph is similar to the Roman numeral for two, and reveals this sign's longing to discover a twin soul. The Cancer glyph may be interpreted as either resembling nurturing breasts or the self-protective claws of the crab. Libra's glyph embodies the duality of the spirit balanced with material reality. The Sagittarius glyph shows that the aspirant must also carry along the earthly animal nature in his quest. The Capricorn sea goat is another symbol with dual emphasis. The goat climbs high yet is always pulled back by the deep waters of the unconscious. Aquarius embodies the double waves of mental detachment, balanced by the desire for connection with others in a friendly way. And finally, the two fishes of Pisces, which are forever tied together, show the duality of the soul and the spirit that must be reconciled.

The Aries Glyph ♈

Since the symbol for Aries is the ram, this glyph's most obvious association is with a ram's horns, which characterize one aspect of the Aries personality—an aggressive, me-first, leaping-headfirst attitude. But the symbol may have other meanings for you, too. Some astrologers liken it to a fountain of energy, which Aries people also embody. The first sign of the zodiac bursts on the scene eagerly, ready to go. Another analogy is to the eyebrows and nose of the human head, which Aries rules, and the thinking power that is initiated in the brain. Another interesting theory is that the symbol represents spirit descending from a higher realm into the mind of man, which would be the point of the V shape in the Aries glyph, corresponding to the center of the eyebrows, the place of the "third eye," which the Hindus mark with a red bindi dot.

The origin of this symbol links it to the Egyptian god Amun, represented by a ram. As Amon-Ra, this god was believed to embody the creator of the universe, the leader of all the other gods. This relates easily to the zodiac, which begins at the spring equinox, a time of the year when nature is renewed.

The Taurus Glyph ♉

This is another easy glyph to draw and identify. It takes little imagination to decipher the bull's head with long, curving horns. Like the bull, the archetypal Taurus is slow to anger but ferocious when provoked, as well as stubborn, steady, and sensual. Another association is the larynx (and thyroid) of the throat area (ruled by Taurus) and the Eustachian tubes (the "horns" of the glyph) running up to the ears, which coincides with the relationship of Taurus to the voice, song, and music. Many famous singers, musicians, and composers have prominent Taurus influences.

Many ancient religions involved a bull as the central figure in fertility rites or initiations, usually symbolizing the victory of man over his animal nature. Another possible origin is in the sacred bull of Egypt, who embodied the incarnate form of Osiris, god of death and resurrection. In early Christian imagery, the Taurean bull, representing St. Luke, appears in many art forms along with symbols of the other fixed signs: the lion (Leo and St. Mark), the man (Aquarius and St. Matthew), and the eagle (Scorpio and St. John).

The Gemini Glyph ♊

The standard glyph immediately calls to mind the Roman numeral for two and the symbol for Gemini, the "twins." In almost all images for this sign, the relationship between two persons is emphasized. This is the sign of communication and human contact, and it manifests the desire to share. Many of the figurative images of Gemini show twins with their arms around each other, emphasizing that they are sharing the same ideas and the same ground. In the glyph, the top line indicates mental communication, while the bottom line indicates shared physical space.

The most famous Gemini legend is that of the twin sons, Castor and Pollux, one of whom had a mortal father, while the other was the son of Zeus, king of the gods. When it came time for the mortal twin to die, his grief-stricken brother pleaded with Zeus, who agreed to let them spend half the year on earth, in mortal form, and half in immortal life, with the gods on Mt. Olympus. This reflects a basic concept of humankind, which possesses an immortal soul, yet is also subject to the limits of mortality.

The Cancer Glyph ♋

Two convenient images relate to the Cancer glyph. The easiest to picture is the curving claws of the Cancer symbol, the crab. Like the crab, Cancer's element is water. This sensitive sign also has a hard protective shell to shield its tender interior. It must be wily to escape predators, scampering sideways and hiding shyly under the rocks. The crab also responds to the cycles of the moon, as do all shellfish. The other image is that of two female breasts, which Cancer rules, showing that this is a sign that nurtures and protects others as well as itself. In ancient Egypt, Cancer was also represented by the scarab beetle, a symbol of regeneration and eternal life.

The Leo Glyph ♌

Lions have belonged to the sign of Leo since earliest times and it is not difficult to imagine the king of beasts with his sweeping mane and curling tail from this glyph. The upward sweep of the glyph easily describes the positive energy of Leos—the flourishing tail of the glyph depicts their flamboyant qualities. Another analogy, which is a stretch, is that of a heart leaping up with joy and enthusiasm, also very typical of Leo. Notice that the Leo glyph seems to be an extension of Cancer's glyph, with a significant difference. In the Cancer glyph, the figures are folding inward, protectively, while the Leo glyph expresses energy outwardly, with no duality in the symbol (or in Leo). In early Christian imagery, the Leo lion represented St. Mark.

The Virgo Glyph ♍

You can read much into this mysterious glyph. For instance, it could represent the initials of "Mary Virgin," or a young woman holding a staff of wheat, or stylized female genitalia, all common interpretations. The "M" shape might also remind you that Virgo is ruled by Mercury. The cross beneath the symbol could indicate the grounded, practical nature of this earth sign.

The earliest zodiacs link Virgo with the Egyptian goddess Isis, who gave birth to the god Horus after her husband Osiris had been killed, in the archetype of a miraculous conception. There are many statues of Isis nursing her baby son, which are reminiscent of medieval Virgin and Child motifs. This sign has also been associated with the image of the Holy Grail, when the Virgo symbol was substituted with a chalice.

The Libra Glyph ♎

It is not difficult to read the standard image for Libra, the scales, into this glyph. There is another meaning, however, that is equally relevant: the setting sun as it descends over the horizon. Libra's natural position on the zodiac wheel is the descendant or sunset position (as Aries' natural position is the ascendant, or rising sign). Both images relate to Libra's personality. Libra is always weighing pros and cons for a balanced decision. In the sunset image, the sun (male) hovers over the horizontal Earth (female) before setting. Libra is the space between these lines, harmonizing yin and yang, spiritual and material, ideal and real worlds. The glyph has also been linked to the kidneys, which are ruled by Libra.

The Scorpio Glyph ♏

With its barbed tail, this glyph is easy to identify with the sign of the Scorpion. It also represents the male sexual parts, over which the sign rules. However, some earlier symbols for Scorpio, such as the Egyptian, represent it as an erect serpent. You can also draw the conclusion that Mars is its ruler by the arrowhead.

Another image for Scorpio, which is not identifiable in this glyph, is the eagle. Scorpios can go to extremes, soaring like the eagle or self-destructing like the Scorpion. In early Christian imagery, which often used zodiacal symbols, the Scorpio eagle was chosen to symbolize the intense apostle St. John the Evangelist.

The Sagittarius Glyph ♐

This glyph is one of the easiest to spot and draw—an upward pointing arrow lifting up a cross. The arrow is pointing skyward, while the cross represents the four elements of the material world, which the arrow must convey. Elevating materiality into spirituality is an important Sagittarius quality, which explains why this sign is associated with higher learning, religion, philosophy, travel—the aspiring professions. Sagittarius can also send barbed arrows of frankness in their pursuit of truth. (This is also the sign of the super-salesman.)

Sagittarius is symbolically represented by the centaur, a mythological creature who is half man, half horse, aiming his arrow toward the skies. Though Sagittarius is motivated by spiritual aspiration, it also must balance the powerful appetites of the animal nature. The centaur Chiron, a figure in Greek mythology, became a wise teacher, after many adventures and world travels.

The Capricorn Glyph ♑

One of the most difficult symbols to draw, this glyph may take some practice. It is a representation of the sea goat: a mythical animal that is a goat with a curving fish's tail.

The goat part of Capricorn wants to leave the waters of the emotions and climb to the elevated areas of life. But the fish tail part of the symbol is the unconscious, the deep chaotic psychic level that draws the goat back. Capricorn is often trying to escape the deep, feeling part of life by submerging himself in work, steadily climbing to the top. To some people, the glyph represents a seated figure with a bent knee, a reminder that Capricorn governs the knee area of the body.

An interesting aspect of this figure is how the sharp pointed horns of the symbol, which represent the penetrating, shrewd, conscious side of Capricorn, contrast with the swishing tail, which represents its serpentine, unconscious, emotional force. One Capricorn legend, which dates from Roman times, tells of the earthly fertility god, Pan, who tried to save himself from uncontrollable sexual desires by jumping into the Nile. His upper body then turned into a goat, while the lower part became a fish. Later, Jupiter gave him a safe haven in the skies, as a constellation.

The Aquarius Glyph ≈

This ancient water symbol can be traced back to an Egyptian hieroglyph representing streams of life force. Symbolized by the water bearer, Aquarius is distributor of the waters of life—the magic liquid of regeneration. The two waves can also be linked to the positive and negative charges of the electrical energy that Aquarius rules, a sort of universal wavelength. Aquarius is tuned in intuitively to higher forces via this electrical force. The duality of the glyph could also refer to the dual nature of Aquarius, a sign that runs hot and cold, is friendly but also detached in the mental world of air signs.

In Greek legends, Aquarius is represented by Ganymede, who was carried to heaven by an eagle in order to become the cup bearer of Zeus, and to supervise the annual flooding of the Nile. The sign became associated with aviation and notions of flight.

The Pisces Glyph)(

Here is an abstraction of the familiar image of Pisces, two fishes swimming in opposite directions, bound together by a cord. The fishes represent spirit, which yearns for the freedom of heaven, while the soul remains attached to the desires of the temporal world. During life on earth, the spirit and the soul are bound together and when they complement each other, instead of pulling in opposite directions, this facilitates the creative expression for which Pisceans are known. The ancient version of this glyph, taken from the Egyptians, had no connecting line, which was added in the fourteenth century.

Another interpretation is that the left fish indicates the direction of involution or the beginning of the cycle, the right-hand fish, the direction of evolution, the way to completion of a cycle. It's an appropriate meaning for Pisces, the last sign of the zodiac.

How Well Do You Know the Glyphs?

Take this test after you've practiced drawing the glyphs.

1. Draw the glyphs of Mercury, Venus, and Mars. How do the differences in form help explain the nature of the planets?
2. How do the glyphs for the sign of Pisces and the planet Uranus relate to the balance of opposites?
3. How do the glyphs for Virgo and Scorpio express sexuality? Can you guess from the Scorpio glyph that Mars was once the ruling planet of Scorpio?
4. What do the central spaces in the Libra and Aquarius glyphs convey?
5. Draw the glyph for Capricorn. Is it the most difficult? Can you see horns and tail of the sea goat in this glyph?
6. Draw the glyphs for Saturn and Jupiter. Can you see how they complement each other?

7. Draw the glyphs for the three horned animals in the zodiac: Aries, Taurus, and Capricorn.
8. Compare the glyphs for the dual signs: the Twins, the Fishes, the Scales.
9. Compare the glyphs of Cancer and Leo. Can you see the Leo glyph as an extension of the Cancer one?
10. What does the dot in the center of the sun glyph mean? Which way is the moon glyph facing?

CHAPTER 5

How to Choose the Right Time

To find out if there is truth to the saying "to every thing there is a season and to every time there is a purpose unto heaven," try using some easy astrological principles to coordinate your schedule with the most beneficial times. When that tricky planet Mercury will be creating havoc with communications, be sure to back up the hard drive on your computer, keep duplicates of your correspondence, record those messages, and read between the lines of contracts. When Venus is in your sign, get a new hairstyle, entertain a VIP client, circulate where you'll be seen and admired.

To mark your own calendar for love, career moves, vacations, and important events, use the information in this chapter and the section in the previous one titled "Look Up Your Planets," as well as the moon sign listing under your daily forecast. Here are the happenings to note on your agenda:

- Dates of your sun sign period. This is a high energy time when you are beginning a new solar cycle. You are "reborn" for the year. A time to get a new lease on life. The sign before yours is a time of gestation, when you are winding up the previous cycle, a good time to review what has happened and make plans for your year ahead. It can be an especially loving time, if there is someone in your life who can provide extra attention now.
- Dates of planets in your sign this year. As each planet enters your sign, it will energize your life in a special way. Mercury will improve communications,

94

Venus will make you more appealing to others, Mars will energize you, Jupiter brings luck and opportunities, Saturn brings tests and discipline, etc.

- Full and new moons. Pay special attention when these fall in your sun sign. This is your axis of beginning and culminating.
- Eclipses. These bring changes in the area of life where they fall.
- When the moon is in your sun sign every month, as well as the moon in the opposite sign. These will be listed in the daily forecasts in the back of the book. Pay special attention to these high and low power times.
- Mercury retrogrades. These happen three times a year.
- Other retrograde periods.

Power Up on Your Birthday!

Every birthday starts a cycle of solar energy for you. You should feel a surge of vitality as the sun enters your sign, the time when predominant energies are most favorable to you. Start new projects, make your big moves. You'll get the recognition you deserve now, because your sun sign is most prominent. The tables in this book will tell you if other planets will also be passing through your sun sign at this time. Venus (love, beauty), Mars (energy, drive), or Mercury (communication, mental sharpness) reinforce the sun, boosting your luck.

Venus will rev up your social and love life, making you attractive to the opposite sex, charming to others. Mars revs up your energy and drive. Mercury fuels your brain power and helps your message reach the right people. Jupiter brings a lucky period of expansion when opportunities could fall into your lap.

There are two "down" times related to the sun. During the month before your birthday period, when you are winding up your annual cycle, you could be feeling especially vulnerable and depleted, so get extra rest, watch your diet, don't overstress yourself: Use this time to gear up for a big "push" when the sun enters your sign. On a positive note, at this time when the creative imagination is strong, your dreams, psychic life, and fantasies can be marvelous. It's a great time to escape the world with someone special on a marvelous vacation.

Another "down" time is when the sun is in the opposite sign (six months from your birthday), when the prevailing energies are very different from yours. You may feel at odds with the world, and things might not come easily. You'll have to work harder for recognition, because the world at large is attuned to the sign opposite yours and might not be receptive to your sun sign personality. However, this could be a good time to work on a team, in cooperation with others or behind the scenes.

Winding Up, Winding Down with the Moon Phases

Working with the moon's phases is as easy as looking up at the night sky. The new moon, when both sun and moon are in the same sign, is the best time to begin new ventures, especially the activities that are favored by the moon's sign. Then you'll naturally be focused outward, toward action. Postpone activities that are associated with the end of a cycle, such as breaking off, terminating, deliberating, reflecting, or activities that require introspection and passive work. Instead, focus on initiating, moving forward.

Get your project under way during the first quarter, then go public at the full moon, a culminating time of high intensity, when feelings come out into the open. This is the time to express yourself. Be aware, however, that because pressures are being released, other people are also letting off steam and confrontations are possible. Things are coming to "light." Traditionally, astrologers often advise against surgery at this time, which could produce heavier bleeding.

From the last quarter to the new moon is a winding-down phase, a time to cut off unproductive relationships, do serious thinking and inward-directed activities.

You'll feel some new and full moons more strongly than others, especially those new moons that fall in your sun sign and full moons in your opposite sign. Because that particular full moon happens at your low-energy time of year, it is likely to be an especially stressful time in a relationship, when hidden problems or unexpressed emotions could surface.

The Year 2001—Full and New Moons

(Note: these are calculated for EST)

JANUARY
Full Moon: January 9—(Lunar Eclipse) Cancer
New Moon: January 24—Aquarius
FEBRUARY
Full Moon: February 8—Leo
New Moon: February 23—Pisces
MARCH
Full Moon: March 9—Virgo
New Moon: March 24—Aries
APRIL
Full Moon: April 7—Libra
New Moon: April 23—Taurus
MAY
Full Moon: May 7—Scorpio
New Moon: May 23—Gemini
JUNE
Full Moon: June 5—Sagittarius
New Moon: June 21—(Solar Eclipse) Cancer
JULY
Full Moon: July 5—(Lunar Eclipse) Capricorn
New Moon: July 20—also in Cancer (as above)
AUGUST
Full Moon: August 4—Aquarius
New Moon: August 18—Leo

SEPTEMBER
Full Moon: September 2—Pisces
New Moon: September 17—Virgo
OCTOBER
Full Moon: October 2—Aries
New Moon: October 16—Libra
NOVEMBER
Full Moon: November 1—Taurus
New Moon: November 15—Scorpio
Full Moon: November 30—Gemini
DECEMBER
New Moon: December 14—(Solar Eclipse) Sagittarius
Full Moon: December 30—(Lunar Eclipse) Cancer

Don't Be Eclipsed!

Both solar and lunar eclipses are times when our natural
rhythms are altered, often producing important changes
in our lives. There are five eclipses this year, which will
affect the houses of your horoscope (areas of life) where
the eclipses fall. If the eclipses fall in your sun sign, especially on or close to your birthday, you may experience
a turning point in your life. This year's eclipses fall in
Cancer, Capricorn, or Sagittarius, and will be felt more
strongly in members of those signs.

Lunar eclipses happen when the Earth is on a level
plane with the sun and moon and moves exactly between
them during the time of the full moon, breaking the powerful monthly cycle of opposition of these two forces.
We might say the Earth "short-circuits" the connection
between them. The effect can be either confusion or clarity, as our subconscious energies, which normally react
to the pull of opposing sun and moon, are turned off.
This momentary "turnoff" could help us turn our lives
around. When we are temporarily freed from the subconscious attachments, we may have "Aha!" insights that
could help us change destructive emotional patterns, such
as addictions. On the other hand, this break in the nor-

mal cycle could cause a bewildering disorientation that intensifies our insecurities.

The solar eclipse occurs during a new moon, when the moon blocks the sun's energies as it passes exactly between the sun and the Earth. This means the objective, conscious force, represented by the sun, will be temporarily darkened. Subconscious lunar forces, activating our deepest emotions, will now dominate, putting us in a highly subjective state. Emotional truths can be revealed or emotions can run wild, as our objectivity is cut off and hidden patterns surface. If your sign is affected, you may find yourself beginning a period of work on a deep inner level, you may have psychic experiences or a surfacing of deep feelings.

You'll start feeling the energies of an upcoming eclipse a few days after the previous new or full moon. The energy continues to intensify until the actual eclipse, then disperses for three or four days. So plan ahead at least a week or more before an eclipse and allow several days afterward for the natural rhythms to return. Try not to make major moves during this period (it's not a great time to get married, change jobs, or buy a home).

Eclipses in 2001

January 9—Lunar Eclipse in Cancer
June 21—Solar Eclipse in Cancer
July 5—Lunar Eclipse in Capricorn
December 14—Solar Eclipse in Sagittarius
December 30—Lunar Eclipse in Cancer

Moon Sign Timing

You can forecast the daily emotional "weather," to determine your monthly high and low days, or to synchronize your activities with the cycles and the sign of the moon. Take note of the moon's daily sign under your daily forecast at the end of the book. Here are some of the activities favored and moods you are likely to encounter under each sign.

Moon in Aries

Get moving! The new moon in Aries is an ideal time to start new projects. Everyone is pushy, raring to go, rather impatient and short-tempered. Leave details and follow-up for later. Competitive sports or martial arts are great ways to let off steam. Quiet types could use some assertiveness, but it's a great day for dynamos. Be careful not to step on too many toes.

Moon in Taurus

It's time to do solid, methodical tasks. This is the time to tackle follow-through or backup work. Lay the foundations for success. Make investments, buy real estate, do appraisals, do some hard bargaining. Attend to your property—get out in the country. Spend some time in your garden. Enjoy creature comforts, music, a good dinner, sensual lovemaking. Forget starting a diet.

Moon in Gemini

Talk means action today. Telephone, write letter, fax! Make new contacts, stay in touch with steady customers. You can handle lots of tasks at once. A great day for mental activity of any kind. Don't try to pin people down—they too are feeling restless. Keep it light. Flirtations and socializing are good. Watch gossip—and don't give away secrets.

Moon in Cancer

This is a moody, sensitive, emotional time. People respond to personal attention, mothering. Stay at home, have a family dinner, call your mother. Nostalgia, memories, and psychic powers are heightened. You'll want to hang on to people and things (don't clean out your closets now). You could have some shrewd insights into what others really need and want now. Pay attention to dreams, intuition, gut reactions.

Moon in Leo

Everybody is in a much more confident, enthusiastic, generous mood. It's a good day to ask for a raise, show what you can do, dress like a star. People will respond to flattery, enjoy a bit of drama and theater. You may be feeling extravagant, so treat yourself royally and show off a bit (but don't break the bank!). Be careful that you don't promise more than you can deliver!

Moon in Virgo

Do practical down-to-earth chores. Review your budget. Make repairs. Be an efficiency expert. (Not a day to ask for a raise.) Have a health checkup. Revamp your diet. Buy vitamins or health food. Make your home spotless. Take care of details, piled-up chores. Reorganize your work and life so they run more smoothly and efficiently. Save money. Be prepared for others to be in a critical, fault-finding mood.

Moon in Libra

Relationships of all kinds are favored. Attend to legal matters. Negotiate contracts. Arbitrate. Do things with your favorite partner. Socialize. Be romantic. Buy a special gift or a beautiful object. Decorate yourself or your surroundings. Buy new clothes. Throw a party. Have an elegant, romantic evening. Smooth over any ruffled feathers. Avoid confrontations, stick to civilized discussions.

Moon in Scorpio

This is a day to do things with passion. You'll have excellent concentration and focus. Try not to get too intense emotionally, however, and avoid sharp exchanges with loved ones. Others many tend to go to extremes, get jealous, overreact. Great for troubleshooting, problem-solving, research, scientific work—and making love. Pay attention to psychic vibes.

Moon in Sagittarius

A great time for travel. Have philosophical discussions. Set long-range career goals. Work out, do sports, or buy athletic equipment. Others will be feeling upbeat, exuberant, adventurous, risk-taking. You may feel like taking a gamble, betting on the horses, visiting a local casino, buying a lottery ticket. Teaching, writing, and spiritual activities also get the green light. Relax outdoors. Take care of animals.

Moon in Capricorn

You can accomplish a lot today, so get on the ball! Issues concerning your basic responsibilities, duties, family, and parents could crop up. You'll be expected to deliver on promises and stick to your schedule now. Weed out the dead wood from your life and attack chores systematically. Get a dental checkup or attend to aching knees.

Moon in Aquarius

A great day for doing things in groups— clubs, meetings, outings, politics, parties. Campaign for your candidate. Work for a worthy cause. Deal with larger issues that affect the welfare of humanity. Buy a computer or electronic gadget. Watch TV. Wear something outrageous. Try something you've never done before. Present an original idea. Don't stick to a rigid schedule—go with the flow. Take a class in meditation, mind control, yoga.

Moon in Pisces

This can be a very creative day, so let your imagination work overtime. Film, theater, music, and ballet could inspire you. Spend some time alone, resting and reflecting, reading, watching a favorite film, or writing poetry. Daydreams can also be profitable. Help those less fortunate or lend a listening ear to someone who may be feeling blue. Don't overindulge in self-pity or escapism via adult beverages, since people are especially vulnerable to substance abuse now. Turn your thoughts to romance and someone special.

When the Planets Seem to Go Backward

All the planets, except for the sun and moon, have times when they appear to move backward—or retrograde—in the sky, or so it seems from our point of view on earth. Astrologers often compare retrograde motion to the optical illusion that occurs when we ride on a train that passes another train traveling at a different speed—the second train appears to be moving in reverse.

At these times, planets do not work as they usually do, so it's best to "take a break" from that planet's energies in our life and do some work on an inner level.

How to Outwit Mercury Mischief

Mercury goes retrograde three times each year, and its effects can be especially irritating, since the Mercury-ruled areas of your life, such as analytical thought processes, communications, scheduling, are subject to all kinds of confusion.

This year Mercury retrogrades in the air signs (Aquarius, Gemini, and Libra), which are associated with mental processes, so expect people to change their minds, renege on commitments. Communications equipment might break down. Schedules must be changed on short notice. People show up late for appointments or don't show up at all. Traffic jams are par for the course. Major purchases may malfunction, not work out, or get delivered in the wrong color. Letters might not arrive or may be sent to the wrong address. Employees make errors that have to be corrected later. Contracts don't work out or must be renegotiated.

Since most of us can't put our lives on "hold" for nine weeks every year (three Mercury retrograde periods), we should learn to tame the trickster and make it work for us. The key is in the prefix "re." This is the time to go back over things in your life. Reflect on what you've done during the previous months. Look for deeper insights, spot errors you've missed, take time to REview and REevaluate what has happened. This time is very good for inner spiritual work and meditations. Rest and reward yourself—it's a good time to take a vacation, especially if you REvisit a favorite place. REorganize your work and finish up projects that are backed up. Clean out your desk and closets. Throw away what you can't REcycle. If you must sign contracts or agreements, do so with a contingency clause that lets you REnegotiate the terms later.

Postpone major purchases or commitments. Don't get married (unless you're RE-marrying the same person). Try not to rely on other people keeping appointments, contracts, or agreements to the letter—have several alternatives. Double-check and read between the lines. Don't buy anything connected with communications or transportation (if you must, be sure to cover yourself). Mercury retrograding through your sun sign will intensify its effect on your life.

If Mercury was retrograde when you were born, you may be one of the lucky people who won't suffer the frustrations of this period. If so, your mind probably works in a very intuitive, insightful way.

The sign Mercury is retrograding through can give you an idea of what's in store—as well as the sun signs that will be especially challenged.

MERCURY RETROGRADE PERIODS IN 2001
February 3–February 25 in Aquarius

June 4–28 in Gemini
October 1–22 in Libra

Venus Retrograde—Make Peace!

Retrograding Venus can cause relationships to take a backward step or it can make you extravagant and impractical. *Not* a good time to redecorate—you'll hate the color of the walls later. Postpone getting a new hairstyle and try not to fall in love. But, if you wish to make amends in an already troubled relationship, make peaceful overtures then. Aries and Libra (its opposite sign) must take special note this year.

VENUS RETROGRADE IN 2001
   March 8–April 19 in Aries

Mars Tips—When to Push and When to Hold Back!

Mars shows how and when to get where you want to go. Timing your moves with Mars on your side can give you a big push. On the other hand, pushing Mars the wrong way can guarantee that you'll run into frustrations in every corner. Your best times to forge ahead are during the weeks when Mars is traveling through your sun sign or your Mars sign (look these up in the chapter on how to find your planets). Also consider times when Mars is in a compatible sign (fire with air signs, or earth with water signs). You'll be sure to have planetary power on your side.

   Hold your fire when Mars retrogrades, especially if you are Sagittarius or Gemini this year. Now is the time to exercise patience, let someone else run with the ball, especially if it's the opposing team. You may feel that you're not accomplishing much, but that's the right idea. Slow down and work off any frustrations at the gym. It's also best to postpone buying mechanical devices, which are Mars-rules, and take extra care when handling sharp objects. Sports, especially those requiring excellent balance, should be played with care. Be sure to use the appropriate protective gear and don't take unnecessary chances. This is not the time for daredevil moves! Pace yourself and pay extra attention to your health, since you may be especially vulnerable at this time.

MARS RETROGRADES IN 2001
May 11–July 19 in Sagittarius

When Other Planets Retrograde

The slower-moving planets stay retrograde for months at a time (Saturn, Jupiter, Neptune, Uranus, and Pluto). When Saturn is retrograde, you may feel more like hanging out than getting things done. It's an uphill battle with self-discipline at this time. Neptune retrograde promotes a dreamy escapism from reality, whereas Uranus retrograde may mean setbacks in areas where there have been sudden changes. Think of this as an adjustment period, a time to think things over and allow new ideas to develop. Pluto retrograde is a time to work on establishing proportion and balance in areas where there have been recent dramatic transformations.

When the planets start moving forward again, there's a shift in the atmosphere. Activities connected with each planet start moving ahead, plans that were stalled get rolling. Make a special note of those days on your calendar and proceed accordingly.

OTHER RETROGRADES IN 2001

- Pluto retrograde: March 17–August 23 in Sagittarius
- Neptune retrograde: May 10–October 17 in Aquarius
- Uranus retrograde: May 29–October 30 in Aquarius
- Saturn retrograde: September 26, 2001–February 7, 2002 in Gemini
- Jupiter retrograde: November 2, 2001–March 1, 2002 in Cancer

CHAPTER 6

Love Clicks and Crashes

Are you a Leo with a fatal attraction to a sexy Scorpio? Or an Aquarius with an immaculate Virgo who complains that you'll rush off leaving a pile of towels on the bathroom floor. Or you're that Virgo, in love with Aquarius, who hadn't bargained for a lifetime of picking up after your mate. Old-fashioned astrologers would say, "This combination is doomed from the start!" It used to be that some sun sign combinations were treated like champagne and tomato juice—never the twain should meet. Others were blessed by the stars as perfectly compatible.

Today we make allowance for the fact that hearts don't follow horoscopes. Although some combinations will be more challenging, too many long-lasting relationships happen between so-called incompatible sun signs to brand ANY combination as totally unworkable. We've gone far beyond stereotyping to respecting and enjoying the differences between people and using astrology to help us get along with them.

Here is a guide to finding out in advance how well you'll get along. Or, if you've already fallen for someone, checking out the potential for clicking long-term or avoiding a crash in the future. Though the comparisons here apply to sun signs, you can apply other planets that could influence your relationship to these sun sign descriptions. The moon (emotions), Mercury (communication), Mars (sex drive), and Venus (allure, tastes) can make a big difference to the longevity of a relationship.

To understand your astrological connection with another person you need to identify the spatial relationship between signs. The sign "next door" is something like your next-door neighbor who loans you his lawn mower or feeds your cats—or disputes your property boundaries. Signs distant from yours also have attitudes based on their "neighborhoods." Since the zodiac is a circle, the signs also relate to each other according to the angle of the distance between them. Between signs of the *same polarity,* but different elements, such as earth signs with water signs or fire and air combinations, energy flows most easily (with one exception: the sign opposite yours). Between signs of *different polarity,* you'll experience tension or challenge (and possibly a very sexy "charge").

Your Sign Mates—It's a Click or a Ho-Hum

Those of your own sign could be the soul mate you've been looking for—one who understands and sympathizes with you like no other sign can! Your sign mate understands your need for space, yet knows how and when to be "there" for you. There are many examples of long-term partnerships between sun sign twins—Roy Rogers and Dale Evans (both Scorpios), Abigail and John Adams (both Scorpios), George and Barbara Bush (both Geminis), Bob and Delores Hope (both Geminis), Frank and Kathie Lee Gifford (both Leos). Working relationships fare especially well when there are common sun signs, though you may have to delegate unwanted tasks to others. In a public lifestyle or one where there is much separation or stimulation, your similarities can also hold you together—there is the feeling of "you and me against the world." The problem is when there is too much of a good thing with no stimulation or challenge—or when there is no "chemistry," which can often happen between signs that share so much. The solution is to bring plenty of outside excitement into your lives.

The Sign Next Door—
Where's the Chemistry?

These signs are your next-door neighbors on the zodiac wheel. Your relationships is based on evolution—you've evolved out of the previous sign carrying energies that have been accumulating and developing through the zodiac cycle. The sign following yours is where your energy is headed, the next step. In a way, it's like sitting at a dinner table and passing the plate from left to right. You receive certain qualities from the previous sign and pass on those, plus your own, to the next.

This is also a sibling relationship where the sign before yours is like a protective older brother or sister, who's "been there," and the next sign is your eager younger sibling. Every sign also has a compensating factor for its predecessor—this sign embodies lessons you should have learned (and which could trip you up if you've forgotten them).

But although both are in the same "family," sibling signs actually have little in common, because you have different basic values (elements), ways of operating (qualities), and types of energy (polarity). You probably won't feel sparks of chemistry or deep rapport unless other planets in your horoscope provide this bond. Instead, the emphasis is on pals, best friends, working partners, who are enhanced by the sibling sign position.

The sign ahead can inspire you—they're where you are heading, but you may be afraid to take the first brave step. For example, to Pisces, Aries embodies dynamic, forceful, self-oriented will—whereas Pisces is the formless, selfless, imaginative state where Aries originated. So Aries energizes Pisces, gets Pisces moving. This sign behind backs you up, supports you. This relationship often makes one of the most lasting and contented unions—a couple of famous examples are the Duke and Duchess of Windsor (Cancer/Gemini), Paul Newman and Joanne Woodward (Aquarius/Pisces).

Your Squared-Off Relationships— Three Signs Away

If you recognize that stress in a relationship often stimulates growth and that sexual tension can be heightened by a challenge, you might succeed with signs that are three signs away from yours. Relationships between these signs, which have a similar quality or way of acting, are charged with erotic energy and sparks of passion. Some of these can thrive on difficulty. But, even though you might declare a truce with this sign, the person probably won't be easy to live with. However, these will also be your least boring partners.

Since you will both operate in the same way, you'll understand how the other acts, though you won't necessarily share the same basic values or type of energy. It often happens that you'll continually confront each other—here is a sign that is just as restless, stubborn, or driven as you are! This person isn't one to provide security, settle down, or back you up. So will you choose to compete or to join forces to forge an equal partnership?

Mutable signs (Gemini, Virgo, Sagittarius, Pisces), which are the most changeable, understand each other's restlessness and low tolerance for boredom. This is a couple that can easily fragment, however, going off in different directions. This union often falls apart under stress, but challenges mutables to make order out of chaos. In other words, get your act together.

Cardinal couples (Aries, Cancer, Libra, Capricorn) with equal drive and energy often are characterized by goal-driven intensity—they never sit still. Fixed signs (Taurus, Leo, Scorpio, Aquarius) can be the most stable partners, or negatively, they can wrestle for control, war over territory, or have a stubborn Mexican standoff.

Positively, this is one of the sexiest aspects—these two signs challenge each other, bring about growth. Here are some of the issues likely to arise between signs that square off:

Aries—Cancer

Aries is forced by Cancer to consider the consequences of actions, particularly those that threaten security and hurt feelings. However, introspection cramps Aries' style—this sign wants perfect freedom to act as they please and has no patience for Cancer's self-pity or self-protectiveness. Although Cancer admires Aries' courage, the interaction will have to confront the conflict between the Aries' out-directed desire to have their own way and Cancer's inward-turning drive to create safety and security.

Cancer—Libra

Cancer is most satisfied by symbiotic, intimate, emotionally dependent relationships. So when you meet someone who is very independent, you feel hurt, rejected, and throw up a defensive shell or get moody and depressed. Unfortunately, you risk this happening with Libra, a romantic, but rather emotionally cool sign. Libras want an equal partner, tend to judge their partner on a detached, idealistic level, by their looks, style, ideas, conversation. Libra recognizes that the best partnerships are between equals, but the issue here is what do you have to share? Libra won't be able to escape emotions through social activities or intellectual analysis here.

Libra—Capricorn

Both of you love the good life, but you may have conflicting ideas about how to get it. Capricorn is a very disciplined, goal-directed, ordered worker who requires concrete results. Libra is more about style, abstract principles, and can be quite self-indulgent. Libran indulgence versus Capricorn discipline could be the cruncher here. Another bone to pick would be differing ideas about what's fair and just. Capricorn often believes that the "end justifies the means." Libra upholds fairness over bottom-line concerns.

Capricorn—Aries

Both are survivors who love to win. But Capricorn works for status and material rewards, while Aries works for glory, heroism, challenge, for the joy of being first. Capricorn wants to stay in control. Aries wants freedom. In a positive way, Aries must grow up with Capricorn, but, in return, it can give this tradition-oriented sign a younger lease on life.

Taurus—Leo

Leo has an insatiable appetite for admiration; Taurus for pleasure. Taurus sensuality can make Leo feel like a star. Leo's romantic gestures appeal to Taurus on a grand scale. Taurus will have to learn courtship and flattery to keep Leo happy—bring on the champagne and caviar! Leo will have to learn not to tease the bull, especially by withholding affection—and to enjoy simple meat-and-potatoes kinds of pleasures as well. Money can be so important here. Leo likes to spend royally; Taurus likes to accumulate and hoard.

Leo—Scorpio

Scorpio wants adventure in the psychic underworld. Leo wants to stay in the throne room. Scorpio challenges Leo to experience life intensely, which can bring out the best in Leo. Leo burns away Scorpio negativity—with low tolerance for dark moods. Scorpio is content to work behind the scenes, giving Leo center stage. But Leo must never mistake a quiet Scorpio for a gentle pussycat. There will be plenty of action behind the scenes. Settle issues of control without playing power games.

Scorpio—Aquarius

Aquarius' love of freedom and Scorpio's possessiveness could clash here. Scorpio wants to own you—Aquarius wants to remain friends. This is one unpredictable sign

Scorpio can't figure out, but has fun trying. Aquarius' flair for group dynamics could bring Scorpio out. However, too many outside interests could put a damper on this combination.

Aquarius—Taurus

Taurus lives in the touchable realm of the earth. Aquarius is in the electric, invisible realm of air, which can't be fenced in. It's anyone's guess if Taurus can ground Aquarius or if Aquarius can uplift Taurus. Taurus' talent as a realist could be the anchor this free spirit needs. Aquarian originality opens new territory to Taurus.

Gemini—Virgo

Nerves can be stimulated or frayed when these Mercury-ruled signs sound off. Both have much to say to each other—from different points of view. Gemini deals in abstractions. Virgo in down-to-earth facts. Common interests could keep this pair focused on each other.

Virgo—Sagittarius

Safety versus risk could be the hallmark of this relationship. Virgo plays it safe and cautious. Sagittarius operates on faith and enthusiasm. You're two natural teachers who have different philosophies and have much to learn from each other. When Virgo picks things apart or gets bogged down in details, Sagittarius urges them to look for the *truth*—the big picture. Sagittarius' lack of organization or follow-through will either drive Virgo crazy or provide a job. Virgo puts Sagittarius down with facts, deflating overblown promises and sales pitches.

Sagittarius—Pisces

There should be many philosophical and spiritual discussions and debates here. When Sagittarius says, "I'm right," Pisces says, "Everything's relative. We're all right and wrong, so what?" Sagittarius is about elevating the self and Pisces is about merging the self, losing the self. On a less cosmic level, these two high-flying signs may never get down to earth. Pisces' supersensitive feelings are easily wounded by Sagittarius' moments of truth-telling. But Sagittarius can help sell those creative Piscean ideas; that is, if you don't wander off in different direction.

Pisces—Gemini

Gemini is always trying to understand, abstract, rationalize. Pisces wants to merge and flow, find a soul mate, go beyond the mind. Pisces' moods get on Gemini's nerves. Gemini runs away from emotional mergers, which really matter to Pisces. Yet Pisces' glamour can intrigue Gemini and Gemini's lightness and wit help Pisces laugh away the blues.

Your Easiest Love Clicks— Too Much of a Good Thing?

Signs of your same element (four signs away from yours) are considered the easiest relationships possible . . . the most compatible partners. But sometimes there is too much of a good thing. These tend to lack dynamism and sexy sparks. They can be too comfortable as you adjust very easily to each other. If it's too easy, you might look for excitement and challenge elsewhere.

Relationships between the three earth signs (Taurus, Virgo, Capricorn) are mutually profitable, both professionally and personally. You won't find the other sign tampering with your financial security, frittering away hard-earned funds, or flirting with danger. You could fulfill your dreams of a comfortable life together. Too much comfort could leave you yawning, however—you need someone to shake you up once in a while.

Fire signs (Aries, Leo, Sagittarius) can ignite each

other, but watch out for temper and jealousy. You both demand exclusive attention, are happiest when your ego is stoked and you feel like number one, so you may have to curb any tendency to flirt. Because you tend to be big risk-takers and free spenders, you may have to delegate the financial caretaking carefully or find an expert adviser.

Water signs (Cancer, Scorpio, Pisces) have found partners who aren't afraid of emotional depths or heights. These are the ones who can understand and sympathize with your moods. This could be your solution to who gives you the emotional security you need. When moods collide, however, you could find it difficult to get each other out of deep water.

Air signs (Gemini, Libra, Aquarius) communicate well together. There is no heavy emotionalism or messy ego or possessiveness to deal with. You both respect the need for freedom and personal space and can make your own rules for an open, equal partnership. Staying in touch is the problem here. You could become so involved in your own pursuits that you let romance fly by or are never there for each other. Be sure to cultivate things in common, because unless there are many shared interests, it is easy to float away.

On Different Wavelengths:
The Potential Crashes

Here are the relationships that challenge your sign the most, where you have to stretch yourself to make this work. You have different basic values (element), ways of acting (quality), kinds of energy (polarity), and unlike your next-door signs, who also have those differences, you don't have the proximity of being next in line. Instead of being beside you, the other sign is off on the other side of the zodiac. On the other hand, this very separateness can have an exotic quality, the attraction of the unknown (and unattainable). This is someone you'll never quite figure out. And this sign also has many threatening traits—if you get into this relationship, there will be risks, you won't quite know what to expect. The relationship is the proverbial square peg and round hole. Even though the stress of making this relationship work can be great, so can the stimulation and creativity that result from trying to find out what makes each other tick.

When positive and negative signs come together, lights go on, as you discover different ways of viewing the world, which can move you out of the doldrums. Here is how your sign relates to these partners.

Aries: Scorpio/Virgo

Scorpio, who tends to be secretive and manipulative, embodies everything that is foreign to Aries. Aries is clear-cut, openly demanding. If an Aries attacks, it will be swift and open. Scorpio will wait for the time when an opponent is most vulnerable—years, if necessary—to deal the lethal blow. Aries burns out much sooner. Yet your very strong differences only make the conquest more exciting.

Virgo thinks the way to solve problems is to get organized, think things through—steamrolling Aries wants fast action, quick results. Both Scorpio and Virgo will challenge Aries to go against the grain—be careful, organized, persevering, delve deeply, look at the long haul. Aries will have to tone down impulsiveness with these signs.

Taurus: Libra/Sagittarius

Libra, also Venus-ruled, is involved with the abstract, idealistic side of the planet, whereas Taurus is involved with the sensual, materialistic, self-indulgent side. Libra challenges Taurus to abstract, to get into the mind as well as the body. Taurus will bring Libra down to earth and provide stability for this sign.

Sagittarius challenges Taurus to expand its territory. Taurus is the most rooted of signs, and can be immobile.

Sagittarius is the happy wanderer. Taurus moves outside its turf with Sagittarius, who challenges it intellectually, spiritually, and physically.

Gemini: Scorpio/Capricorn

Here, playful, verbal, mental Gemini is confronted by the failure to probe, the failure to deal with passion. Gemini gets into deep real emotional stuff with Scorpio. Contact with Scorpio often precipitates a crisis in Gemini's life, as this sign realizes there is something powerful it's been missing. Scorpio challenges Gemini to delve deeply and make commitments rather than deals.

Capricorn makes Gemini develop discipline, set goals, and do practical bottom-line things the sign is not prepared to do. Capricorn has no tolerance for fragmented efforts and forces Gemini to focus and produce.

Cancer: Sagittarius/Aquarius

Fearful, frugal Cancer must take risks to make a relationship work with Sagittarius, who loves to gamble, has faith in the universe. Everyone's buddy, Aquarius makes Cancer give love with an open hand, placing less emphasis on personal security, property.

Cancer must give up possessiveness with both these signs, who actually enjoy the kind of freedom (insecurity) that Cancer most fears. In these relationships, Cancer's expectations of what a relationship should be have to change. It gets no protection from either sign and its favorite sympathy-winning techniques (playing "poor little me," whining, clinging, or complaining) only alienate these signs further. In the process of coping with these distant signs however, Cancer can eventually become more independent and truly secure within itself.

Leo: Capricorn/Pisces

Capricorn demands that Leo deliver on promises. With this down-to-earth sign, Leo can't coast for long on looks and star power. Capricorn wants results, pushes Leo to produce, casts a cold eye on shows of ego, and sees through bluffs. Conversely, both enjoy many of the same things, such as a high-profile lifestyle, if for different reasons.

Pisces is on another planet from solar Leo—the Neptunian embodies all that is not-self. This is a sign that devalues the ego. Pisces teaches Leo to be unselfish, to exercise compassion and empathy, to walk in others' shoes. Leo has to give up arrogance and false pride for a lasting relationship with Pisces.

Virgo: Aquarius/Aries

Aquarius sheds light on Virgo's problem without getting bogged down in details. Interaction with Aquarius expands Virgo, prepares this sign for the unpredictable, the sudden, the unexpected. Aquarius gets Virgo to broaden scope—to risk experimenting. Aries gives Virgo positive energy and draws Virgo away from self-criticism and out into the world.

Libra: Pisces/Taurus

Looking for a decision-maker—Libra won't find it in Pisces! Pisces and Libra both share an artistic nature, but executed in a different way. Libra can't project its need for direction onto Pisces. Libra says, "What should I do?" Pisces says, "I know how you feel. It's tough not knowing what to do." Pisces challenges Libra to go within, to understand where others are coming from, rather than expecting them to conform to an abstract ideal.

Taurus brings Libra into the practical material world and gives this sign ground, but Taurus will also insist on material value. Taurus will ask, "How much does it cost?" Libra says, "I don't care, it's so pretty." Libra would rather not worry about function and operations, which become Taurus' task. Libra will either desperately need Taurus' practicality or find it a drag.

Scorpio: Aries/Gemini

Listen for the clanking of iron shields on a Mars-ruled Aries and Scorpio get-together. Both of you thrive on challenge and find it in each other. The issue here: who's the conqueror when neither will give in or give up? You'll have to respect each other's courage and bravery, and enjoy the sparks.

Gemini is the sign you can never pin down or possess—and this is super-fascinating for Scorpio. Their quicksilver wit and ability to juggle many people and things are talents not found in the Scorpio repertoire. Scorpios never stop trying to fathom the power of Gemini. Just when they've almost got them pegged, Gemini's onto something or someone else! As long as you don't expect devotion, you won't be disappointed.

Sagittarius: Taurus/Cancer

This is a dialogue between the rooted and the rootless. Both Taurus and Cancer are the most home-loving signs of the zodiac, while Sagittarius is the eternal wanderer—mentally, physically, or both. Will they be content to keep the home fires burning for Sagittarius? Another sticky point: both signs are very careful with money. However, these two financially savvy signs could help Sagittarius achieve miracles instead of talking about them. Sagittarius will have to learn patience with Taurus, who will inevitably try to tie Sagittarius down. Cancer could dampen Sagittarius' spirits with self-pity if they feel neglected in any way. Sagittarius will have to learn sensitivity to feelings. If Sagittarius can give up the position as teacher and become a student, these relationships might last.

Capricorn: Gemini/Leo

Both of these signs are social charmers who need organization, which is Capricorn's forte. They can help Capricorn get a desired position with Gemini's deft charm or

Leo's warmth and poise. The trade-off is that Capricorn will have to learn to take life less seriously, be as devoted to the partnership as to work. Otherwise, these two signs will look for amusement elsewhere. Gemini should inspire Capricorn to diversify, communicate, and spread wings socially. Leo adds confidence, authority, status. They'll appreciate Capricorn's adding structure to their lives.

Aquarius: Cancer/Virgo

Aquarius, the most freedom-loving sign, here encounters two different dimensions, both of which tend to bring this sign back to the realities of operating on a day-to-day level (Virgo) and honoring emotional attachments, the level of feeling (Cancer). Cancer is the home-loving sign who values security, family, emotional connections—an area often dismissed by Aquarius. Virgo is about organization, critical judgment, efficiency—which enhance Aquarius' accomplishments.

Pisces: Leo/Libra

With Leo, Pisces learns to find and project itself. Leo enjoys Pisces' talent and often profits by it. In return, Leo gives this often-insecure sign confidence. With Leo, Pisces can't hide any longer, must come out from the depths—but Leo will not sympathize or indulge Pisces' blue moods or self-pity. Pisces has to give up negativity with Leo.

Libra's instinct is to separate and analyze. Pisces wants an emotional merger with no boundaries. However, the more Pisces gets emotional, the more Libra becomes cool and detached. On a more positive note, Pisces can gain objectivity from this relationship, which insists on seeing both sides of any matter equally. Libra can provide the balance that keeps Pisces from drowning in the emotional depths.

Opposites Click or Freeze Up

This sign opposite yours is your other half, who manifests qualities that you think you don't have. There are many marriages between "opposite numbers," because one sign expresses what the other suppresses.

Because most lasting relationships are between equals, the attraction to your "opposite number" could backfire, if you suddenly develop strength in the opposite sign's own stronghold. What happens if you're an easygoing Aquarius married to a star-quality Leo and you decide it's time to show off your natural charisma on center stage? Or a disorganized Pisces with an efficient Virgo partner who goes on a cleanup, shape-up program and out-organizes the Virgo? No longer does the opposite partner have exclusive rights to certain talents or attitudes. If they can make adjustments to the new you, fine. Otherwise, someone could be out of a job.

It's an excellent idea to ask yourself if you are attracting your opposite sign in relationships, what the signs are acting out for you. It could be a clue to a side of your character you need to develop. Sometimes, after the initial chemistry dies down, and two opposite signs actually begin living together, you'll be irritated by the same qualities that at first attracted you. That's because they reveal the part you are afraid of within yourself— the part you haven't really claimed for yourself, and you resent this other person taking it over. Here's how it works out with opposite numbers: the more you learn to express "both sides of the same coin," the better chance your relationship will have.

Aries—Libra

Aries brings out Libra's placating, accommodating talents. And, at first, Libra is happy to play the charmer, in exchange for Aries' decisiveness. Aries revels in the chance to take charge and to be so openly needed. But in close quarters, Aries seems too pushy, too bossy. And when Libra decided to make its own decisions, Aries had better learn to charm.

Taurus—Scorpio

This is one of the most powerful attractions and is often found in marriages and long-term relationships. Some of these couples manage to balance out their differences nicely; others are just too stubborn to give up or give in. The uncomplicated, earthy, sensual Taurus likes safety, comfort, pleasurable physical things. Scorpio, who enjoys the challenges and dangers of intense feelings (and could live in a monk's cell), is often attracted to danger and risk. Scorpio wants a deep powerful merger. Taurus likes to stay aboveground, enjoying innocent pleasures. Both are possessive and jealous, with a need to control their own territory. Scorpio marvels at the uncomplicated basic drives of Taurus—couldn't they get into trouble together? Taurus enjoys teasing Scorpio with promises of innocent pleasure, but learns that Scorpios will sting when teased. Settle issues of control early on—and never underestimate each other's strength.

Gemini—Sagittarius

Gemini is the eager student of the world. Sagittarius is the perfect guide, only too happy to teach, enlighten, and expound. This is a very stimulating combination. Sagittarius enjoys telling others what to believe, however, and Gemini can't be bossed. Gemini also turns off fiery confrontations and absolute declarations of truth, and may deflate Sagittarius with barbs of wit. On a positive note, this could be a wonderful combination both socially and professionally. Romantically it works best if they can be both student and teacher to each other.

Cancer—Capricorn

Both of these signs have strong defense mechanisms. Cancer's is a protective shell. Capricorn's is a cold stony wall. In a relationship, both of these defenses play off each other. Cancer shows weakness (complains, whines) as a means of getting protection, which dovetails nicely with Capricorn's need to play the authoritarian parental father figure (even when it's a female) who takes responsibility for the vulnerable child (Cancer). But if Capricorn shows vulnerability, such as a fear of not being "right," Cancer panics, becomes insecure, and erects a self-protective shell. On the other hand, if Capricorn takes over Cancer's life, this active cardinal sign gets crabby. Learning to "parent" each other and reinforce strong traditional values could be the key to happiness here.

Leo—Aquarius

Both are stubborn fixed signs with opposite points of view. Leo is "me-oriented" and does not like to share. Aquarius is "them-oriented" and identifies with others. The Leo charisma comes from projecting the self—others are there for applause, while Aquarius shines as the symbol or spokesperson of a group, which reflects self-importance. Aquarius is the talk-show host, working from the audience. Leo is the guest star, on stage. Leo is not about to become one of the Aquarius crowd (especially if the crowd includes Aquarius' ex-lovers). Aquarius will not confine interests to Leo (become an exclusive Leo fan). If Leo can learn to share and Aquarius can give one-on-one attention, these opposites could balance out.

Virgo—Pisces

In Pisces, Virgo finds someone who apparently needs their services badly. Virgo in turn is attracted to Pisces because this sign can deal with the tricky side of life that can't be organized or made to run on schedule. Sensitive Pisces seems to need Virgo's clarity, orderliness, and practicality to keep together and in line. You can see how easy it is for this to become a bargain between the helper and the apparently helpless. When Pisces gets organized and Virgo gets in touch with their own irrational side, these two could form a more solid relationship.

Will Your Romance Click or Crash? Take This Quiz to Find Out

1. How many signs away are your sun signs?
2. How many signs away are your moon signs? This reflects your emotional compatibility.
3. How many signs away are your Venus signs? This reflects compatible tastes.
4. How many signs away are your Mercury signs? This reflects the way you'll communicate.
5. How many signs away are your Mars signs? This reflects your temper and your drive.

Score

Same sign: 7
Adjacent sign: 5
Two signs away: 8
Three signs away: 4
Four signs away: 10
Five signs away: 3
Opposite your sign: 7

High scores: 55–77 Plenty of clicks! A winner. Minimum compromises, but is there enough excitement?

Medium scores: 35–55 Crashes or freezes. Be sure you are willing to compromise.

Low scores: 21–35 A maximum compromise relationship. Lots of sparks but plenty of adjustments to make.

CHAPTER 7

What Makes Your Horoscope Special—Your Rising Sign

It's often said that every horoscope is unique. But you may wonder why, since many people were born on your same birthday. Most of your high school class will have the slow-moving planets (Uranus, Neptune, Pluto) and very possibly Jupiter and Saturn in the same sign as you do. What makes you truly special is your rising sign. It's the key to your specific horoscope, since it sets up the sequence of the houses of your chart.

What is a rising sign? At the moment you were born, when you assumed an independent physical body, one of the signs of the zodiac (that is, a thirty-degree slice of the sky) was just passing over the eastern horizon. In astrology, this is called the rising sign, often referred to as the ascendant. Other babies who were born later or earlier in the day, in the same hospital as you were born, might have planets in the same signs as you do, but would have a different rising sign, because as the earth turns, a different sign rises over the horizon every two hours. Therefore the planets would be in a different place or "house" in their horoscopes, accentuating different areas of their lives.

On the circular wheel of the horoscope, the other signs follow the rising signs in sequence, rotating counterclockwise. The rising sign marks the first house, which represents your first presentation to the world, your physical body, how you come across to others. It has been called your "shop window," the first impression you give to others. After the rising sign is determined, then each "house" or area of your chart will be influenced by the signs following it.

Without a valid rising sign, your collection of planets would have no "homes." Once the rising sign is established, it becomes possible to analyze a chart accurately because the astrologer knows in which area of life (house) the planet will operate. For instance, if Mars is in Gemini and your rising sign is Taurus, then Mars will be active in the second or financial house of your chart. If your rising sign is Virgo, then Mars will energize the career portion of your horoscope. That is why many astrologers insist on knowing the exact time of a client's birth, before they analyze a chart.

Your rising sign has an important relationship with your sun sign. Some will complement the sun sign; others hide the sun under a totally different mask, as if playing an entirely different role, so it is often difficult to guess the person's sun sign from outer appearances. For example, a Leo with a conservative Capricorn ascendant would come across as much less flamboyant than a Leo with a fiery Aries or Sagittarius ascendant. The exception is when the sun sign is reinforced by other planets; then, with other planets on its side, the sun may assert its personality much more strongly, overcoming the image of a contradictory rising sign. For example, a Leo with Venus and Jupiter also in Leo might counteract the conservative image of the Capricorn ascendant, in the above example. However, in most cases, the ascendant is the ingredient most strongly reflected in the first impression you make.

Rising signs change every two hours with the Earth's rotation. Those born early in the morning when the sun was on the horizon will most likely project the image of their sun sign. These people are often called a "double Aries" or a "double Virgo," because the same sun sign and ascendant reinforce each other.

Look up your rising sign on the chart at the end of this chapter. Since rising signs change every two hours, it is important to know your birth time as close to the minute as possible. Even a few minutes difference could change the rising sign and therefore the setup of your chart. If you are unsure about the exact time, but know within a few hours, check the following descriptions to see which is most like the personality you project.

Aries Rising—Fiery Emotions

You are the most aggressive version of your sun sign, with boundless energy that can be used productively. Watch a tendency to overreact emotionally and blow your top. You come across as openly competitive, a positive asset in business or sports. Be on guard against impatience, which could lead to head injuries. Your walk and bearing could have the telltale head forward Aries posture. You may wear more bright colors, especially red, than others of your sign. You may also have a tendency to drive your car faster.

Taurus Rising—The Earth Mother

You'll exude a protective nurturing quality, even if you're male, which draws those in need of TLC and support. You're slow-moving, with a beautiful (or distinctive) speaking or singing voice that can be especially soothing or melodious. You probably surround yourself with comfort, good food, luxurious surroundings, sensual pleasures, and prefer welcoming others into your home to gadding about. You may have a talent for business, especially in trading, appraising, real estate. This ascendant gives a well-padded physique that gains weight easily.

Gemini Rising—Expressive Talents

You're naturally sociable, with lighter, more ethereal mannerisms than others of your sign, especially if you're female. You love to communicate with people and express your ideas and feelings easily. You may have writing or public speaking talent. You thrive on a constantly changing scenario with many different characters, though you may be far more sympathetic and caring than you project. You will probably travel widely, changing partners and jobs several times (or juggle two at once). Physically, you should cultivate a calm, tranquil atmosphere, because your nerves are quite sensitive.

Cancer Rising—Sensitive Antenna

You easily pick up others' needs and feelings, a great gift in business, the arts, and personal relationships, but guard against overreacting or taking things too personally especially during full moon periods. Find creative outlets for your natural nurturing gifts, such as helping the less fortunate, particularly children. Your insights would be useful in psychology, your desire to feed and care for others in the restaurant, hotel, or child-care industry. You may be especially fond of wearing romantic old clothes, collecting antiques, and, of course, good food. Since your body may retain fluids, pay attention to your diet. To relax, escape to places near water.

Leo Rising—The Scene Player

You may come across as more poised than you really feel; however, you play it to the hilt, projecting a proud royal presence. This ascendant gives you a natural flair for drama. You'll also project a much more outgoing, optimistic, sunny personality than others of your sign. You take care to please your public by always projecting your best star quality, probably tossing a luxuriant mane of hair or, if you're female, dazzling with a spectacular jewelry collection. Since you may have a strong parental nature, you could well be the regal family matriarch or patriarch.

Virgo Rising—Cool and Calculating

Virgo rising masks your inner nature with a practical, analytical outer image. You seem neat, orderly, more particular than others of your sign. Others in your life may feel they must live up to your high standards.

Though at times you may be openly critical, this masks a well-meaning desire to have only the best for loved ones. Your sharp eye for details could be used in the financial world, or your literary skills could draw you to teaching or publishing. The healing arts, health care, and service-oriented professions attract many with this Virgo emphasis in their chart. Physically, you may have a very sensitive digestive system.

Libra Rising—The Charmer

Libra rising makes you appear as a charmer, more of a social, public person than others of your sign. Your private life will extend beyond your home and family to include an active social life. You may tend to avoid confrontations in relationships, preferring to smooth the way or negotiate diplomatically, rather than give in to an emotional reaction. Because you are interested in all aspects of a situation, you may be slow to reach decisions. Physically, you'll have good proportions and pleasing symmetry. You're likely to have pleasing, if not beautiful, facial features. You move gracefully, and you have a winning smile and good taste in your clothes and home decor. Legal, diplomatic, or public relations professions could draw your interest.

Scorpio Rising—Magnetic Power

You project an intriguing air of mystery when Scorpio's secretiveness and sense of underlying power combines with your sign. You can project the image of a master manipulator, always in control and moving comfortably in the world of power. Your physical look comes across as intense and many of you have remarkable eyes, with a direct, penetrating gaze. But you'll never reveal your private agenda and you tend to keep your true feelings under wraps (watch a tendency toward paranoia). You may have an interesting romantic history with secret love affairs. Many of you heighten your air of mystery by wearing black. You're happiest near water and should provide yourself with a seaside retreat.

Sagittarius Rising—The Wanderer

You travel with this ascendant. You may also be a more outdoor, sportive type, with an athletic, casual, outgoing air. Your moods are camouflaged with cheerful optimism or a philosophical attitude. Though you don't hesitate to speak your mind, you can also laugh at your troubles or crack a joke more easily than others of your sign. This ascendant can also draw you to the field of higher education or to spiritual life. You'll seem to have less attachment to things and people and may travel widely. Your strong, fast legs are a physical bonus.

Capricorn Rising—Serious Business

This rising sign makes you come across as serious, goal-oriented, disciplined, and careful with cash. You are not one of the zodiac's big spenders, though you might splurge occasionally on items with good investment value. You're the traditional, conservative type in dress and environment, and you might come across as quite formal and businesslike. You'll function well in a structured or corporate environment where you can climb to the top. (You are always aware of who's the boss.) In your personal life, you could be a loner or a single parent who is "father and mother" to your children.

Aquarius Rising—One of a Kind

You come across as less concerned about what others think and could even be a bit eccentric. You're more at ease with groups of people than others in your sign, and may be attracted to public life. Your appearance may be unique, either unconventional or unimportant to you. Those with the sun in a water sign (Cancer, Scorpio, Pisces) may exercise your nurturing qualities with a large group, an extended family, a day-care or community center.

Pisces Rising—Romantic Roles

Your creative, nurturing talents are heightened and so is your ability to project emotional drama. And your dreamy eyes and poetic air bring out the protective instinct in others. You could be attracted to the arts, especially theater, dance, film, or photography, or to psychology, spiritual, or charity work. Since you are vulnerable to up and down mood swings, it is especially important for you to find interesting, creative work where you can express your talents and boost your self-esteem. Accentuate the positive and be wary of escapist tendencies, particularly involving alcohol or drugs, to which you are supersensitive.

Rising Sign Quiz

Can You Guess the Rising Sign of These Celebrities?

1. Bill Clinton and John F. Kennedy. Their charming smiles and easy social manner charmed the ladies.
2. Marilyn Monroe. Born to take center stage.
3. Madonna. Conscious of health, diet, and exercise.
4. Paul Newman. Rejected the Hollywood scene for a quiet life in Connecticut. Looks great in gray hair.
5. Candice Bergen. A world traveler. Outspoken Murphy Brown was her best-known role.
6. Bill Gates. Acquisitive, possessive, private, a moneymaker.
7. Drew Barrymore. Light, lively, a life of changes.
8. Diana Ross. Extreme, gutsy, a survivor.
9. Robert Redford. Remote, imaginative filmmaker.
10. Audrey Hepburn. Unique appearance, crusader for a worthy cause.

11. Bette Midler. Exciting, fiery redhead, confrontational, dynamic energy, expressive face.
12. Wilt Chamberlain. "Wilt the Stilt," 7'1", powerful body image, big moneymaker, huge appetites—claimed he slept with 20,000 women.

Answers:

1. Libra
2. Leo
3. Virgo
4. Capricorn
5. Sagittarius
6. Cancer
7. Gemini
8. Scorpio
9. Pisces
10. Aquarius
11. Aries
12. Taurus

RISING SIGNS—A.M. BIRTHS

	1 AM	2 AM	3 AM	4 AM	5 AM	6 AM	7 AM	8 AM	9 AM	10 AM	11 AM	12 NOON
Jan 1	Lib	Sc	Sc	Sc	Sag	Sag	Cap	Cap	Aq	Aq	Pis	Ar
Jan 9	Lib	Sc	Sc	Sag	Sag	Sag	Cap	Cap	Aq	Pis	Ar	Tau
Jan 17	Sc	Sc	Sc	Sag	Sag	Cap	Cap	Aq	Aq	Pis	Ar	Tau
Jan 25	Sc	Sc	Sag	Sag	Sag	Cap	Cap	Aq	Pis	Ar	Tau	Tau
Feb 2	Sc	Sc	Sag	Sag	Cap	Cap	Aq	Pis	Pis	Ar	Tau	Gem
Feb 10	Sc	Sag	Sag	Sag	Cap	Cap	Aq	Pis	Ar	Tau	Tau	Gem
Feb 18	Sc	Sag	Sag	Cap	Cap	Aq	Pis	Pis	Ar	Tau	Gem	Gem
Feb 26	Sag	Sag	Sag	Cap	Aq	Aq	Pis	Ar	Tau	Tau	Gem	Gem
Mar 6	Sag	Sag	Cap	Cap	Aq	Pis	Pis	Ar	Tau	Gem	Gem	Can
Mar 14	Sag	Cap	Cap	Aq	Aq	Pis	Ar	Tau	Tau	Gem	Gem	Can
Mar 22	Sag	Cap	Cap	Aq	Pis	Ar	Ar	Tau	Gem	Gem	Can	Can
Mar 30	Cap	Cap	Aq	Pis	Pis	Ar	Tau	Tau	Gem	Can	Can	Can
Apr 7	Cap	Cap	Aq	Pis	Ar	Ar	Tau	Tau	Gem	Gem	Can	Leo
Apr 14	Cap	Aq	Aq	Pis	Ar	Tau	Tau	Gem	Gem	Gem	Can	Leo
Apr 22	Cap	Aq	Pis	Ar	Ar	Tau	Gem	Gem	Gem	Can	Leo	Leo
Apr 30	Aq	Aq	Pis	Ar	Tau	Tau	Gem	Can	Can	Can	Leo	Leo
May 8	Aq	Pis	Ar	Ar	Tau	Gem	Gem	Can	Can	Leo	Leo	Leo
May 16	Aq	Pis	Ar	Tau	Gem	Gem	Can	Can	Can	Leo	Leo	Vir
May 24	Pis	Ar	Ar	Tau	Gem	Gem	Can	Can	Leo	Leo	Leo	Vir
June 1	Pis	Ar	Tau	Gem	Gem	Can	Can	Can	Leo	Leo	Vir	Vir
June 9	Ar	Ar	Tau	Gem	Gem	Can	Can	Leo	Leo	Leo	Vir	Vir
June 17	Ar	Tau	Gem	Gem	Can	Can	Can	Leo	Leo	Vir	Vir	Vir
June 25	Tau	Tau	Gem	Can	Can	Can	Leo	Leo	Leo	Vir	Vir	Lib
July 3	Tau	Gem	Gem	Can	Can	Can	Leo	Leo	Vir	Vir	Vir	Lib
July 11	Tau	Gem	Gem	Can	Can	Leo	Leo	Leo	Vir	Vir	Lib	Lib
July 18	Gem	Gem	Can	Can	Can	Leo	Leo	Vir	Vir	Vir	Lib	Lib
July 26	Gem	Gem	Can	Can	Leo	Leo	Vir	Vir	Vir	Lib	Lib	Lib
Aug 3	Gem	Can	Can	Can	Leo	Leo	Vir	Vir	Vir	Lib	Lib	Sc
Aug 11	Gem	Can	Can	Leo	Leo	Leo	Vir	Vir	Lib	Lib	Lib	Sc
Aug 18	Can	Can	Can	Leo	Leo	Vir	Vir	Vir	Lib	Lib	Sc	Sc
Aug 27	Can	Can	Leo	Leo	Leo	Vir	Vir	Lib	Lib	Sc	Sc	Sc
Sept 4	Can	Can	Leo	Leo	Leo	Vir	Vir	Vir	Lib	Lib	Sc	Sc
Sept 12	Can	Leo	Leo	Leo	Vir	Vir	Vir	Lib	Lib	Lib	Sc	Sag
Sept 20	Leo	Leo	Leo	Vir	Vir	Vir	Lib	Lib	Sc	Sc	Sc	Sag
Sept 28	Leo	Leo	Leo	Vir	Vir	Lib	Lib	Lib	Sc	Sc	Sag	Sag
Oct 6	Leo	Leo	Vir	Vir	Vir	Lib	Lib	Sc	Sc	Sc	Sag	Sag
Oct 14	Leo	Vir	Vir	Vir	Lib	Lib	Lib	Sc	Sc	Sag	Sag	Cap
Oct 22	Leo	Vir	Vir	Lib	Lib	Lib	Sc	Sc	Sc	Sag	Sag	Cap
Oct 30	Vir	Vir	Vir	Lib	Lib	Sc	Sc	Sc	Sag	Sag	Cap	Cap
Nov 7	Vir	Vir	Lib	Lib	Lib	Sc	Sc	Sc	Sag	Sag	Cap	Cap
Nov 15	Vir	Vir	Lib	Lib	Sc	Sc	Sc	Sag	Sag	Cap	Cap	Aq
Nov 23	Vir	Lib	Lib	Lib	Sc	Sc	Sag	Sag	Sag	Cap	Cap	Aq
Dec 1	Vir	Lib	Lib	Sc	Sc	Sc	Sag	Sag	Cap	Cap	Aq	Aq
Dec 9	Lib	Lib	Lib	Sc	Sc	Sc	Sag	Sag	Cap	Cap	Aq	Pis
Dec 18	Lib	Lib	Sc	Sc	Sc	Sag	Sag	Cap	Cap	Aq	Aq	Pis
Dec 28	Lib	Lib	Sc	Sc	Sag	Sag	Sag	Cap	Aq	Aq	Pis	Ar

RISING SIGNS—P.M. BIRTHS

	1 PM	2 PM	3 PM	4 PM	5 PM	6 PM	7 PM	8 PM	9 PM	10 PM	11 PM	12 MIDNIGHT
Jan 1	Tau	Gem	Gem	Can	Can	Can	Leo	Leo	Vir	Vir	Vir	Lib
Jan 9	Tau	Gem	Gem	Can	Can	Leo	Leo	Leo	Vir	Vir	Vir	Lib
Jan 17	Gem	Gem	Can	Can	Can	Leo	Leo	Vir	Vir	Vir	Lib	Lib
Jan 25	Gem	Gem	Can	Can	Leo	Leo	Leo	Vir	Vir	Lib	Lib	Lib
Feb 2	Gem	Can	Can	Can	Leo	Leo	Vir	Vir	Vir	Lib	Lib	Sc
Feb 10	Gem	Can	Can	Leo	Leo	Leo	Vir	Vir	Lib	Lib	Lib	Sc
Feb 18	Can	Can	Can	Leo	Leo	Vir	Vir	Vir	Lib	Lib	Sc	Sc
Feb 26	Can	Can	Leo	Leo	Leo	Vir	Vir	Lib	Lib	Lib	Sc	Sc
Mar 6	Can	Leo	Leo	Leo	Vir	Vir	Vir	Lib	Lib	Sc	Sc	Sc
Mar 14	Can	Leo	Leo	Vir	Vir	Vir	Lib	Lib	Lib	Sc	Sc	Sag
Mar 22	Leo	Leo	Leo	Vir	Vir	Lib	Lib	Lib	Sc	Sc	Sc	Sag
Mar 30	Leo	Leo	Vir	Vir	Vir	Lib	Lib	Sc	Sc	Sc	Sag	Sag
Apr 7	Leo	Leo	Vir	Vir	Lib	Lib	Lib	Sc	Sc	Sc	Sag	Sag
Apr 14	Leo	Vir	Vir	Vir	Lib	Lib	Sc	Sc	Sc	Sag	Sag	Cap
Apr 22	Leo	Vir	Vir	Lib	Lib	Lib	Sc	Sc	Sc	Sag	Sag	Cap
Apr 30	Vir	Vir	Vir	Lib	Lib	Sc	Sc	Sc	Sag	Sag	Cap	Cap
May 8	Vir	Vir	Lib	Lib	Lib	Sc	Sc	Sag	Sag	Sag	Cap	Cap
May 16	Vir	Vir	Lib	Lib	Sc	Sc	Sc	Sag	Sag	Cap	Cap	Aq
May 24	Vir	Lib	Lib	Lib	Sc	Sc	Sag	Sag	Sag	Cap	Cap	Aq
June 1	Vir	Lib	Lib	Sc	Sc	Sc	Sag	Sag	Cap	Cap	Aq	Aq
June 9	Lib	Lib	Lib	Sc	Sc	Sag	Sag	Sag	Cap	Aq	Aq	Pis
June 17	Lib	Lib	Sc	Sc	Sc	Sag	Sag	Cap	Cap	Aq	Aq	Pis
June 25	Lib	Lib	Sc	Sc	Sag	Sag	Sag	Cap	Cap	Aq	Pis	Ar
July 3	Lib	Sc	Sc	Sc	Sag	Sag	Cap	Cap	Aq	Aq	Pis	Ar
July 11	Lib	Sc	Sc	Sc	Sag	Sag	Cap	Cap	Aq	Pis	Ar	Tau
July 18	Sc	Sc	Sc	Sag	Sag	Cap	Cap	Aq	Aq	Pis	Ar	Tau
July 26	Sc	Sc	Sag	Sag	Sag	Cap	Cap	Aq	Pis	Ar	Tau	Tau
Aug 3	Sc	Sc	Sag	Sag	Cap	Cap	Aq	Aq	Pis	Ar	Tau	Gem
Aug 11	Sc	Sag	Sag	Sag	Cap	Cap	Aq	Pis	Ar	Tau	Tau	Gem
Aug 18	Sc	Sag	Sag	Cap	Cap	Aq	Pis	Pis	Ar	Tau	Gem	Gem
Aug 27	Sag	Sag	Sag	Cap	Cap	Aq	Pis	Ar	Tau	Tau	Gem	Gem
Sept 4	Sag	Sag	Cap	Cap	Aq	Pis	Pis	Ar	Tau	Gem	Gem	Can
Sept 12	Sag	Sag	Cap	Aq	Aq	Pis	Ar	Tau	Tau	Gem	Gem	Can
Sept 20	Sag	Cap	Cap	Aq	Pis	Pis	Ar	Tau	Gem	Gem	Can	Can
Sept 28	Cap	Cap	Aq	Aq	Pis	Ar	Tau	Tau	Gem	Gem	Can	Can
Oct 6	Cap	Cap	Aq	Pis	Ar	Ar	Tau	Gem	Gem	Can	Can	Leo
Oct 14	Cap	Aq	Aq	Pis	Ar	Tau	Tau	Gem	Gem	Can	Can	Leo
Oct 22	Cap	Aq	Pis	Ar	Ar	Tau	Gem	Gem	Can	Can	Leo	Leo
Oct 30	Aq	Aq	Pis	Ar	Tau	Tau	Gem	Can	Can	Can	Leo	Leo
Nov 7	Aq	Aq	Pis	Ar	Tau	Tau	Gem	Can	Can	Can	Leo	Leo
Nov 15	Aq	Pis	Ar	Tau	Gem	Gem	Can	Can	Can	Leo	Leo	Vir
Nov 23	Pis	Ar	Ar	Tau	Gem	Gem	Can	Can	Leo	Leo	Leo	Vir
Dec 1	Pis	Ar	Tau	Gem	Gem	Can	Can	Can	Leo	Leo	Vir	Vir
Dec 9	Ar	Tau	Tau	Gem	Gem	Can	Can	Leo	Leo	Leo	Vir	Vir
Dec 18	Ar	Tau	Gem	Gem	Can	Can	Can	Leo	Leo	Vir	Vir	Vir
Dec 28	Tau	Tau	Gem	Gem	Can	Can	Leo	Leo	Vir	Vir	Vir	Lib

CHAPTER 8

Your Axis of Action—The Secrets of Timing by the Moon

Would you like to predict your most significant trends for the months ahead, as astrologers do? You can, by using the rising sign table in this book and simply looking up at the moon!

Though it might seem obvious to some moon-watchers, many of us have never stopped to think that in each sun sign period (note: we do not mean the calendar month), the new moon will be in the same sign as the sun, while the full moon will fall in the opposite sign, creating a polarized axis. The issues governed by the houses where the moon falls will have special importance over the upcoming month. In the new moon's house are the issues that are beginning. In the full moon's house are culminations, things coming to light. Sometimes the new moon in this axis of action comes first, at other times it comes after the full moon (as it does this fall), creating a different dynamic. Once in a while there are two new or full moons in the same sign, as happens this summer, which can reverse the order of the axis.

The object here is to find the houses (or area of life) on the axis where the new moon and full moon fall in your horoscope. First, look up your rising sign in the chart in this book on pages 133–134. This is actually an approximate rising sign for you, because it is impossible to be precise without knowing your exact time of birth. The sequence of houses that follows after your rising sign will most likely have the signs on the cusp (or beginning of the house) in sequential order. For example, if your rising sign is Scorpio, the second house cusp would be Sagittarius, the third house cusp Capricorn, the fourth Aquarius, and so on. However, to be on the safe side, consult the polarity of the previous sign as well. That's because there is a possibility that the degree of your rising sign may be so far along in the sign that the moon falls in the previous house. For instance, taking the above example, if your rising sign is fifteen degrees of Scorpio and the new moon falls at ten degrees Scorpio, it would be in the previous or twelfth house, rather than the first house. (Note: If you do not know your rising sign, assume that it is the same as your sun sign. Though the forecast will not be as accurate, it will still be relevant.)

The areas of your life covered by the twelve houses are actually six pairs of polarities. For example, the first house deals with independent action (it's the "me" house) while the opposite house, the seventh, deals with relationships (it's the "you" house). The second house deals with your possessions, the income you earn by yourself, what is "mine"; the opposite, eighth house, deals with joint resources, issues of power, or control, what is "ours." Here's how they line up:

First House (Rising Sign)/Seventh House Polarity

This polarity usually brings up issues of me versus you, independence versus dependence, freedom versus closeness, solo ventures versus partnerships, as well as the ability to commit and to form a contractual relationship. This could bring up issues in your marital or partnership life. If the new moon falls in your seventh house, you may be making a new commitment or you may meet someone who becomes a marital or business partner. If the new moon falls in your first house, you'll begin an independent venture and you'll be feeling very much on your own. Legal issues (seventh house) and court cases also happen at this time.

Second House/Eighth House

This polarity deals with what you own by yourself versus what you own with others (insurance, bank loans, taxes, inheritance, joint property), and with buying and selling. This polarity also brings up issues of your physical body, which "you own" versus sexual activity, which is joint physical activity.

Third House/Ninth House

This polarity will deal with issues in your local area versus the world at large, with neighbors versus people of a different background, with students versus higher education and with writing letters versus writing books. Your immediate, outgoing communications and thoughts versus your expansive thoughts and your philosophy of life are also considered. So are hobbies, skills, and students versus higher education and teachers, as well as how your mind works in everyday matters versus how your mind receives higher ideas. You may be traveling and dealing with issues of education, writing, publishing, and religion, or you may be very much on the go in your local area, involved with relatives—the third house rules siblings.

Fourth House/Tenth House

This is the axis of your private (fourth) versus your public life (tenth). It concerns your home life versus your life outside the home (career), and the nurturing side of your life versus the authority figures. Issues of prestige and status versus domestic situations, family, and "roots" will come up.

Fifth House/Eleventh House

The fifth is your house of personal self-expression, what you create (including your children) versus the eleventh house, where you express yourself through a group. The eleventh is your clubs, your labor union, your political party, your teams, and the goals and ideals you identify with. Your contribution to society is here as well. Vying with those interests are your personal projects and what you want to do to express your own interests. Here also are your romantic love affairs (the ones that might not lead to commitment). Along this axis, issues arise involving your love life, or what you want to do for yourself balanced with what your group or society wants. It's about what "I" want versus what "they" want.

Sixth House/Twelfth House

This is where you deal with the reality functions of the material world versus situations where you leave the material world behind. The sixth house is where you organize, maintain your body in working order, work with the world in a structured way versus the twelfth house where you go with the flow, surrendering, giving up something. It's an area of order (function) versus chaos (creativity).

This is also the polarity of addiction (twelfth house) versus codependency (sixth). It's the polarity, too, of the conscious (sixth) versus the unconscious (twelfth). The sixth house is where you are in situations of responsibility, where you are the caretaker, versus the twelfth house, where you have no responsibility, where you are taken care of (prisons, hospitals, institutions). The twelfth house is often called the house of self-undoing, because it is the area where you have no brakes or boundaries. The sixth house is where you set up the structures and boundaries that will later enable you to function in the twelfth house . . . you must learn the scales and techniques (sixth) before you can play the concerto (twelfth).

The House Game

Put the following in the appropriate houses:
  A. An attractive person you're flirting with
  B. Your mate
  C. A hospital stay

D. A philosophy course
E. IRS payments
F. Making the baseball team
G. Your new boss
H. Medical checkups
I. A letter from your sister
J. A family dinner
K. Your gold necklace
L. A solo trip

Answers:

A. Fifth house
B. Seventh house
C. Twelfth house
D. Ninth house
E. Eighth house
F. Eleventh house
G. Tenth house
H. Sixth house
I. Third house
J. Fourth house
K. Second house
L. First house

If There's an Eclipse on the Axis

Eclipses tend to throw the new moon/full moon axis off balance, as if there were a temporary short circuit of the usual cyclical energy. So be prepared for the unexpected in whatever you do in that house area. (There are five eclipses this year.)

Recap—How to Find Your Lunar Axis of Action

1. Look up your rising sign in the chart on pages 133–134. Example: For the following explanations, we'll assume your rising sign is Leo.

2. Determine the sequence of the twelve houses, following the rising sign.
Example: First house, Leo. Second house, Virgo. Third house, Libra. Fourth house, Scorpio. Fifth house, Sagittarius. Sixth house, Capricorn. Seventh house, Aquarius. Eighth house, Pisces. Ninth house, Aries. Tenth house, Taurus. Eleventh house, Gemini. Twelfth house, Cancer.
3. Determine the signs of houses that are opposite each other.
Example: First house Leo is opposite seventh house Aquarius, second house Virgo is opposite eighth house Pisces.
4. Look up the current new and full moon in the chart at the end of this chapter.
Example: The new moon on January 24 falls in Aquarius, the following full moon in Leo happens on February 8.
5. Determine the issues that are reflected by the new and full moon. For someone with Leo rising, the Leo/Aquarius axis would indicate issues involving the first and seventh house, personal freedom versus relationships.

New and Full Moons for 2001

(Note: these are calculated for EST)

JANUARY
Full Moon: January 9—(Lunar Eclipse) Cancer
New Moon: January 24—Aquarius
FEBRUARY
Full Moon: February 8—Leo
New Moon: February 23—Pisces
MARCH
Full Moon: March 9—Virgo
New Moon: March 24—Aries
APRIL
Full Moon: April 7—Libra
New Moon: April 23—Taurus

MAY
Full Moon: May 7—Scorpio
New Moon: May 23—Gemini
JUNE
Full Moon: June 5—Sagittarius
New Moon: June 21—(Solar Eclipse) Cancer
JULY
Full Moon: July 5—(Lunar Eclipse) Capricorn
New Moon: July 20—also in Cancer
AUGUST
Full Moon: August 4—Aquarius
New Moon: August 18—Leo
SEPTEMBER
Full Moon: September 2—Pisces
New Moon: September 17—Virgo
OCTOBER
Full Moon: October 2—Aries
New Moon: October 16—Libra
NOVEMBER
Full Moon: November 1—Taurus
New Moon: November 15—Scorpio
Full Moon: November 30—Gemini
DECEMBER
New Moon: December 14—(Solar Eclipse) Sagittarius
Full Moon: December 30—(Lunar Eclipse) Cancer

CHAPTER 9

Meet Your Astrologer!
What a Personal Reading Can—
and Can't—Do for You

If you're at a crossroads in your life and have been wondering whether an astrological reading could help you make the right decisions, it might be time for a personal consultation. But should you choose a telephone reading, a celebrity-endorsed astrologer, have a chat room reading on the Internet, buy a personalized computer printout that promises many pages of deep insights, or find an astrologer in your city? The dizzying variety of options available today makes choosing a reading a confusing dilemma. The following basic guidelines can help you sort out your options to find the reading that's right for you.

The One-on-One Reading

Nothing compares to a one-on-one consultation with a professional astrologer who has analyzed thousands of charts and can pinpoint the potential in yours. During your reading, you can get your specific questions answered. For instance, how to get along better with your mate or coworker. There are many astrologers who now combine their skills with training in psychology and are well suited to help you examine your alternatives.

To give you an accurate reading, an astrologer needs certain information from you. Before your reading, a reputable astrologer should ask for the date, time, and place of birth of the subject of the reading. (A horoscope can be cast about anything that has a specific time and place.) Most astrologers will then enter this information into a computer, which will calculate a chart in seconds. From the resulting chart, the astrologer will do an interpretation.

If you don't know your exact birth time, you can usually locate it at the Bureau of Vital Statistics at the city hall or county seat of the state where you were born. If you still have no success in getting your time of birth, some astrologers can estimate an approximate birth time by using past events in your life to determine the chart.

How to Find a Good Astrologer

Your first priority should be to choose a qualified astrologer. Rather than relying on word of mouth or grandiose advertising claims, do this with the same care you would choose any trusted adviser such as a doctor, lawyer, or banker. Unfortunately, anyone can claim to be an astrologer—to date, there is no licensing of astrologers or established professional criteria. However, there are nationwide organizations of serious, committed astrologers that can help you in your search.

Good places to start your investigation are organizations such as the American Federation of Astrologers or the National Council for Geocosmic Research (NCGR), which offers a program of study and certification. If you live near a major city, there is sure to be an active NCGR chapter or astrology club in your area—many are listed in astrology magazines available at your local newsstand. In response to many requests for referrals, the NCGR has compiled a directory of professional astrologers, which includes a glossary of terms and an explanation of specialties within the astrological field. Contact the NCGR headquarters (see the resource list in this book) for information.

Be Aware of When to Beware

As a potentially lucrative freelance business, astrology has always attracted self-styled experts who may not have the knowledge or the counseling experience to give a helpful reading. These astrologers can range from the well-meaning amateur to the charlatan or street-corner gypsy who has for many years given astrology a bad name. Be very wary of astrologers who claim to have occult powers or who make pretentious claims of celebrated clients or miraculous achievements. You can often tell from the initial phone conversation if the astrologer is legitimate. He or she should ask for your birthday, time and place and conduct the conversation in a professional manner. Any astrologer who gives a reading based only on your sun sign is highly suspect.

When you arrive at the reading, the astrologer should be prepared. The consultation should be conducted in a private, quiet place. The astrologer should be interested in your problems of the moment. A good reading involves feedback on your part, so if the reading is not relating to your concerns, you should let the astrologer know. You should feel free to ask questions and get clarifications of technical terms. The reading should be an interaction between two people, rather than a solo performance. The more you actively participate, rather than expecting the astrologer to carry the reading or come forth with oracular predictions, the more meaningful your experience will be. An astrologer should help you validate your current experience and be frank about possible negative happenings, but suggest a positive course of action.

In their approach to a reading, some astrologers may be more literal, others more intuitive. Those who have had counseling training may take a more psychological approach. Though some astrologers may seem to have an almost psychic ability, extrasensory perception or any other parapsychological talent is not essential. A very accurate picture can be drawn from the data in your horoscope chart.

An astrologer may do several charts for each client, including one for the time of birth and a "progressed chart," showing the evolution from birth to the present time. According to your individual needs, there are many other possibilities, such as a chart for a different location, if you are contemplating a change of place. Relationships between any two people, things, or events can be interpreted with a chart that compares one partner's horoscope with the other's. A composite chart, which uses the midpoint between planets in two individuals charts to describe the relationship, is another commonly used device.

An astrologer will be particularly interested in transits—times when planets will pass over the planets or sensitive points in your birth chart, which signal important events in your life.

Many astrologers offer tape-recorded readings, another option to consider. In this case, you'll be mailed a taped reading based on your birth chart. This type of reading is more personal than a computer printout and can give you valuable insights, but it is not equivalent to a live reading, when you can have a face-to-face dialogue with the astrologer and discuss your specific interests and issues of the moment.

Phone Readings—Real or Phony?

Telephone readings come in two varieties . . . one is a dial-in taped reading, usually by a well-known astrologer. The other is a live consultation with an "astrologer" on the other end of the line. The taped readings are general daily or weekly forecasts, applied to all members of your sign and charged by the minute. The quality depends on the astrologer. One caution: be aware that these readings can run up quite a telephone bill, especially if you get into the habit of calling every day. Be sure that you are aware of the per-minute cost of each call beforehand.

Live telephone readings also vary with the expertise of the astrologer. Ideally the astrologer at the other end

of the line enters your birth data into a computer that
calculates your chart. This chart will then be referred to
during the consultation. The advantage of a live telephone reading is that your individual chart is used and
you can ask about a specific problem. However, before
you invest in any reading, be sure that your astrologer
is qualified and that you fully understand in advance how
much you will be charged.

About Computer Readings

Companies that offer computer programs (such as ACS,
Matrix, Astrolabe) also offer a variety of computer-
generated horoscope readings. These can be quite com-
prehensive, offering a beautiful printout of the chart plus
many pages of detailed information about each planet
and aspect of the chart. You can then study your chart
at your convenience, since the details of the chart are
interpreted in a very understandable way. Of course, the
interpretations will be general, since there is no personal
input from you, and may not cover your immediate concerns. Since computer-generated horoscopes are much
lower in cost than live consultations, you might consider
them as either a supplement or preparation for an even-
tual live reading. You'll then be more familiar with your
chart and able to plan specific questions in advance. They
also make a terrific gift for astrology fans. There are
several companies in our "Yellow Pages" chapter that
offer computerized readings prepared by reputable
astrologers.

CHAPTER 10

The Sydney Omarr Yellow Pages

Have you caught the "astrology bug"? If so, you'll want to meet other astrology fans, attend conferences, buy a program for your computer, maybe even attend a college devoted to astrology. In this chapter, we'll give you the information you need to locate the latest products and services available, as well as the top astrology organizations that hold meetings and conferences in your area.

There are organized groups of astrologers all over the country who are dedicated to promoting the image of astrology in the most positive way. The National Council for Geocosmic Research (NCGR) is one nationwide group that is dedicated to bringing astrologers together, promoting fellowship and high-quality education. Their accredited course system promotes a systematized study of all the different facets of astrology. Whether you'd like to know more about such specialties as financial astrology or techniques for timing events, or if you'd prefer the psychological or mythological approach, you'll find the leading experts at NCGR conferences.

Your computer can be a terrific tool for connecting with other astrology fans at all levels of expertise, as we explore in the Internet chapter in this book. Even if you are using a "dinosaur" from the eighties, there are still calculation and interpretation programs available for DOS and MAC formats. They may not have all the bells and whistles or exciting graphics, but they'll get the job done!

Newcomers to astrology should learn some of the basics, including the glyphs (astrology's special shorthand language), before you invest in a complex computer program. Use the chapter in this book to help you learn the symbols easily, so you'll be able to read the charts without consulting the "help" section of your program every time. Several programs such as Astrolabe's "Solar Fire," have pop-up definitions to help you decipher the meanings of planets and aspects. Just click your mouse on a glyph or an icon on the screen and a window with an instant definition appears.

You may be pleasantly surprised that you don't have to spend a fortune to get a perfectly adequate astrology program. In fact, if you are connected to the Internet, you can download one free. Astrology software is available at all price levels, from a sophisticated free application like "Astrolog," which you can download from a Web site, to inexpensive programs for under $100 such as Halloran's "Astrology for Windows," to the more expensive astrology programs such as "Winstar," "Solar Fire," or "Io" (for the Mac), which are used by serious students and professionals. Before you make an investment, it's a good idea to download a sample from the company's Web site or order a demo disk. If you just want to have fun, investigate an inexpensive program such as Matrix Software's "Kaleidoscope," an interactive application with lots of fun graphics. If you're baffled by the variety of software available, most of the companies on our list will be happy to help you find the right application for your needs.

If you live in an out-of-the-way place or are unable to fit classes into your schedule, you have several options. There are on-line courses offered at astrology Web sites, such as *www.panplanet.com*. Some astrology teachers will send you a series of audiotapes or you can order audio-taped seminars of recent conferences; other teachers offer correspondence courses that use their workbooks or computer printouts.

Nationwide Astrology Organizations and Conferences

Contact these organizations for information on conferences, workshops, local meetings, conference tapes, or referrals:

National Council for Geocosmic Research

Educational workshops, tapes, conferences, and a directory of professional astrologers are available from this nationwide organization devoted to promoting astrological education. For a $35 annual membership fee, you get their excellent publications and newsletters, plus the opportunity to network with other astrology buffs at local chapter events (there are chapters in twenty states). For general information about NCGR, contact:

NCGR
P.O. Box 38866
Los Angeles, CA 90038
Telephone: (818) 705-0797

At this writing, the contact for new memberships is:

Linda Fei, Membership Director
1359 Sargent Ave.
St. Paul, MN 55105
E-mail: LindaFei@aol.com
Telephone: (651) 698-1691

Or visit their Web page: *http://www.geocosmic.org* for updates and local events.

American Federation of Astrologers (A.F.A.)

One of the oldest astrological organizations in the United States, established 1938. It offers conferences, conventions, and a correspondence course. It will refer you to an accredited A.F.A. astrologer.

A.F.A.
P.O. Box 22040
Tempe, AZ 85285-2040
Telephone: (480) 838-1751
Fax: (480) 838-8293

A.F.A.N. (Association for Astrological Networking)

Did you know that astrologers are still being arrested for practicing in some states? A.F.A.N. provides support, legal information, works toward improving the public image of astrology. Here are the people who will go to bat for astrology when it is attacked in the media. Everyone who cares about astrology should join!

A.F.A.N.
8306 Wilshire Blvd, Suite 537
Beverley Hills, CA 90211

ARC Directory

(Listing of Astrologers Worldwide)
2920 E. Monte Vista
Tucson, AZ 85716
Telephone: (602) 321-1114

Pegasus Tapes

(Lectures, Conference tapes)
P.O. Box 419
Santa Ysabel, CA 92070

International Society for Astrological Research

(Lectures, Workshops, Seminars)
P.O. Box 38613
Los Angeles, CA 90038

ISIS Institute

(Newsletter, Conferences, Astrology tapes, Catalog)
P.O. Box 21222
El Sobrante, CA 94820–1222
Telephone (800) 924-4747 or (510) 222-9436
Fax: (510) 222-2202

Astrology Software

Astrolabe

Box 1750–R
Brewster, MA 02631
Telephone: (800) 843-6682

Check out the latest version of their powerful "Solar Fire" software for Windows—it's a breeze to use and will grow with your increasing knowledge of astrology to the most sophisticated levels. This company also markets a variety of programs for all levels of expertise, a wide selection of computer astrology readings, and Mac programs. A good resource for innovative software as well as applications for older computers.

Matrix Software

315 Marion Ave.
Big Rapids, MI 49307
Telephone: (800) PLANETS

You'll find a wide variety of software in all price ranges, demo disks at student and advanced levels, and lots of interesting readings. Check out "Kaleidoscope," an inexpensive program with beautiful graphics, and "Winstar Plus," their powerful professional software, if you're planning to study astrology seriously.

Astro Communications Services

Dept. AF693, PO Box 34487
San Diego, CA 92163–4487
Telephone: (800) 888-9983

You'll find books, software for Mac and IBM compatibles, individual charts, and telephone readings. Also find technical astrology materials here, such as "The American Ephemeris." They will calculate charts for you if you do not have a computer.

Air Software

115 Caya Avenue
West Hartford, CT 06110
Telephone: (800) 659-1247

Powerful, creative astrology software, like their award-winning "Star Trax." For beginners, check out "Father Time," which finds your best days. Or "Nostradamus," which answers all your questions. Also, financial astrology programs for investors.

Time Cycles Research—For Mac Users!!!

375 Willets Avenue
Waterford, CT 06385
Fax: (869) 442-0626
E-mail: *astrology@timecycles.com*
Internet: *http://www.timecycles.com*

Yes, there are astrologers who use Macs! This is where they come to for astrology software that's as sophisticated as it gets. If you have a Mac, you'll love their beautiful graphic IO Series programs.

Astro-Cartography

(Charts for location changes)
Astro-Numeric Service Box 336–B
Ashland, OR 97520
Telephone: (800) MAPPING

Astrology Magazines

In addition to articles by top astrologers, most have listings of astrology conferences, events, and local happenings.

AMERICAN ASTROLOGY
475 Park Avenue South
New York, NY 10016

DELL HOROSCOPE
P.O. Box 53352
Boulder, CO 89321–3342

PLANET EARTH
The Great Bear
P.O. Box 5164
Eugene, OR 97405

THE MOUNTAIN ASTROLOGER
P.O. Box 11292
Berkeley, CA 94701

ASPECTS
Aquarius Workshops
P.O. Box 260556
Encino, CA 91426

Astrology Schools

Though there are many correspondence courses available through private teachers and astrological organizations, up until now, there has never been an accredited college of astrology. That is why the address below is so important.

The Kepler College of Astrological Arts and Sciences

Kepler College, the first institution of its kind to combine an accredited liberal arts education with extensive astrological studies, should now be in operation. A degree-granting college that is also a center of astrology has long been the dream of the astrological community and will be a giant step forward in providing credibility to the profession.
For more information:

The Kepler College of Astrological Arts and Sciences
P.O. Box 77511
Seattle, WA 98177–0511
Telephone: (206) 706-0658
or *http://www.keplercollege.org*

CHAPTER 11

The Best Clicks to Hot Astrology Spots On-line

How to Surf the Internet for Free Software, Meet Top Astrologers, and Connect with Other Astrology Fans.

Once upon a time, you had to live in a big city to find other astrology fans. Otherwise, you had to travel to conferences to study with the best teachers or buy astrology books. Now the world of astrology is just a few clicks away, if you own or have access to a computer. There's a global community of astrologers on-line with sites that offer everything from chart services to chat rooms to individual readings. Even better, many of the most exciting sites offer *free* software, *free* charts, *free* articles to download. You can virtually get an education in astrology from your computer screen, share your insights with new astrology-minded pals in a chat room or on a mailing list, later meet them in person at one of the hundreds of conferences around the world.

So if you're curious to see a copy of your chart (or someone else's), want to study astrology in depth, or chat with another astrology fan, log on!

One caveat, however: since the Internet is constantly changing and growing, some of these sites may have changed addresses or content by the time this book is published, even though this selection was chosen with an eye to longevity. Sites were also chosen for general interest among the many thousands of astrology-oriented places on the net. Most have links to other sites for further exploration.

Free Charts

Do you want to see what your chart looks like? Want to practice reading the glyphs? Or would you like to check out the chart of that cool Aquarius you've just met in Mexico. If you've got access to the Internet (or there's an Internet café nearby), just click to one of these addresses:

ASTROLABE Software at *http://www.alabe.com* distributes some of the most creative and user-friendly programs now available, like "Solar Fire," a favorite of top astrologers. Visitors are greeted with a chart of the time when you log on. They will also E-mail a copy of your chart (or anyone else's chart) to you. Though you can't read it immediately at the site, it's worth waiting for.

For an instant chart displayed on the screen, surf to this address: *http://www.astro.ch/* and check into "ASTRO-DIENST," also home of a world atlas that will give you the accurate longitude and latitude worldwide. After entering your birthday and place of birth, you can print out your chart in a range of chart formats. One handy feature for beginners: the planetary placement is written out in an easy-to-read list alongside the chart (a real timesaver, if you haven't yet learned to read the astrology glyphs).

Free Software

Software manufacturers on the Web are generous with free downloads of demo versions of their software. You may then calculate charts using their data. This makes sense if you're considering investing serious money in astrology software and want to see how the program works in advance. You'll find a demo preview of ASTROLABE Software programs that are favored by many professional astrologers at *http://www.alabe. com/*. Check out the latest demo version of "Solar Fire," one of the most user-friendly astrology programs available—you'll be impressed!

For a fully functional astrology program:

Walter Pullen's amazingly complete ASTROLOGY program is offered absolutely free at this site: *http://www.magitech.com/~cruiser1/astrolog.htm.*

This ultra-sophisticated program comes in versions for all formats—DOS, WINDOWS, MAC, UNIX—and has some cool features such as a revolving globe and a constellation map. A "must" for those who want to get involved with astrology, without paying big bucks for a professional caliber program. Or for those who want to add ASTROLOG's unique features to their astrology software library. This program has it all!

Another great resource for software is Astro Computing Services. Their Web site has free demos of several excellent programs. Note especially their "Electronic Astrologer," one of the most effective and reasonably priced programs on the market. Go to *http://www.astrocom.com* for ACS software, books, readings, chart services, and software demos.

Go to another *http://www.astroscan.ca* for a free program called ASTROSCAN. Stunning graphics and ease of use make this a winner. It seems too good to be free!

At Halloran Software's site, *http://www.halloran.com,* there are four levels of Windows astrology software from which to choose. The "Astrology for Windows" shareware program is available in unregistered demo form as a free download and in registered form for $26.50. The calculations in this program may be all that an astrology hobbyist needs. The price for the full-service program is certainly reasonable.

Improve Your Social Life

Join a News Group or Mailing List!

You'll never feel lonely again, but you will be very busy reading the letters that overflow your mailbox every day. Be prepared! Of the many news groups, there are several devoted to astrology. The most popular is "alt.astrology." Here's your chance to connect with astrologers worldwide, exchange information, answer some of the skeptics who frequent this news group. Your mailbox will be jammed with letters from astrologers from everywhere on the planet, sharing charts of current events, special techniques, and personal problems.

Free Screen Saver and More

The Astrology Matrix offers a way to put your sign in view with a beautifully designed graphic screen saver downloadable at this site. There are also many other diversions at this site, so spend some enjoyable hours here. If a problem's got you stumped, find the answer via a variety of oracles. After you've consulted the stars, the I Ching, the runes, and the Tarot, you'll be sure to have the answer. Then consult their almanac to help you schedule the best day to sign on the dotted line, ask for a raise, or plant your rosebush. Address: *http://thenewage.com/*.

Free Astrology Course

Schedule a long visit to: *http://www.panplanet.com/,* where you will find the Canopus Academy of Astrology, a site loaded with goodies. For the experienced astrologer there are excellent articles from top astrologers. They've done the work for you when it comes to picking the best astrology links on the Web, so be sure to check out those bestowed with the Canopus Award of Excellence.

Astrologer Linda Reid, an accomplished astrology teacher and author, offers a complete on-line curriculum for all levels of astrology study plus individual tutoring. To get your feet wet, Linda is offering an excellent biginners' course at this site. A terrific way to get well grounded in astrology.

Visit an Astro Mall

Surf to *http://www.astronet.com* for the Internet's equivalent of an Astrology Mall.

ASTRONET offers interactive fun for everyone. At this writing, there's a special area for teenage astrology fans, access to popular astrology magazines like *American Astrology,* advice to the lovelorn, plus a grab bag of horoscopes, featured guests, a shopping area for books, reports, software, even jewelry.

Find an Astrologer Here

Metalog Directory of Astrology
http://www.astrologer.com

Looking for an astrologer in your local area? Perhaps you're planning a vacation in Australia or France and would like to meet astrologers or combine your activities with an astrology conference there? Go no further than this well-maintained resource. Here is an extensive worldwide list of astrologers and astrology sites. There is also an agenda of astrology conferences and seminars all over the world.

The A.F.A. Web Site
http://www.astrologers.com

This is the interesting Web site of the prestigious American Federation of Astrologers. The A.F.A. has a very similar address to the Metalog Directory and also has a directory of astrologers, restricted to those who meet their stringent requirements. Check out their correspondence course, if you would like to study astrology in depth.

Tools Every Astrologer Needs Are On-line:

Internet Atlas
http://www.astro.ch/atlas/

Find the geographic longitude and latitude and the correct time zone for any city worldwide. You'll need this information to calculate a chart.

The Exact Time, Anywhere in the World
http://www.timeticker.com

A fun site to find the exact time anywhere in the world. Click on the world map and the correct time and zone for that place lights up.

The Zodiacal Zephyr
http://www.zodiacal.com

A great jumping-off place for an astrology tour of the Internet. There's a good selection of articles, plus tools such as a U.S. and world atlas, celebrity birth data, information on conferences, software, and tapes. The links at this site will send you off in the right direction.

Astrology World
http://astrology-world.com

Astrologer Deborah Houlding has gathered some of the finest European astrologers on this terrific Web site. Great freebies, links, and lists of conferences. A "must," especially if you're traveling to the U.K.!

Astrology Alive
http://www.astrologyalive.com/

Barbara Schermer has one of the most creative approaches to astrology. She's an innovator in the field and was one of the first astrologers to go on-line, so there's always a "cutting edge" to this site. Great list of links.

National Council for Geocosmic Research (NCGR)
http://www.geocosmic.org/

A key stop on any astrological tour of the Net. Here's where you can find local chapters in your area, get information on the NCGR testing and certification programs, get a conference schedule. You can also order lecture tapes from their nationwide conferences, or get complete lists of conference topics, to study at home. Good links to resources.

Where to Find Charts of the Famous

When the news is breaking, you can bet Lois Rodden will be the first to get accurate birthdays of the headline-makers, and put up their charts on her Web site: *www.astrodatabank.com*. Rodden's research is astrology's most reliable source for data of the famous and infamous. Her new Web site features birthdays and charts of current newsmakers, political figures, international celebrities. It's also the place where you can purchase her database of thousands of birthdays of the famous, a must for astrological researchers.

Another site with birthdays and charts of famous people to download is *http://www.astropro.com*

You can get the sun and moon signs, plus a biography of the hottest new film stars here: *www.mrshowbiz.com*.

Another good source of celebrity birthdates is *http://www.metamaze.com/bdays/*. You can find some interesting offbeat celebs here like Matt Drudge and Joey Buttafuoco.

For Astrology Books

National Clearing House for Astrology Books

A wide selection of books on all aspects of astrology, from basics to advanced. Many hard-to-find books. Surf to: *http://www.astroamerica.com*

These addresses also have a good selection of astrology books, some of which are unique to the site.

http://www.panplanet.com
http://thenewage.com
http://www.astrocom.com

Browse the huge astrology list of the on-line bookstore Amazon.com at *http:www.amazon.com/*.

Astrology Tapes

Pegasus Tapes
http://www.pegasustape.com

You can study at home with world-famous astrologers via audiocassette recordings from Pegasus Tapes. There's a great selection taped from conferences, classes, lectures, and seminars. An especially good source for astrologers who emphasize psychological and mythological themes.

Your Questions Answered

Astrology FAQ
(Frequently Asked Questions)
http://www.magitech.com/pub/astrology/ info/faq.txt

Here are answers to questions that are on everyone's mind. Especially useful information, if you're countering astrology-bashers.

History and Mythology of Astrology
http://www.elore.com

Be sure to visit the astrology section of this gorgeous site, dedicated to the history and mythology of many traditions. One of the most beautifully designed sites we've seen.

The Mountain Astrologer
http://www.mountainastrologer.com/

A favorite magazine of astrology fans, *The Mountain Astrologer* has an interesting Web site featuring the latest news from an astrological point of view, plus feature articles from the magazine.

Financial Astrology

Find out how financial astrologers play the market. Here are hot picks, newsletters, specialized financial astrology software, and mutual funds run by astrology seers.

Go to *www.afund.com* or *www.alphee.com* for tips and forecasts from two top financial astrologers.

CHAPTER 12

Are You a Typical Leo?

"Regal, enthusiastic, dramatic, a natural leader" . . . does that sound like you? Some of you will agree wholeheartedly with the description of your typical Leo sun sign characteristics. Others might say, "Hey, wait a minute, I'm a couch potato who loves to stay home." Or "I'm really shy and don't like the spotlight." What we're talking about, when we say you're a "Leo," is the sign the sun was passing through at the time of your birth. But there are 10 other planets that also color your horoscope. For example, if only the sun was in Leo and the moon was passing through quiet, serious Capricorn at the time you were born, you're likely to have a more conservative personality than the typical Leo. So, the more Leo planets you have, the more likely the following descriptions will resemble your personality.

The Leo Man—Think Big

The Leo man behaves like a king, regardless of your bank statement or position in life. Everything Leo does has a larger-than-life quality, as if it is to be viewed on a giant movie screen. You're a scene-stealer, whether you're naturally impressive physically, like Arnold Schwarzenegger, or by sheer force of personality, like Bill Clinton or Mick Jagger. However, your greatest pleasure is sharing your wealth and prestige with loyal followers, treating them to a first-class trip, then picking up the tab.

Behind your self-confidence, however, is a tireless

worker who believes in what he is doing. And it is that belief that generates the enthusiasm that makes you a super-salesman. As it has been written about Arnold Schwarzenegger: "He believes with a vengeance, and that belief is compelling." You are able to radiate a kind of positive energy that draws others to you. You also believe in living on the offensive. After facing an obstacle that would knock down others, you astonish by your ability to move on, pick up your life, and go forward.

Your confidence and natural dignity seem to attract wealth and fame, even if your ascendant (rising sign) makes you seem a bit shy and retiring. Once there is a chance to step into the spotlight, you'll do so with natural flair. If you can't perform in front of an audience of some sort, you'll grab headlines as an impresario or entrepreneur. Your love of applause might lead you to cultivate those who admire you and ignore those who could offer constructive criticism.

A child at heart, Leo enjoys the perks of your position to the fullest. Many wealthy Leos, like the late tycoon Malcolm Forbes, have a collection of adult toys (yachts, motorcycles, balloons, and estates), which they love to share with others. This is one sign that truly enjoys and shares wealth, but never hoards it. But the Leo who feels he is not getting his fair share of attention is an unhappy lion who can hide in his lair, suffering from wounded pride.

In a Relationship

The king of the zodiac naturally wants a glamorous royal queen as a consort. Many Leos marry "princess" types, glamorous women of prestigious pedigree. You want a mate you can show off, yet she must always remember to put you first in her life. You'll revel in her successes, as long as she doesn't become a rival. You'll make sure she has the best of everything (even if you can't afford the tab). In return, you expect to be treated like lord of the manor, awarded the loyalty, respect, and loud applause you deserve.

Many famous Leos have wives who are equally famous, like Arnold Schwarzenegger (Maria Shriver), Frank Gifford (Kathie Lee Gifford), Gerald McRaney (Delta Burke), and President Bill Clinton. The secret of the successful Leo relationship seems to be that each has separate territory and the Leo male gets his lion's share of the limelight. If he is eclipsed by his wife in any way, he is very likely to find solace elsewhere. When a married Leo man runs into trouble, it is usually because he is not getting enough attention from his wife and craves an ego-boost from an attractive admirer, and the charismatic Leo man usually has plenty of eager female fans to choose from.

The Leo Woman—Always On Stage

The proud Leo woman is always conscious of your audience—you know how to keep entertained and fascinated. You'll keep your fans guessing, like Madonna or Jacqueline Onassis, whose changes in personal style kept her far ahead of the pack. When under intense pressure, your dignity and poise can move the world. Some Leos in the public eye have the power to move us even after death, such as the tragic little Jon Benet Ramsey. And you'll project your own unique personality regardless of the scene you're required to play. (Instantly recognizable, Leos are often first-name celebrities, such as Jackee, Madonna, Jackie O., and Iman.)

Like a playful, exuberant child, you have a show-off quality that basks in the attention and admiration of others. Your career is the stage where your talent can shine, especially in fields such as politics, where you thrive on being constantly in the public eye. You make excellent teachers and excel in any kind of sales work, where you can express your natural enthusiasm. Your desire to set others' lives on a more positive course often draws you to healing and counseling work.

A natural delegator, you surround yourself with a dream team of creative people and admirers who support you and help you look your best. (It's a rare Leo who doesn't have a hairdresser on call.) But while using your team to best advantage, you'll return favors by boosting their confidence and sometimes rewarding them with sumptuous gifts.

A Leo woman holds her head high no matter what life offers her. Your stellar qualities are nowhere more evident than in difficult times, when you have the strength to surmount impossible odds, thanks to the power of your positive mental outlook. Circumstances that could devastate anyone else are often conquered by the powerful solar energy of your Leo personality.

Two of your best professional assets are your stamina and confidence. Your radiant, positive energy is sure to get you noticed, like Julia Child, whose television debut in the 1950s on an obscure Boston station made her the Queen of Cuisine. Or Martha Stewart, who turned a small local catering venture into a huge business empire. Although you can be very demanding and imperious at times, your warmhearted nature usually wins defectors back to your side.

In a Relationship

Most Leo women prefer not to live alone, because you need admiring company. Your ideal companion would be a man as powerful, loyal, and devoted as you are, one who will not stint on lavishing you with adoration and attention. You love nothing more than to have a strong, handsome, and attentive husband on your arm, and return his attention by helping him look and feel his best and by building up his social status. However, Leo often picks men who are not your equal and who may disappoint you in the long run. You often prefer the flatterers and hangers-on who are drawn to your radiant self-confidence and positive energy. Many Leo women end up as heads of their own families, because their marriage could not take the strain of two stars, or because Leo's husband felt eclipsed by her strong personality. When you do find the right partner, however, you'll remain loyal, even in difficult times using your positive outlook to turn things around for the better. Ultimately, you may attain the relationship you've always longed for, one based on mutual respect and friendship, as well as admiration.

Your Role in the Family

The Leo Parent

Your strong, positive sign is considered one of the natural parenting signs of the zodiac. Children blossom under Leo's radiant energy, because no one encourages self-confidence and self-esteem like you do, praising them to the limit, and encouraging them to express their talents. You want only the best for your children and will give them the best education you can afford. Although you are naturally protective, you raise your children to be strong and independent, to meet your super-high standards. Sometimes you can be quite demanding, but your children are inspired to reach royal heights and often attain them.

The Leo parent usually finds ways to include children in your activities, sharing interesting aspects of your professional life with them and taking them along on trips as Kathie Lee Gifford, Madonna, and Bill Clinton do. You'll coach your children in how to handle themselves in the spotlight with poise and flair and loudly applaud any achievements and awards.

The Leo Stepparent

Stepchildren respond to your warmth at a difficult transition in their lives and often become as close to you as your own children are, retaining this closeness after they've left the nest. Your natural generosity is your greatest asset as a stepparent. You'll reach out warmly to your extended family—you enjoy having even more cubs around. At the same time, however, you'll make it very clear who rules the roost. But at a time of indecision, your strong, confident personality can provide direction and stability, while your poise and confidence rub off on socially insecure youngsters. To bring your extended family together, you'll plan gala occasions and be equally generous with presents and praise to all loved ones.

The Leo Grandparent

You command royal respect as a grandparent, holding court at family gatherings, bursting with pride over the youngest generation, especially when you see them well dressed and well mannered. Though you delegate child-rearing responsibilities to parents, you'll generously offer help with education, buy them the prettiest party dresses, and coach them in social poise and grooming. Getting together with a Leo grandparent is a special occasion, whether you're the honored guest at sports outings or playing the superlative host, taking your grandchildren to the best restaurant in town. You'll happily preside at weddings, bar mitzvahs, and anniversaries, looking every inch the family matriarch or patriarch.

CHAPTER 13

Live the Leo Way Every Day!

Your sun sign influences the styles that suit you best, the colors and sounds that lift your mood, even the places you might enjoy visiting. So try putting more of your sun sign in your daily life and see the happy difference.

Light Up Your Life

The ideal Leo environment sets off your star quality like the setting of a precious jewel. You decorate with the Midas touch, using the finest materials, plus a bit of glitter, glamour, and gold trim, wherever possible. There should be a great room for entertaining friends lavishly. Mirrored walls and antique French furniture (or good reproductions) make you feel like Louis XIV at Versailles. Photos and portraits (of guess who!) and trophies of your achievements should be prominently displayed. You love touches of fur, or feline-print rugs and bedspreads. A big, impressive bedroom, with lots of mirrors and a dramatic bed, is the perfect resting place for lazy lions. You should have a well-equipped entertainment center to bring the theater to you. Because sun-ruled Leo needs bright light, big windows and a dramatic spotlight here and there keep your mood sunny. Your decorator? Leo Martha Stewart, whose books, magazines, and TV shows should help you create a beautiful ambience and treat yourself to "good things," as Martha would do.

Hear the Leo Beat!

The Leo sound track features the scores of great Broadway hits and movie musicals. Big band sounds, opera, hundreds of serenading strings, and sweeping symphonies appeal to Leo's big-time tastes. The music of superstars Madonna, Whitney Houston, Mick Jagger, and Belinda Carlisle delight Leo rock fans. Plan your music menu to complement the many moods of your life by making a special tape of your favorite songs to use as background music for brunch and dinner parties, or to set the scene for seduction. Leos with video equipment might like to make their own multimedia shows. If you have a musical talent, or if your friends do, be sure to include live entertainment in your party plans. A talent show, with you as the MC, would be fun for all.

What a Trip! Awesome
Leo Places to Go

The three "s" words for Leo places are sun, service, and social life. Leo likes to shine in the sun, and, like actor George Hamilton, many of you are famous for your year-round tans. Pampering places like spas and plush resorts that treat you royally are Leo favorites. Glamorous cruises on the *QE II* or the Princess lines appeal to Leo explorers who like to see the world in style, without giving up any luxurious amenities. (Glamorous Leo spokesperson Kathie Lee Gifford was the perfect choice for cruise line commercials!) Adventurous Leos might visit the big cats on a safari. Choose your dream vacation destination from among these lion-favored places: the South Pacific, the Alps, Bombay, Rome, Sicily, Prague, and Zanzibar.

Leos should plan their packing carefully. Select luggage that organizes your wardrobe so you can unpack quickly. Lots of tissue paper and plastic packs keep designer clothes looking their regal best. One well-traveled Leo star packs a bag for each city she'll visit, with the appropriate clothes and accessories in each bag. Locate a good hairdresser in the city (ask someone who travels there frequently), or book your hair appointments immediately after you board a cruise ship. Since Leos rarely travel light, you should consider luggage with wheels or a sturdy folding luggage cart for those times when porters are not available.

Your Leo Colors

All shades of yellow and gold. Coral and mauve are other Leo favorites, or, like Mae West, you could shine in all white, lit up with lots of gold jewelry.

Style Setting the Leo Way

You are a great entrance maker, who steals the show every time. (But be careful not to overdo the glitz.) Yes, you can be stunning without hitting everyone over the head with your glamour. Take a cue from Jacqueline Onassis or Kathie Lee Gifford. Your hair is a focal point, and a bouffant, but immaculately groomed, mane looks best.

You can pile on the gold jewelry: It looks right on you! But don't forget your best fashion asset—your radiant smile.

Leo Fashion Leaders

Consider the glamorous designs of Yves St. Laurent. A Chanel suit also suits you fine.

The Leo Gourmet

Go somewhere you'll be treated like a queen and seated wherever you want, either to be noticed or to have a very private tête-à-tête. Next, consider the food. Basically, Leo is a traditionalist. Experimental cuisine or anything too avant-garde is not for you. You'll love a glamorous setting, either traditional with fine antiques or very theatrical with good lighting and lots of gold accents. The service should be discreet and very attentive. Dine at a grand hotel or resort in your area, which is sure to have an impressive dining room. Private country clubs are also a good bet. Some Leos, like Mae West, Madonna, or Arnold Schwarzenegger insist on health-conscious cuisine, the better to maintain the body beautiful.

CHAPTER 14

The Leo Way to Good Health

Leo rules the upper back and heart, two important areas to guard throughout your life. Be sure you have a good mattress to support the vulnerable Leo spine and learn some therapeutic exercises to strengthen and protect it. Aerobic exercises that benefit the heart and lungs are also "musts" for Leo.

Ruled by the sun, you're one sign that usually loves to tan, like Leo George Hamilton. However, considering the permanent damage sun exposure can cause, you may elect to remain porcelain white, like Madonna or the ever-beautiful Arlene Dahl. So don't leave home without a big hat, umbrella, and sunblock formulated for your skin type.

Leos are proud of your body and usually take excellent care of it. To maintain your public image, you'll summon up great discipline and determination, including sticking to a healthy diet. Your downfall could be your preference for the finer things in life, which might include dining on gourmet food at the best restaurants. Indulge yourself now and then, but balance this with regular exercise. And a lion who is not getting the love and attention you need can easily turn to food for consolation. Learn to give yourself the royal treatment in non-food ways, such as an extra trip to the beauty salon for some pampering or a massage.

Like Esther Williams, Leos love showing off a beautiful body in a swimsuit. To glorify the body beautiful, why not consider what a body-building regimen could do for you. Be sure any exercise routine you choose emphasizes good posture . . . the way you carry yourself can make the most of your figure type and dramatically affect your energy level. Get that regal bearing!

CHAPTER 15

Scoping Out Leo on the Job

When choosing a career, Leo must be careful to select an atmosphere where your talents will shine brightly. You'll get noticed, no matter what, but a strong push from a supportive mentor will send you soaring quickly. Office politics, senior executives locked into their positions, and a low-key atmosphere can dampen your spirits, so look for a company with *room at the top.* Because you work for glory as well as security, you need praise and recognition in the form of job perks.

Your business should be one that arouses your enthusiasm, and all the better if your job has as an impressive title. *Aim for a job that is be up front,* rather than behind the scenes, since you are not one to stay in the background for long. You best bets are sales, management, public relations or advertising, politics, personnel training, or teaching—all of which bring you before the public. Show business in its many forms is a Leo natural. Choose a company that thinks big, with a generous expense account and impressive offices; avoid those with gloomy working conditions, meager expense accounts, or discounted, low-status products.

Leo in Charge

You understand naturally one of the most important qualities of a leader: the art of delegating. You enjoy your prestige position to the fullest, taking advantage of all the perks. You are always visible, playing the role with style, conducting meetings with flair and a sense of drama. You make a great presentation and understand how to project the image of success with your wardrobe, posture, and gestures. You'll demand loyalty from underlings, and can be very generous to those you favor, as long as they do not outshine you or threaten your territory. You enjoy doing things in a big way, which could put a strain on your expense account, but you'll find many ways to combine business with pleasure to the greater glory of both.

Leo Teamwork

Even when working in a group, Leo will gravitate toward the most public position and will delegate lesser chores or behind-the-scenes activities as soon as possible. You are a natural self-promoter, which may cause friction with less assertive members of the team; however, you take great pride in your work and deliver full value for your time. You are careful to fulfill job requirements, even when it means working very long hours. The more recognition you get, the harder you will work, so it behooves your employer to dish out praise and perks. Sharing the spotlight can be a problem on the Leo team (particularly if there are two Leos in the group). This can be circumvented in a job that has well-defined territory and that gives you a chance to prove what you can do.

To Get Ahead Fast:

Pick a job where you'll get attention and recognition and play up these talents:

Your enthusiasm for the company's products
Style and flair
Poise and confidence
Salesmanship
Stamina

Optimism and sincerity
Ability to manage others and delegate responsibility
Big time ideas

Leo Career Role Models

Study the success stories of these highly successful Leo entrepreneurs. You might get some useful tips for moving ahead on the fast track.

Saul Steinberg
Malcolm Forbes
President Bill Clinton
Adnan Kashoggi
Madonna
Martha Stewart
Henry Ford
Mick Jagger
Julia Child
Whitney Houston
Yves St. Laurent
Coco Chanel
Dino DeLaurentiis

CHAPTER 16

The Leo Hall of Fame

We're fascinated by reading tabloids and gossip about the rich, famous, and infamous in the post-Millennium, but astrology can tell you more about your heroes than most magazine articles. Like what really turns them on (check their Venus). Or what gets them rattled (scope their Saturn). Compare similarities and differences between the celebrities who embody the typical Leo sun sign traits and those who seem untypical. Then look up other planets in the horoscope of your favorites, using the charts in this book, to find other influences in the horoscope. It's a fun way to get your education in astrology.

Woody Harrelson (7/23/61)
Stephanie Seymour (7/23/68)
Monica Lewinsky (7/23/73)
Jennifer Lopez (7/24/70)
Barry Bonds (7/24/64)
Michael Richards (7/24/49)
Lynda Carter (7/24/51)
Iman (7/25/55)
Estelle Getty (7/25/23)
Sandra Bullock (7/26/64)
Mick Jagger (7/26/43)
Susan George (7/26/50)
Blake Edwards (7/26/22)
Stanley Kubrick (7/26/28)
Dorothy Hamill (7/26/56)
Peggy Fleming (7/27/48)
Sally Struthers (7/28/48)

Peter Jennings (7/29/38)
Michael Spinks (7/29/56)
Henry Ford (7/30/1863)
Lisa Kudrow (7/30/63)
Arnold Schwarzenegger (7/30/47)
Delta Burke (7/30/56)
Paul Anka (7/30/41)
Dean Cain (7/31/66)
Geraldine Chaplin (7/31/44)
Wesley Snipes (7/31/63)
Jerry Garcia (8/1/42)
Giancarlo Giannini (8/1/42)
Yves St. Laurent (8/1/36)
Dom DeLuise (8/1/33)
Carroll O'Connor (8/2/24)
Peter O'Toole (8/2/32)
Tony Bennett (8/3/36)
Martin Sheen (8/3/40)
The Queen Mother Elizabeth (8/4/1900)
Neil Armstrong (8/5/30)
Loni Anderson (8/5/46)
"Ginger Spice" Geri Halliwell (8/6/72)
Robert Mitchum (8/6/17)
Abbey Lincoln (8/6/30)
David Duchovny (8/7/60)
Alberto Salazar (8/7/58)
Dustin Hoffman (8/8/37)
Esther Williams (8/8/23)
Gillian Anderson (8/9/68)
Sam Elliott (8/9/44)
Whitney Houston (8/9/63)
Melanie Griffith (8/9/57)
Antonio Banderas (8/10/60)
Eddie Fisher (8/10/28)
Rosanna Arquette (8/10/59)
Arlene Dahl (8/11/28)
Ben Affleck (8/12/72)
George Hamilton (8/12/39)
John Derek (8/12/26)
Kathleen Battle (8/13/48)

Fidel Castro (8/13/26)
Don Ho (8/13/30)
Jane Wyatt (8/13/12)
Halle Berry (8/14/68)
Jennifer Flavin (8/14/68)
Jackee (8/14/56)
Danielle Steel (8/14/47)
Steve Martin (8/14/45)
Magic Johnson (8/14/59)
Susan St. James (8/14/46)
Abby Dalton (8/15/35)
Julia Child (8/15/12)
Napoleon (8/15/1769)
Wendy Hiller (8/15/12)
Ethel Barrymore (8/15/1879)
Princess Anne of England (8/15/50)
Linda Ellerbee (8/15/45)
Angela Bassett (8/16/58)
Madonna (8/16/58)
Frank Gifford (8/16/30)
Kathie Lee Gifford (8/16/54)
Lesley Ann Warren (8/16/46)
Timothy Hutton (8/16/60)
Belinda Carlisle (8/17/58)
Robert De Niro (8/17/43)
Sean Penn (8/17/60)
Maureen O'Hara (8/17/21)
Mae West (8/17/1893)
Ed Norton (8/18/69)
Christian Slater (8/18/69)
Rosalyn Carter (8/18/27)
Roman Polanski (8/18/33)
Robert Redford (8/18/36)
Shelley Winters (8/18/22)
Patrick Swayze (8/18/54)
Gerald McRaney (8/19/40)
Jill St. John (8/19/40)
Malcolm Forbes (8/19/19)
Willie Shoemaker (8/19/31)
John Stamos (8/19/63)

Ron Darling (8/19/60)
Connie Chung (8/20/46)
Jacqueline Susann (8/20/21)
Jim McMahon (8/21/59)
Kenny Rogers (8/21/58)
Wilt Chamberlain (8/21/36)
Princess Margaret (8/21/30)
Count Basie (8/21/06)
Norman Schwarzkopf (8/22/34)
Ray Bradbury (8/22/20)
Valerie Harper (8/22/40)
Cindy Williams (8/22/47)

CHAPTER 17

Leo Partnership Potential— How You Get Along with Every Other Sign

Are you thinking about teaming up with someone either romantically or professionally? Here are the pluses and minuses of every combination, so you'll know what to expect before you commit. Bear in mind that we're all a combination of many different planets, most likely in other signs, so be tolerant of your choices. There could be another planet in the picture that will make a big difference in how well (or not) you get along.

Leo/Aries

PLUSES:
The heat's on with this pair of romantics who share high hopes, high energy, and high ideals. You can express your finest qualities, if you learn to feed each other's egos and co-star, rather than take over center stage. This could be a long-run relationship.

MINUSES:
The problems appear when romance turns to reality. Both of you are delegators—neither likes to do nitty-gritty follow-through. If either of you gets overly bossy, this romance could explode. Leo may long to be fussed over, while Aries will want to feel like number one once in a while.

These two self-centered signs have to learn to give and occasionally give in to each other.

Leo/Taurus

PLUSES:
Leo passion meets Taurus sensuality and there's a volcanic physical attraction, as you test each other's strength. Both lovers of beauty and comfort, you also have high ideas, fidelity, love of good food and music going for you. Taurus money management could provide Leo with a royal lifestyle.

MINUSES:
Tensions between these two fixed signs are inevitable. Leo plays dangerous games here, such as denying each other affection or sex. Focus on building emotional security and avoiding no-win emotional showdowns. Leo's extravagance and Taurus' possessiveness could be bones of contention.

Leo/Gemini

PLUSES:
Gemini's good humor, ready wit, and social skills delight and complement Leo. Here is someone who can share the spotlight without trying to steal the show from the regal lion. This is one of the most entertaining combinations. Steady Leo provides the focus Gemini often lacks and directs the twins toward achieving goals and status.

MINUSES:
Gemini loves to flirt and flit among many interests, romantic and otherwise, which is sure to irritate the lion, who does one thing at a time and does it well. Gemini might be a bit bored with Leo's self-promotion and might poke fun at this sign's notorious vanity. The resulting feline roar will be no laughing matter.

Leo/Cancer

PLUSES:
These neighboring signs come through for each other like good buddies. Cancer gives Leo total attention, backup support, and the VIP treatment the lion craves. Here is someone who won't fight for the spotlight. Leo gives Cancer confidence, and this sign's positive mental outlook is good medicine for Cancer moods.

MINUSES:
Cancer's blue moods and tendency to cling tenaciously can weight Leo down, while Leo can steamroll sensitive Cancer feelings with high-handed behavior.

Leo/Leo

PLUSES:
This mirror-image couple can be a mutual admiration society. You'll love showing each other off, spotlighting each other's talents and radiating confidence, warmth, and optimism. If you can get the right working dynamics, you'll move ahead together socially and professionally.

MINUSES:
You may be too dazzled to deal with practical realities. Popularity won't take the place of long-range goals and clear priorities. You could burn out from high living or eclipse each other if you don't learn to share the stage and take turns boosting each other.

Leo/Virgo

PLUSES:
Leo confidence, sales power, and optimism, as well as aristocratic presence, is a big Virgo draw. Virgo will have a ready-made job efficiently running the mechanical parts

of Leo's life—which Leo is only too happy to delegate. And Leo's social poise brings Virgo into the public eye—and can help this shy sign bloom! Both are faithful and loyal signs who find much to admire in each other.

MINUSES:
You may not appreciate each other's point of view. Virgo is more likely to dole out well-meaning criticism and vitamins than the admiration and applause Leo craves. Virgo will also protest leonine high-handedness with the budget. Virgo makes the house rules, but Leo is above them, a rule unto yourself. Leo always looks at the big picture, Virgo at the nitty-gritty details. You might dampen each other's spirits, unless you find a way to work this out early in the relationship.

Leo/Libra

PLUSES:
Libra is the perfect audience for Leo theatrics. And this sign knows how to package you for stardom. You both love the best things in life, are intelligent, stylish, and social. Since you have similar priorities, and stroke each other the right way, you could have a long-lasting relationship.

MINUSES:
Getting the financial area of your life under control could be a problem for these two big spenders. Since you both love to make an elegant impression, you may find yourself perennially living beyond your means. You are both flirts, which is easier for Libra to tolerate than Leo, who could unleash lethal jealousy.

Leo/Scorpio

PLUSES:
Scorpio's innate power and Leo's confidence and authority can make a fascinating high-profile combination like

Leo Arnold Schwarzenegger and Scorpio Maria Shriver. There is great mutual respect and loyalty here, as well as sexual dynamite. You two magnetic, unconquerable heroes offer each other enough challenges to keep the sparks flying.

MINUSES:
Scorpio's natural secretiveness and Leo's openness could conflict, especially if Scorpio reveals their powerful will and need for control underneath a deceptively quiet facade. And Leo is often surprised by the sheer intensity of Scorpio's drive and willpower. Though Scorpio won't fight for the spotlight, they will often control behind the scenes. When these two intense, stubborn, demanding signs collide, it's a no-win situation.
Celebrity Couples: Leo Arnold Schwarzenegger and Scorpio Maria Shriver

Leo/Sagittarius

PLUSES:
Under Sagittarius' optimism and good humor, Leo's luck soars. You both inspire each other and boost each other creatively. If you like the outdoor life, have a spirit of adventure, and love to travel, you're a winning combination that could feel fated to be together.

MINUSES:
Sagittarius is not one to pour on the flattery Leo loves, nor is this sign known for monogamy. When both your fiery tempers explode, Leo roars and Sagittarius heads for the door. Leo must tone down bossiness and give Sagittarius a very long leash. Sag must learn to coddle the Leo ego and keep that blazing temper on hold.

Leo/Capricorn

PLUSES:
Here's the perfect mix of business and pleasure. Dignified, refined Capricorn has energy and discipline to

match Leo's. However, Leo comes to the rescue of this ambitious workaholic, adding confidence, poise, and joie de vivre. Capricorn reciprocates with the royal treatment.

MINUSES:
Capricorn prefers underplayed elegance to glitz and glamour, so you may have to tone down your showoff style. Capricorn cuts off the cash flow when Leo becomes extravagant and may not pour out the megadoses of affection that Leo requires. Leo can't stand a partner who is stingy with love or money.

Leo/Aquarius

PLUSES:
Love at first sight often happens between these magnetic zodiac opposites. You both flourish in the public eye and enjoy sharing your life with admiring fans. You enjoy taking on big projects and helping humanity together. Leo warmth is a social plus for Aquarius. And Aquarius vision tunes in to Leo's spiritual side.

MINUSES:
Cool, detached Aquarius may not give Leos the devotion they demand, and may need to devote more time and attention to stroking Leo's ego. Aquarius likes an open relationship, with lots of freedom to roam—although not necessarily to stray. You will need to put this sign on a very long leash.

Leo/Pisces

PLUSES:
Highly sensitive Pisces admires Leo's radiant confidence and gains stability under your warm encouraging protection. Leo will gain an adoring admirer who easily shows affection and satisfies Leo's constant craving for ro-

mance. This is a noncompetitive mutual admiration society where you promote each other enthusiastically.

MINUSES:
Pisces also loves to flirt, but, unlike Leo, is not basically monogamous. Sticklers for loyalty, Leo may try to keep the Pisces dancing attendance by strong-arm tactics. Pisces operates best in free-flowing waters—swims off when this sign senses a "hook."

CHAPTER 18

Astrological Outlook for
Leo in 2001

There will be rough spots this year, as the Saturn keynote attempts to blot out your sun ruler. There will be love affairs and obstacles. You could be musing, "What has happened; are the gods against me?" For a time, you will decide: "What is the use, perhaps I should hand 'em up." Then, like a bolt out of the blue, you recall the words of one of your favorite authors, Capricorn Jack London. The famous author put forth this philosophy: "The purpose of life is to live, not to exist."

Saturn will be in Taurus until April, when it goes into Gemini, and this emphasizes career, ambition, defeat, victory, as if on an escalator. As Jack London prescribes, however, victory or defeat, you will be living, not merely existing.

People who play important roles in your life this year will include Capricorn and Cancer, and are likely to have these letters or initials in their names: H, Q, Z.

In matters of speculation, you will have luck with these numbers: 8, 2, 9.

It Could Happen

Someone from your past will once again play a role in your life. The person is likely to be an older Capricorn willing to share the benefit of experience. Part of that experience will be to share information about a business partnership or marriage.

Even in victory, including winning a contest, there

could be an aura of sadness. While Saturn is in your eleventh house, starting in April and going back and forth, problems are solved financially by the winning of money. Saturn will not let you forget; haunting memories blend with victory celebrations.

Highlights

A change of marital status, good fortune in finance, romance, the acquisition of an art object made of heavy steel, promotion in your career, being in charge of production, standing tall for your principles, gaining acceptance and rejection from the public at large.

In the following pages, you will be reading your diary in advance. You will be provided with lucky lottery numbers, racetrack results, the joy of love and agony of rejection. It is time to begin reading, so please start now!

CHAPTER 19

Eighteen Months of Day-by-Day Predictions—July 2000 to December 2001

JULY 2000

Saturday, July 1 (Moon in Cancer)   The realization hits home that you have much information to dispense, but there are restrictions and you must hold back to some degree. The new moon, solar eclipse, falls in Cancer, which relates to your twelfth house, covering secret information that, for the time being, must be kept secret. Your lucky number is 6.

Sunday, July 2 (Moon in Cancer to Leo 10:39 p.m.)   On this Sunday, there's plenty of time for reflection, as Cancer and Pisces with the letters G, P, Y in their names play leading roles. This Sunday will feature self-revelation. A Virgo steps into your scenario, saying, "I know everything about what you need legally!"

Monday, July 3 (Moon in Leo)   Tomorrow's holiday will find you gaining enthusiasm and sharing information unabashedly. Relate to quotations from Washington, Jefferson, and other leaders who promoted independence. Capricorn is involved.

Tuesday, July 4 (Moon in Leo to Virgo 11:20 p.m.)   Take special care while handling explosives, including fireworks. It's an excellent time to be the center of attention, without hogging the spotlight. Some people will be extremely sensitive or even jealous. Know it, and be sure to praise those who display a unique talent. Make this holiday memorable and joyful!

Wednesday, July 5 (Moon in Virgo)   What was taken by mistake will be returned. It's a very good day for reading and writing, teaching, and disseminating information. Although tired, you will emit an aura of personal magnetism, sensuality, and sex appeal. Another Leo plays a dynamic role. Your lucky number is 1.

Thursday, July 6 (Moon in Virgo)   For racing luck, these selections apply to all tracks: post-position special—number 6 p.p. in the fifth race. Pick six: 2, 3, 4, 1, 6, 5. Look for these letters in the names of potential winning horses or jockeys: B, K, T. Hot daily doubles: 2 and 3, 1 and 1, 6 and 6. Cancer-born jockeys will ride favorites into the Winner's Circle.

Friday, July 7 (Moon in Virgo to Libra 2:48 a.m.)   Go slow, because your forces tend to be scattered. The information you need will be handed to you on a silver platter—but don't rush it! Special: Be wary in traffic, as careless drivers could cause you to be injured as result of frustration. A Gemini figures prominently.

Saturday, July 8 (Moon in Libra)   Lucky lottery: 8, 16, 14, 6, 7, 12. Your source material requires scrutiny, for figures have been juggled—deliberately or otherwise. Strive for balance, including your budget. An aggressive Scorpio tends to tell you all about everything—but most of the talk is frivolous.

Sunday, July 9 (Moon in Libra to Scorpio 9:49 a.m.) Within 24 hours, you'll learn more about property and long-term negotiations, and you'll see where you fit in with a real estate activity. Be willing to revise, review, and to tear down in order to rebuild on a more suitable structure. Gemini, Virgo, and Sagittarius are in this picture, and have these letters in their names—E, N, W.

Monday, July 10 (Moon in Scorpio)   Attention revolves around what happens at home. A family member, not conscious of budget, insists on decorating and bringing your color coordination into focus. In order to keep the peace, make an intelligent compromise. No matter how long you wait, the facts of life eventually will have to be articulated.

Tuesday, July 11 (Moon in Scorpio to Sagittarius 8:06 p.m.)   You've waited for this—and today a special package finally arrives. The contents will help you to prove a major thesis. Define your terms, outline your boundaries, and play the waiting game. Try to perfect your techniques and streamline your procedures. Pisces and Virgo are represented.

Wednesday, July 12 (Moon in Sagittarius)   Lucky lottery: 8, 9, 3, 14, 12, 22. Intensity! The spotlight is on time, timing, and a relationship that grows hotter by the moment. If you are single, a decision about marriage looms large; if you're married, the two of you agree to go into business for yourselves. Capricorn plays a role.

Thursday, July 13 (Moon in Sagittarius)   For racing luck, these selections apply at all tracks: post-position special—number 8 p.p. in the first race. Pick six: 8, 5, 4, 4, 6, 7. Look for these letters in the names of potential winning horses or jockeys: I and R. Hot daily doubles: 8 and 5, 3 and 6, 4 and 4. Aries and Libra jockeys win and pay good prices.

Friday, July 14 (Moon in Sagittarius to Capricorn 8:28 a.m.)   Lucky numbers: 4, 14, 7. Within 24 hours, you receive your marching orders. Mainly, you get what you ask for, so keep your independent stance and imprint your style. It's not necessary to take a backseat to anyone. Aquarius and another Leo dominate the scenario.

Saturday, July 15 (Moon in Capricorn) Make resolutions about your home, family, and future prospects. What must be done will be made crystal clear. Your security is at stake, so insist on quality material and maintain creative control of a project. Cancer and Capricorn are featured, and have these letters in their names— B, K, T.

Sunday, July 16 (Moon in Capricorn to Aquarius 9:27 p.m.) The full moon, lunar eclipse, falls in Capricorn. This represents a shakeup in your routine, especially in connection with employment. Attention: Household pets require more care than usual. Your own health factors necessitate a change of plans. Those little aches and pains might not be so little if you continue to ignore them.

Monday, July 17 (Moon in Aquarius) The Aquarian moon relates to your partnership, legal documents, public relations, and marital status. It seems that today people you meet and situations you experience will be completely unusual. Taurus, Scorpio, and another Leo involve you in fascinating discussions.

Tuesday, July 18 (Moon in Aquarius) You'll be musing, "Very unusual Tuesday!" The Aquarian moon tells of surprises, as well as the consummation of deals that apparently were cold. A relationship that at first you did not take seriously could lead to partnership or marriage. Sagittarian plays a top role.

Wednesday, July 19 (Moon in Aquarius to Pisces 9:45 a.m.) Attention revolves around your home, family relationships, income potential, and questions about your home, your companions, and your marital status. Be diplomatic and avoid forcing issues. Purchase a gift for special person—an art object or a luxury item. Flowers and music are involved. Lucky number is 6.

Thursday, July 20 (Moon in Pisces) For racing luck these selections apply to all tracks: post-position special—number 1 p.p. in the sixth race. Pick six: 1, 7, 4, 2, 5, 1. Watch for these letters in the names of potential winning horses or jockeys: G, P, Y. Hot daily doubles: 1 and 7, 3 and 3, 5 and 8. Upset winners! Horses that run well in mud will win, and Pisces jockeys are outstanding.

Friday, July 21 (Moon in Pisces to Aries 8:10 p.m.)   Dig deep for information! What you need to learn is contained in arcane literature. By devoting some time to investigation, you might reap a handsome reward. Focus on time, a deadline, and on an intense and controversial relationship. Someone in a position of authority decides to test you.

Saturday, July 22 (Moon in Aries)   On this Saturday, your sense of perception becomes razor sharp. You are capable of predicting the future and making it come true—to your vision and advantage. A project is completed; you are grateful to be finished with an unsavory situation. You'll have luck with the number 9.

Sunday, July 23 (Moon in Aries)   The Aries moon relates to your education, knowledge, and awareness of spiritual values. The answer to your question: Yes, make a fresh start, exercising independence of thought and action. Do your own thing; don't follow others. Stress your pioneering spirit. A love relationship smolders!

Monday, July 24 (Moon in Aries to Taurus 3:45 a.m.) Lucky numbers: 2, 4, 20. Someone with a reputation for being a strict disciplinarian shows appreciation for your ability. The spotlight falls on promotion, production, and initiative. Capricorn and Cancer play outstanding roles, and have these letters in their names—B, K, T.

Tuesday, July 25 (Moon in Taurus)   For racing luck, these selections apply to all tracks: post-position special—number 5 p.p. in the seventh race. Pick six: 3, 7, 6, 4, 1, 5. Look for these letters in the names of potential winning horses or jockeys: C, L, U. Hot daily doubles: 3

and 7, 3 and 3, 4 and 8. Sagittarian jockeys ride and win with long shots—expect big payoffs!

Wednesday, July 26 (Moon in Taurus to Gemini 8:03 a.m.)   Lucky lottery: 2, 4, 24, 1, 5, 50. Mechanical objects act up so check your car water and oil, and take care when handling electrical outlets at home. Taurus, Scorpio, and another Leo play fantastic roles, and will have these letters in their names—D, M, V.

Thursday, July 27 (Moon in Gemini)   Thursday will be a day featuring creative activity. Be on the move, focusing on discovery and exploration. Permit a flirtation to lend spice to your life. What was lost 24 hours ago will reappear, almost as if by magic. Gemini and Virgo are in the picture.

Friday, July 28 (Moon in Gemini to Cancer 9:31 a.m.)   Attention revolves around domestic relationships that include your friends and your marital status. There's more music in your life. Romantic dining by candlelight makes you slightly uncomfortable, but is rewarding. A Libra plays a featured role. In matters of speculation, stick with the number 6.

Saturday, July 29 (Moon in Cancer)   For racing luck, these selections apply at all tracks: post-position special—number 1 p.p. in the sixth race. Pick six: 7, 3, 8, 4, 1, 1. Watch for these letters in the names of potential winning horses or jockeys: G, P. Y. Hot daily doubles: 7 and 3, 4 and 8, 1 and 3. Pisces jockeys are in danger of injury. Horses that run well in mud will win.

Sunday, July 30 (Moon in Cancer to Leo 9:24 a.m.) Private information comes into your hands. Following hours of confusion you will know what to do and will benefit from this action. The emphasis is on secrets and the need for discretion. Get your priorities in order. Show off your ability to function well under pressure. A Cancer is involved.

Monday, July 31 (Moon in Leo)   The blue moon and
solar eclipse fall in your sign, so your actions and reactions will be closely observed. An opportunity exists to
let go of restrictions, to travel, and to pursue romance.
Added recognition could equate to fame and fortune. An
Aries will play an instrumental role.

AUGUST 2000

***Tuesday, August 1 (Moon in Leo to Virgo 9:28
a.m.)***   You start off this month with the moon in your
own sign, with the Neptune keynote and every prospect
for a harmonious, romantic, prosperous month. Despite
obstacles, you'll be in charge of your own destiny. Your
judgment and intuition will be on target. Another Leo
plays a key role.

Wednesday, August 2 (Moon in Virgo)   Lucky lottery: 8, 12, 50, 7, 17, 6. The Virgo moon relates to payments, collections, and your earning power. What was
lost will be returned. The entire incident was a blend of
humor and embarrassment. Focus on a business transac-
tion closely related to your partnership or marriage. Capricorn is involved.

Thursday, August 3 (Moon in Virgo to Libra 11:32 a.m.)
Loosen up! Keep your plans flexible, for you could be
called on to travel at the drop of a hat. A relationship
is tested, and it could be the beginning or end. Do not
let yourself become an emotional punching bag. Aries
and Libra figure in this scenario, and will have these
letters in their names—I and R.

Friday, August 4 (Moon in Libra)   What you've been
waiting for will arrive within hours of reading these
words. Take the initiative in making a fresh start in a
new direction, but be sure to take precautions to protect
your right eye from a possible injury. Your lucky number
is 1.

Saturday, August 5 (Moon in Libra to Scorpio 5:05 p.m.) You'll be dubbed a dashing figure. People are drawn to your charm, as well as to your knowledge of fashion and current events. Others say you are urbane. Warning: Don't break too many hearts! Focus on direction, motivation, and major questions about marriage. A Cancer is involved.

Sunday, August 6 (Moon in Scorpio) Focus on your family, and on a declaration of your principles. You'll win friends and influence people, largely as a result of your ability to laugh at your own foibles. An argument at home will conclude with passionate lovemaking. Gemini and Sagittarius are in this picture.

Monday, August 7 (Moon in Scorpio) Lucky numbers: 4, 10, 12. The Scorpio moon relates to your home and property values, and to your ability to handle a temperamental outburst of a relative who shouts, "Nobody ever listens to me!" Taurus, Scorpio, and another Leo play astounding roles, and will have these letters in their names—D, M, V.

Tuesday, August 8 (Moon in Scorpio to Sagittarius 2:31 a.m.) For racing luck, these selections apply to all tracks: post-position special—number 3 p.p. in the second race. Pick six: 6, 3, 1, 4, 2, 8. Watch for these letters in the names of potential winning horses or jockeys: E, N, W. Hot daily doubles: 6 and 3, 1 and 5, 4 and 5. Longshot winners, Gemini jockeys provide outstanding rides.

Wednesday, August 9 (Moon in Sagittarius) Lucky lottery: 6, 51, 4, 12, 18, 33. The Sagittarian moon coincides with creativity, romance, challenge, flirtation, and physical attraction. The spotlight is on your home, and on serious discussions with your family about your income potential and your marriage. Taurus and Libra could dominate this scenario.

Thursday, August 10 (Moon in Sagittarius to Capricorn 2:45 p.m.) On this Thursday, you'll be saying, "I don't know exactly why, but I feel like a night out!" In any project, maintain your creative control, taking advantage of the fact that many consider you a mysterious figure. Capitalize on it—don't tell how your tricks are done!

Friday, August 11 (Moon in Capricorn) Your intuition rings true—don't be "touted off" winners. A working relationship with someone not socially acceptable will ultimately prove beneficial. The spotlight is on priorities, the element of time, and the need to meet a deadline. Capricorn plays a distinguished role.

Saturday, August 12 (Moon in Capricorn) For racing luck, these selections apply to all tracks: post-position special—number 8 p.p. in the first race. Pick six: 8, 1, 4, 4, 7, 3. Look for these letters in the names of potential winning horses or jockeys: I and R. Hot daily doubles: 8 and 1, 3 and 6, 8 and 8. Aries jockeys do very well, especially those riding horses from foreign lands.

Sunday, August 13 (Moon in Capricorn to Aquarius 3:44 a.m.) No matter that it is Sunday—love and romance dominate. The Aquarian moon is in a section of the horoscope associated with your marriage. The sun keynote encourages independence, daring, the courage of your convictions, and a willingness to make a fresh start in a new direction. An Aquarian plays a role.

Monday, August 14 (Moon in Aquarius) All indications point to your public appearances, displays of products, partnerships, and marriage. The answer to your question: It's good, but this is not quite the same—please wait! Correct a plumbing problem. Cancer and Capricorn play astonishing roles, and have these initials in their names—B, K, T.

Tuesday, August 15 (Moon in Aquarius to Pisces 3:42 p.m.)   The full moon is in an area of your chart associated with a relationship that grows intense, romantic, and sensual. Marriage is possible. Keep up to date on international news, vitamins and fitness, and travel and humor. A Sagittarian plays a major role. Your lucky number is 3.

Wednesday, August 16 (Moon in Pisces)   The moon position emphasizes interest in the occult and your ability to do well when handling other people's money—this includes the stock market. Taurus, Scorpio, and another Leo play dramatic roles, and will have these letters in their names: D, M, V. Your lucky number is 4.

Thursday, August 17 (Moon in Pisces)   You'll be commenting on the element of time; the subject of changing times will figure prominently. People seek your opinion, but be careful of envious persons who want only to argue about nothing. Gemini, Virgo, and Sagittarius play fascinating roles, and will have these letters in their names—E, N, W.

Friday, August 18 (Moon in Pisces to Aries 1:45 a.m.)   Go slow, letting family member learn what has been going on while away. Travel talk is prominent. The Aries moon relates to your ninth house, that section of chart associated with spiritual affairs, travel, publishing, and getting your message across.

Saturday, August 19 (Moon in Aries)   Toss aside false premises, refusing to substitute wishful thinking for facts and figures. Someone who promises something for nothing has exactly that to offer—nothing! Get your promises in writing and be sure to insist on background material and references. Pisces is involved.

Sunday, August 20 (Moon in Aries to Taurus 9:32 a.m.)   The end of a long wait! A promise of promotion and production will finally be fulfilled. You will have proof that something solid is being done to keep promises and fulfill obligations. A top executive declares, "We know your worth; you are appreciated and we will reward you!"

Monday, August 21 (Moon in Taurus)   Universal appeal! What goes around comes around. You could be on a journey that combines business with pleasure. Focus on photography, publishing, and expressing feelings in a unique, original way. An important relationship could be beginning—or ending. Aries is involved.

Tuesday, August 22 (Moon in Taurus to Gemini 2:56 p.m.)   You get the proverbial second chance—what fell flat one month ago will be revived to your advantage. The moon position highlights your career, promotion, and prestige, as well as a conference with community leaders. Special: Take care while dining on foods that contain bones—you might be in danger of choking. Know it, and prevent it—forewarned is forearmed!

Wednesday, August 23 (Moon in Gemini)   Talk revolves around a close call you experienced 24 hours ago. Tonight, emphasis will be on deciding about the purchase or sale of property, home environment, and rules and regulations concerning tax and license requirements. A Cancer brings the subject of marriage to the forefront.

Thursday, August 24 (Moon in Gemini to Cancer 6 p.m.)   Focus on diversity, versatility, and your ability to use your powers of persuasion. Your Leo charm enables you to win friends and influence people among those who have influence. You'll have good fortune in matters of finance and romance. A Gemini comes up with profitable surprise.

Friday, August 25 (Moon in Cancer)   Your memory is tested! People talk about the past and you might meet a former lover who declares, "I thought you would never forget me, but I see you have!" Maintain your humor and your emotional equilibrium. Don't take what others say or claim too seriously. Scorpio is involved.

Saturday, August 26 (Moon in Cancer to Leo 7:17 p.m.)   What you have been trying to get away from will not let you go! You're haunted by past promises and obligations. A sensual person asserts, "Try as you may, you won't get away!" All of this is said and done with a smile. A secret and romantic meeting will finally settle burning issues.

Sunday, August 27 (Moon in Leo)   An aura of calm prevails. Your cycle is high; you'll once again be in charge of your own fate and destiny. Attention revolves around your family, home, property value, income, and the music in your life. A recent throat irritation will be cured. Keep your resolutions about exercise, diet, and nutrition.

Monday, August 28 (Moon in Leo to Virgo 7:56 p.m.)   Refuse to be discouraged by a broken promise. Someone who made a promise is sincere and in the long run, will not let you down. What happens should be regarded as a blessing in disguise. Pisces and Virgo play leading roles, and will have these letters in their names— G, P, Y.

Tuesday, August 29 (Moon in Virgo)   The new moon in Virgo symbolizes a fresh chance to recoup a financial loss. Be aware of statistical evidence and ride with the tide. Your cycle remains high and you could emerge as a big winner. Capricorn and Cancer play outstanding roles, and have these letters in their names—H, Q, Z.

Wednesday, August 30 (Moon in Virgo to Libra 9:34 p.m.)   For racing luck, these selections apply to all tracks: post-position special—number 8 p.p. in the first race. Pick six: 8, 3, 4, 1, 7, 8. Watch for these letters in the names of potential winning horses or jockeys: I and

R. Hot daily doubles: 8 and 3, 3 and 6, 5 and 5. Aries and Libra jockeys ride the long shots and win!

Thursday, August 31 (Moon in Libra)   Answer: Affirmative. Take the initiative when making a new start, promoting a new product, or encouraging a new kind of love. On this last day of August, imprint your style, wearing bright colors and making personal appearances. Aquarius, Libra, and another Leo play fantastic roles, and will have these letters in their names—A, S, J. Lucky number is 1.

SEPTEMBER 2000

Friday, September 1 (Moon in Libra)   On this first day of September, with the moon in Libra and a Saturn keynote, you'll nail down professional and personal agreements. A relative, mostly absent from your life, insists, "We must see more of each other!" A Capricorn plays a dynamic role.

Saturday, September 2 (Moon in Libra to Scorpio 1:56 a.m.)   What you have been waiting for will arrive—in the form of answers to your questions. Your writing skills are highlighted, so express your ideas on paper and submit your format. Someone of the opposite sex declares, "You have more talent in your little finger than most people have in both of their hands!"

Sunday, September 3 (Moon in Scorpio)   An exciting Sunday! Attention revolves around your home base, and you receive rapt observation from those who are usually disinterested. Seize the moment! Take the initiative, highlighting your originality, and letting others know, "There are two ways to do things, the wrong way and my way!" Ignore those who claim you are arrogant.

Monday, September 4 (Moon in Scorpio to Sagittarius 10:10 a.m.)   Within 24 hours, your love life is revived in a substantial way. Focus on discovery, intellectual curiosity, charm, humor, and physical attraction. The emphasis is on direction, motivation, the sight of your ultimate goal, and the knowledge of what to do when it is reached. A Cancer is involved.

Tuesday, September 5 (Moon in Sagittarius)   Refuse to take a backseat to a slick person who knows the price of everything, but the value of nothing. The Sagittarian moon coincides with creativity, style, and an aura of sensuality and sex appeal. Gemini and Sagittarius play dramatic roles, and have these letters in their names—C, L, U.

Wednesday, September 6 (Moon in Sagittarius to Capricorn 10:10 a.m.)   For racing luck, these selections apply to all tracks: post-position special—number 4 p.p. in the eighth race. Pick six: 2, 6, 4, 1, 3, 5. Watch for these letters in the names of potential winning horses or jockeys: D, M, V. Hot daily doubles: 2 and 6, 4 and 4, 3 and 8. Taurus, Leo, and Scorpio jockeys will be in the Winner's Circle!

Thursday, September 7 (Moon in Capricorn)   The subject of Libra writer, Thomas Wolfe, is brought up during a literary discussion. There is talk about home, marriage, where you belong, and your purpose in life. That will bring forth the title of Wolfe's work *Look Homeward, Angel*. Gemini, Virgo, and Sagittarius are involved, and have these letters in their names—E, N, W.

Friday, September 8 (Moon in Capricorn)   You'll muse, "It was refreshing yesterday to talk about art and literature and that strange, burly writer, Wolfe!" Interest will be in connection with home, family, security, earning power, and marriage. You'll decide, "From now on, I'm dancing to my own tune!" Your lucky number is 6.

Saturday, September 9 (Moon in Capricorn to Aquarius 10:46 a.m.)   Lucky lottery: 10, 11, 8, 22, 44, 5. Hold tight to your possessions, for someone is trying to talk you out of something of value. Be perceptive enough to recognize meaningless chatter. Pisces and Virgo figure in this fascinating scenario, and have these letters in their names—G, P, Y.

Sunday, September 10 (Moon in Aquarius) A serious discussion revolves around a legal agreement, public relations, and the possibility of a partnership or marriage. The Saturn keynote depicts reality, lasting power, and the need to work overtime to meet and beat a deadline. About a relationship, you'll ask: "Is it worth it?"

Monday, September 11 (Moon in Aquarius to Pisces 10:35 p.m.) Maintain your aura of mystery—although you are not hiding anything, people will perceive that you have a secret and are not revealing it. A barrage of questions represents tests of your veracity. Tell the whole truth, but don't be afraid to embellish it—just a little!

Tuesday, September 12 (Moon in Pisces) The answer to your question: Yes, this is the time for a new start, provided you have looked behind the scenes and stay aware of potential traps. Imprint your own style and refuse to follow others. Material regarded as occult can be used to definite advantage. An Aquarian plays a role.

Wednesday, September 13 (Moon in Pisces) Lucky lottery: The full moon in Pisces encourages these numbers—2, 20, 12, 7, 19, 4. Check accounting procedures and be careful when handling money belonging to others. Taking bets at this time would not be wise. Capricorn and Cancer play outstanding roles, and have these initials in their names—B, K, T.

Thursday, September 14 (Moon in Pisces to Aries 8:01 a.m.) Lucky numbers: 3, 12, 9. Before the day is finished, you'll be offered a promotion or project that requires skill, originality—or both. Maintain your aplomb and your emotional equilibrium, and make sure you are granted creative control. A Sagittarian plays a distinctive role.

Friday, September 15 (Moon in Aries) You'll know what to do and when to do it—a long-distance communication provides the guideline. Proofreading is necessary, so verify references and bring your source material up to date. Your prestige is at stake—you come through with flying colors! Taurus will play a dramatic role.

Saturday, September 16 (Moon in Aries to Taurus 3:06 p.m.) For racing luck, these selections apply to all tracks: post-position special—number 3 p.p. in the second race. Pick six: 7, 3, 1, 2, 2, 5. Look for these letters in the names of potential winning horses or jockeys: E, N, W. Hot daily doubles: 7 and 3, 5 and 5, 2 and 8. Speed horses get out in front and win—Gemini jockeys bring in long shots.

Sunday, September 17 (Moon in Taurus) You get a crystal-clear view of where you are, your potential, how far you will go, and what you will win as a result. The lunar position highlights your career and conferences with leaders. Attention revolves around your lifestyle, giving and receiving love, beautifying your surroundings, and your marital status.

Monday, September 18 (Moon in Taurus to Gemini 8:23 p.m.) Avoid self-deception! A jealous person who says you get all the breaks tries to put the brakes on you. Make it clear that you don't mind working alone and steer clear of nefarious schemes. Your psychic impression is valid—pay heed! Pisces and Virgo are represented.

Tuesday, September 19 (Moon in Gemini) At last! What you've been waiting for—a kind of cycle during which you win friends and influence powerful people. You hit emotional and financial jackpots—some member of the opposite sex will positively swoon! Attention: Listen, Leo, don't break too many hearts!

Wednesday, September 20 (Moon in Gemini to Cancer 12:16 p.m.)   What goes around comes around—someone who cheated will confess, apologize, and plead for forgiveness. Look beyond the immediate. Your facility with language and words will be featured—to your advantage. Lucky lottery: 9, 12, 32, 19, 22, 33.

Thursday, September 21 (Moon in Cancer)   On this Thursday, you make a mark! Your actions are noticed by people connected with communications—newspaper, television, or radio. Languidly reply to your questions, "After all, aren't records made to be broken!" Another Leo is in this picture.

Friday, September 22 (Moon in Cancer)   You'll be asking, "Is this déjà vu?" Today's scenario highlights familiar places and faces. A family member acts in a strange way. Nothing seems to taste good until at least seven tonight. You'll swear this has happened to you before at another time and in another land.

Saturday, September 23 (Moon in Cancer to Leo 3:01 a.m.)   For racing luck, these selections apply at all tracks: post-position special—number 5 p.p. in the second race. Pick six: 1, 5, 3, 8, 4, 4. Look for these letters in the names of potential winning horses or jockeys: C, L, U. Hot daily doubles: 1 and 5, 3 and 3, 7 and 4. Racing luck enables Sagittarius jockeys to win photo finishes and bring good prices!

Sunday, September 24 (Moon in Leo)   Your cycle is high, so objections to procedures are overcome. You have your way. Taurus, Scorpio, and another Leo play fascinating roles, and could have these letters in their names—D, M, V. Fuel is required for mechanical objects and your car.

Monday, September 25 (Moon in Leo to Virgo 5:03 a.m.) You'll have extrasensory perception. Mercury dominates, so focus on reading, writing, and disseminating information. Some people will claim, "You must be a mind reader!" Make inquiries, giving full play to your intellectual curiosity. Your lucky number is 5.

Tuesday, September 26 (Moon in Virgo) Listen to music. Stay close to familiar ground. Highlight diplomacy, not weakness. The financial picture is bright—there are some puzzles to be solved, but they won't stand in the way of your ultimate success. Taurus, Libra, and Aries figure in this dynamic scenario, and have these letters in their names—F, O, X.

Wednesday, September 27 (Moon in Virgo to Libra 7:23 a.m.) The new moon in Libra relates to trips, visits, and a new attitude expressed by your siblings. You'll enjoy this day! Your imagination soars; you will put across ideas and concepts that are mysterious, entertaining, and educational. Lucky lottery: 12, 10, 7, 1, 2, 4.

Thursday, September 28 (Moon in Libra) Focus on industrial development. Promote ideas aimed at saving time, money. A young person declares, "In a way, you are ahead of your time!" Accept the compliment without undue modesty. Capricorn and Cancer figure in this profitable, dynamic scenario.

Friday, September 29 (Moon in Libra to Scorpio 11:31 a.m.) Within 24 hours, a price will be settled regarding property value. A family member declares, "Let's take the money and run!" Maintain your principles; steer clear of a shady operation. Aries and Libra play cards close to the chest and might have something to hide—ask questions!

Saturday, September 30 (Moon in Scorpio) On this last day of September, let others know you have been here. Lead the way, refusing to follow others. Special:

Protect your right eye from danger! Another Leo—romantic, impulsive, and headstrong—could steer you into the rocks. Being forewarned is forearmed—so be careful!

OCTOBER 2000

Sunday, October 1 (Moon in Scorpio to Sagittarius 6:51 p.m.) On this first day of October, you lay out plans for the future. Almost as if by magic, you perceive potential and what must be done to fulfill it. Pay almost immediate attention to a project that has lingered—by finishing it, you could hit a home run.

Monday, October 2 (Moon in Sagittarius) Make a fresh start, maintain your confidence, and realize that you are charming and sophisticated. Emphasize the new and the inventive. Celebrate your pioneering spirit, and the courage of your convictions. An Aquarius and another Leo are featured, with these letters in their names—A, S, J.

Tuesday, October 3 (Moon in Sagittarius) For racing luck, these selections apply to all tracks: post-position special—number 6 p.p. in the fifth race. Pick six: 5, 2, 1, 3, 6, 4. Watch for these letters in the names of potential winning horses or jockeys: B, K, T. Hot daily doubles: 5 and 2, 1 and 4, 3 and 6. Favorites come in the money. Cancer-born jockeys provide wonderful rides!

Wednesday, October 4 (Moon in Sagittarius to Capricorn 5:44 a.m.) Lucky lottery: 3, 30, 1, 10, 8, 4. Accelerate your social activity, and try to learn more about politics and international news. What you take as fun is apt to be regarded seriously by others. Be up to date regarding fashion, and keep recent resolutions about diet and nutrition.

Thursday, October 5 (Moon in Capricorn) Your work methods are revised, so get accustomed to a different schedule. A Scorpio talks about settling down. Be sure that your toolbox contains what is needed for instant repairs. Taurus, Scorpio, and another Leo play fascinating roles, and will have these letters in their names—D, M, V.

Friday, October 6 (Moon in Capricorn to Aquarius 6:34 p.m.) Get your thoughts on paper. You gain via writing. A Capricorn proves loyalty, and will be at your side during a possible crisis. A communication is received from afar that relates to distance, language, and the possibility of a product display. Virgo and Sagittarius are also in featured roles.

Saturday, October 7 (Moon in Aquarius) Lucky lottery: 6, 12, 11, 22, 18, 32. Attention revolves around your lifestyle, an important domestic adjustment involving beautifying your surroundings, and your marital status. Those who counted you out will be in for a rude awakening. Aries plays a sensational role.

Sunday, October 8 (Moon in Aquarius) You are not out of step! Others are missing a beat, and some accuse you of deliberately creating confusion. Your response: "If you are confused that easily, then you better see to your mental well-being!" Pisces and Virgo play instrumental roles, and will have these initials in their names—G, P, Y.

Monday, October 9 (Moon in Aquarius to Pisces 6:37 a.m.) You have more responsibility than you originally anticipated—and a greater chance for hitting the financial jackpot. Someone in a position of authority takes a liking to you. Promotion and more money is a distinct possibility. Capricorn and Cancer people figure prominently.

Tuesday, October 10 (Moon in Pisces) What had run amuck will once again get back to normal. You'll be saying, "Now I've seen everything and survived it!" The question of riding and racing horses is the subject of conversation. Aries and Libra play astounding roles, and have these letters in their names—I and R.

Wednesday, October 11 (Moon in Pisces to Aries 3:52 p.m.)   Make a fresh start. Within 24 hours, you'll have a new outlook in connection with foreign exchange rates, travel, and language. Imprint your style, stressing independence and inventiveness. Don't fight the fact that you exude sex appeal! Lucky lottery: 1, 12, 20, 51, 6, 7.

Thursday, October 12 (Moon in Aries)   The Aries moon relates to philosophy, publishing, communication, and your ability to get your message across. Subjects of discussion will include Edgar Cayce, Daniel Dunglas Home, and Harry Houdini. Questions invariably arise about the possibility of the survival of human personality after bodily death.

Friday, October 13 (Moon in Aries to Taurus 10:06 p.m.)   The full moon, plus the Jupiter keynote, all relate to this date—Friday the 13th. It will be lucky for you, as people comment, "You most certainly have a good hold on your emotional and mental self!" Gemini and Sagittarius figure in this scenario, with these initials in their names—C, L, U.

Saturday, October 14 (Moon in Taurus)   Obstacles are present during this weekend, especially tonight. Ultimately, this proves favorable. A Taurus who is at first competitive could become your valuable ally. A Scorpio enlightens you about account procedures, property value, investments, and tax and license requirements. Your lucky number is 4.

Sunday, October 15 (Moon in Taurus)   Valuable information is gathered by reading—Gemini talks about flirting, travel, and putting across ideas. You learn more about money and how to earn it. Taurus, Virgo, and

Sagittarius play outstanding roles. You will have luck with the number 5.

Monday, October 16 (Moon in Taurus to Gemini 2:19 a.m.)   People around you are restless and filled with nervous energy. You will provide a soothing effect that includes music, color coordination, and design. A family member declares, "You are an emotional Rock of Gibraltar." A Sagittarian will play a fascinating role.

Tuesday, October 17 (Moon in Gemini)   Define your terms and realize your own power. The lunar position highlights your ability to win friends and influence people. The world could be your Trilby. You pull strings. The scenario features fun and frolic. Pisces and Virgo play creative roles and will have these letters in their names—G, P, Y.

Wednesday, October 18 (Moon in Gemini to Cancer 5:38 a.m.)   For racing luck, these selections apply to all tracks: post-position special—number 8 p.p. in the eighth race. Pick six: 2, 1, 7, 8, 5, 3. Watch for these letters in the names of potential winning horses or jockeys: H, Q, Z. Hot daily doubles: 2 and 1, 3 and 5, 8 and 8. Veteran jockeys ride favorites into the Winner's Circle.

Thursday, October 19 (Moon in Cancer)   People consult you in a quiet way. Some individuals reveal confidential information, including intimate facts about their love life. Special: Let go of a burden you have no right to assume in the first place! Aries and Libra dominate today's exciting scenario.

Friday, October 20 (Moon in Cancer to Leo 8:43 a.m.)   You've waited for this day! Emotional debris is put aside as you get to the heart of matters. You are told by a very special person that you truly are loved. Be original, independent, and inventive. Another Leo is involved.

Saturday, October 21 (Moon in Leo)   Lucky lottery: 2, 20, 5, 50, 10, 12. Your cycle is high, so designate where the action will be and refuse to follow others. Set the pace and do things your way, wearing yellow and gold, speaking up, and present your views dramatically. Capricorn and Cancer will not let you down.

Sunday, October 22 (Moon in Leo to Virgo 11:54 a.m.)   On this Sunday, the key is relaxation, along with discussions about religious miracles. A long-distance communication relates to a possible journey to attend an educational institution. Gemini and Sagittarius make themselves known in a conspicuous way. You will have luck with the number 3.

Monday, October 23 (Moon in Virgo)   Lucky numbers: 4, 16, 16. The financial picture is bright; an investment that at first seemed to be a loss will rebound in your favor. A critical newspaper review of a play contains information that you can use constructively. Scorpio figures prominently.

Tuesday, October 24 (Moon in Virgo to Libra 3:31 p.m.)   News you have been holding can be released, and you'll be complimented on keeping a promise about a device that uses voice commands. Accept accolades without undue modesty. Add this: "I only did what any decent person would do!"

Wednesday, October 25 (Moon in Libra)   Lucky lottery: 6, 12, 18, 22, 33, 4. The Libra moon tells of emergency messages. Your presence is requested by a restless Libra relative who states, "I always feel so much better when you are near!" Be receptive but not gullible. Taurus will play a top role.

Thursday, October 26 (Moon in Libra to Scorpio 8:25 p.m.)   Many people insist, "Tell us your secret!" In truth, your secret is universal and well known to everyone. Say it that way; tell people that the harder you work, the luckier you get. Pisces and Virgo play interesting roles, will have these letters in their names—G, P, Y.

Friday, October 27 (Moon in Scorpio)   The Scorpio new moon throws light on property value and your residence, as well as a decision regarding marriage. Emotions could run rampant, so give logic equal time. Passionate lovemaking is evanescent, but lacks staying power. Taurus and Scorpio will play fantastic roles.

Saturday, October 28 (Moon in Scorpio)   Learn more about National Magic Day, held on the 31st in memory of Harry Houdini. While most people will be celebrating Halloween, you will discuss, lecture, and dig deep for facts about the extraordinary life of the fabulous escape artist. In three days, you should be with people who express intellectual curiosity about magic in general and specifically the life of Houdini.

Sunday, October 29—Daylight Saving Time Ends (Moon in Scorpio to Sagittarius 2:42 a.m.)   Let go of the status quo. The Sagittarian moon relates to creativity, challenge, change, variety, and sex appeal. Do not follow others. At the risk of being unpopular, set your own pace. In the long run, you'll win fame and fortune. An Aquarian plays the top role.

Monday, October 30 (Moon in Sagittarius)   Attention revolves around your lifestyle, where you live, cooperative efforts, and publicity regarding a community project. Focus will be on direction, motivation, and a decision relating to the sale or purchase of property. There's exquisite dining tonight. A Cancer—naturally—will be in charge.

Tuesday, October 31 (Moon in Sagittarius to Capricorn 1:03 p.m.)   It is all right to celebrate Halloween, but don't overlook National Magic Day. Three days ago, on the 28th, you spoke to people about joining a discussion group. Many will express gratitude and astonishment, as facts about Houdini and his life evolve. Sagittarius is in this picture.

NOVEMBER 2000

Wednesday, November 1 (Moon in Capricorn) Lucky numbers: 1, 10, 8. The answer to your question: Affirmative. Take the initiative in making a fresh start in a new direction. Special: Avoid heavy lifting. Realize that what might begin as a harmless flirtation could go too far and cost you plenty! Another Leo is in the picture.

Thursday, November 2 (Moon in Capricorn) A fitness report needs scrutiny—take nothing for granted, especially where your health is concerned. A minor digestive problem could become major if neglected. Capricorn and Cancer figure prominently, and could have these letters in their names—B, K, T.

Friday, November 3 (Moon in Capricorn to Aquarius 1:41 a.m.) The moon position highlights public appearances, legal rights, your reputation, and your ability to do the right thing when nobody is looking. Today's Jupiter keynote emphasizes participation in charitable campaigns; stresses popularity; and accents exploration, publishing, advertising. A Gemini figures prominently.

Saturday, November 4 (Moon in Aquarius) Lucky lottery: 4, 40, 11, 22, 7, 9. The Aquarian moon emphasizes cooperative efforts and your ability to keep your plans flexible. Questions concerning marriage loom large. Another Leo talks about your sales program, showmanship, and advertising—don't ignore it!

Sunday, November 5 (Moon in Aquarius to Pisces 2:15 p.m.) Within 24 hours, you'll have access to privileged information. Today the emphasis is on dissemination of information. You gain as a result of displaying

215

your writing skills. Lively people play key roles, including Gemini, Virgo, and Sagittarius. You will have luck with the number 5.

Monday, November 6 (Moon in Pisces) Attention revolves around investments concerning your home, insurance, and property, and a special gift for a special person. The spotlight falls on your home, decorating and remodeling, letting the sunlight in, and listening to music. People comment on your voice—they say, "You sound different today—sultry and sexy!"

Tuesday, November 7 (Moon in Pisces) An aura of mystery surrounds you—people claim you are psychic. Some individuals, attempting to be scientific, probe with questions, many of which are nonsensical. Use showmanship to fend off pests. Pisces and Virgo play fascinating roles, and will have these letters in their names—G, P, Y.

Wednesday, November 8 (Moon in Pisces to Aries 12:03 a.m.) For racing luck, these selections apply to all tracks: post-position special—number 8 p.p. in the eighth race. Pick six: 2, 8, 1, 1, 5, 3. Look for these letters in the names of potential winning horses or jockeys: H, Q, Z. Hot daily doubles: 2 and 8, 3 and 3, 4 and 6. Veteran jockeys bring back memories of the great one. Favorites win!

Thursday, November 9 (Moon in Aries) The lunar position highlights philosophy, travel, communication, and an awareness of spirituality. Reach beyond the immediate to get in touch with idealistic, bilingual. A series of events causes you to ponder, "Could this be déjà vu?" Aries plays a top role.

Friday, November 10 (Moon in Aries to Taurus 6:13 a.m.) Make a fresh start in a new direction, and contact a Taurus who has assumed a leadership role. Shiny objects figure in this scenario; some represent a gift or part of a special collection. Aquarius and another Leo play decisive roles, and will have these letters in their names—A, S, J.

Saturday, November 11 (Moon in Taurus)   The full moon relates to that part of your life associated with ambition, promotion, production, and getting recognition long denied. A very romantic Saturday night, with excellent wine, food, and music. You might hear these words in whispered tones, "I love so much being with you!"

Sunday, November 12 (Moon in Taurus to Gemini 9:29 a.m.)   Diversify and keep plans flexible. Within 24 hours, you might be asking, "Could this really be happening to me?" Tonight, you get the facts and figures concerning accounting procedures, earnings, and expenses. Gemini and Sagittarius play leading roles, and have these initials in their names—C, L, U.

Monday, November 13 (Moon in Gemini)   On this Monday, a series of stunning events coincides with the passing parade. The Gemini moon in your eleventh house relates to good fortune in matters of finance and romance. During this cycle, you win friends and influence people—many are powerful.

Tuesday, November 14 (Moon in Gemini to Cancer 11:22 a.m.)   The Mercury keynote emphasizes sleight of hand, written material, and contacts with people who quote poetry. You'll enjoy the day and night. Some promises will be broken, but are subject to repair. Gemini, Virgo, and Sagittarius play interesting roles, and have these initials in their names—E, N, W.

Wednesday, November 15 (Moon in Cancer)   Lucky lottery: 6, 12, 14, 2, 22, 30. Attention revolves around harmony and a reunion with a family member who once declared, "I don't really care if I ever see you again!" If you are diplomatic, differences over money will be amicably settled. Gourmet dining tonight helps salve emotional wounds.

Thursday, November 16 (Moon in Cancer to Leo 1:20 p.m.) Secrets involving your family will be revealed. Events transpire to bring you closer to your ultimate goal as circumstances move in your favor. Play the waiting game, defining terms and refusing to be coerced into making a snap decision. A Pisces plays a key role.

Friday, November 17 (Moon in Leo) A power play day! Your judgment and intuition are on target—don't be discouraged by someone who knows the price of everything but the value of nothing. Rely on your past experience. A personal relationship can best be described as uncertain. A Capricorn figures prominently.

Saturday, November 18 (Moon in Leo to Virgo 4:17 p.m.) The moon in your sign highlights your personality, personal magnetism, sensuality, and sex appeal. Wear yellow and gold; make known your views; and highlight showmanship, entertainment, and advertising. An envious person attempts to start a vicious rumor. Lucky lottery: 12, 13, 18, 22, 33, 5.

Sunday, November 19 (Moon in Virgo) Questions are answered about lost articles, financial compensation, and accounting methods. Don't be shy about expressing your views. Those who claim you are self-absorbed are merely envious. Aquarius and another Leo play fascinating roles, and they could have these letters in their names—A, S, J.

Monday, November 20 (Moon in Virgo to Libra 8:36 p.m.) You're being pulled in two directions—this involves your family and money. Evaluate your property and repair broken images. This means renew your faith in yourself and your ability to prophesize your future. Cancer and Capricorn play dynamic roles and will have these letters in their names—B, K, T.

Tuesday, November 21 (Moon in Libra) For racing luck, these selections apply at all tracks: post-position special—number 5 p.p. in the seventh race. Pick six: 1, 5, 4, 2, 7, 8. Watch for these letters in the names of potential winning horses or jockeys: C, L, U. Hot daily doubles: 1 and 5, 3 and 3, 6 and 4. Sagittarian jockeys win photo finishes—and pay big prices!

Wednesday, November 22 (Moon in Libra)   Lucky lottery: 4, 7, 12, 6, 16, 50. The Libra moon emphasizes contacts with people who are on the move. A charming Libra salesperson causes you to think twice about buying and selling. An obstacle will be removed, so do some proofreading, check your references and research carefully.

Thursday, November 23 (Moon in Libra to Scorpio 2:34 a.m.)   Thanksgiving! The Scorpio moon indicates lively discussions at home, where everyone seems to have an appetite. An aura of creativity and sensuality surrounds you and people with whom you share the holiday spirit. Gemini, Virgo, and Sagittarius will tell tall tales. Your lucky number is 5.

Friday, November 24 (Moon in Scorpio)   A Scorpio expresses gratitude for sharing Thanksgiving, thanking you so often that it borders on being embarrassing. Focus on home, property, and a passionate interest in a unique subject that involves the occult or sacred writings. Taurus and Libra play roles.

Saturday, November 25 (Moon in Scorpio to Sagittarius 10:34 a.m.)   The new moon position emphasizes creativity, style, children, change, and a variety of experiences and sensations. A member of the opposite sex talks about a faraway land and whets the appetite for language, food, and romantic customs. Pisces and Virgo figure in this scenario, and will have these letters in their names—G, P, Y.

Sunday, November 26 (Moon in Sagittarius)   Learn from experience! You'll be intrigued by someone who flatters while acting available and elusive. Don't permit distance or language barriers to create a discouraging atmosphere. Stand tall for your beliefs and as a result, you'll be loved even more.

Monday, November 27 (Moon in Sagittarius to Capricorn 8:58 p.m.)   Questions about your occupation will be settled within 24 hours. The Mars keynote tells of travel, contacts with people from foreign lands, and an assignment or opportunity involving publishing or photography. Aries and Libra play outstanding roles, and will have these letters in their names—I and R.

Tuesday, November 28 (Moon in Capricorn)   The Capricorn moon relates to fitness, work methods, and completing necessary repairs. Someone who advocates shortcuts should be politely ignored. Use your own initiative, emphasizing independence of thought and action. If it can be avoided, do not lift heavy objects!

Wednesday, November 29 (Moon in Capricorn)   Focus on direction, motivation, plumbing repairs in your home, and welcoming a Cancer who promises, "I'm going to prepare you a meal tonight you won't soon forget!" For your part, present a gift to the chef. You will have luck with the number 2.

Thursday, November 30 (Moon in Capricorn to Aquarius 9:27 a.m.)   On this last day of November, with a Jupiter keynote and the moon getting ready to enter Aquarius, you'll have happy thoughts and memories, and you will be optimistic about the future. Gemini and Sagittarius play dramatic roles and will have these letters in their names—C, L, U.

DECEMBER 2000

Friday, December 1 (Moon in Aquarius)   On this Friday, you'll begin making plans for the upcoming holidays.

Originally, you had no thoughts of considering Christmas or New Year's this early in the month. Circumstances change, however, due to family relationships, moving, marriage, and business commitments. Another Leo plays a role.

Saturday, December 2 (Moon in Aquarius to Pisces 10:24 p.m.)   This is the time for a fresh start, for entertainment, and for touching base with friends and relatives. Circumstances move in your favor; you'll overcome the odds; you exude personal magnetism and an aura of sensuality and sex appeal. Gemini and Sagittarius play outstanding roles and will have these letters in their names—C, L, U. Your lucky number is 3.

Sunday, December 3 (Moon in Pisces)   What seems the same will turn out to be entirely different. Avoid over-confidence; don't shout to the rooftops, "How bored I am!" A major opportunity slips through your fingers unless you're alert, dynamic, and lively. Taurus and Scorpio will play exciting roles.

Monday, December 4 (Moon in Pisces)   Keep your plans flexible and be ready for a travel invitation or for communication from a relative who is constantly on the go. It seems you no longer can call yourself forgotten. People remember—all at once! Gemini, Virgo, and Sagittarius play roles, and have these initials in their names—E, N, W.

Tuesday, December 5 (Moon in Pisces to Aries 9:19 a.m.)   The Pisces moon relates to the occult and to mystery, as well as how much money someone close to you has saved—including your partner or mate. Attention revolves around your lifestyle and residence, and a gift representing a strong token of love. Music is involved.

Wednesday, December 6 (Moon in Aries)   Lucky lottery: 7, 17, 1, 10, 12, 14. The moon position accents publishing, communication, spirituality, and the desire to learn a language. What had been in disarray will fall into an orderly process. You get credit for doing much, but in truth, it was accomplished almost effortlessly. Virgo is involved.

Thursday, December 7 (Moon in Aries to Taurus 4:28 p.m.)   For racing luck, these selections apply at all tracks: post-position special—number 8 p.p. in the eighth race. Pick six: 4, 4, 1, 7, 3, 5. Watch for these letters in the names of potential winning horses or jockeys: H, Q, Z. Hot daily doubles: 4 and 4, 8 and 8, 5 and 1. Veteran jockeys mount favorites and bring them in the money.

Friday, December 8 (Moon in Taurus)   On this Friday, news is received that elevates your morale—you gain recognition, especially from an Aries you feared had entirely forgotten you. The key is to finish what you start, to keep the faith, and to realize that a delay or postponement should not be regarded as a defeat.

Saturday, December 9 (Moon in Taurus to Gemini 7:52 p.m.)   On this Saturday you'll be asking yourself, "Could it be true? Has my vitality returned, or is this some kind of delayed adolescence?" It's Saturday night, and you'll be lively, as your introduction to another Leo could be the start of something big. Lucky lottery: 42, 8, 12, 1, 10, 5.

Sunday, December 10 (Moon in Gemini)   The focus is on decisions relating to building material, plumbing, a business partnership, or your marital status. There's a gourmet dinner tonight, but keep your resolutions and be moderate. A Cancer introduces you to fine wine. Capricorn will play an astounding role—very entertaining!

Monday, December 11 (Moon in Gemini to Cancer 8:50 p.m.)   The full moon position emphasizes your ability to make your dreams come true. A romantic interlude with Gemini could be the start of a blazing romance.

222

Meditation is necessary, lest the full moon encourages a tendency to brood. A Sagittarian comes up with an innovative concept, but like all things—it will cost money.

Tuesday, December 12 (Moon in Cancer) On this Tuesday, repair work should be done, including testing the electrical outlets in your home and car. Focus on rewriting, proofreading, revising material, and submitting it to the right people. Taurus, Scorpio, and another Leo figure in this scenario, and have these letters in their names—D, M, V.

Wednesday, December 13 (Moon in Cancer to Leo 9:10 p.m.) Today marks a blend of practicality with emotionalism and creativity. A deadline exists, so set priorities and don't make promises you cannot fulfill. You can beat the odds if you stay focused and refuse to be coerced off track by someone who has a clever way with words and a hidden agenda. Be diplomatic with Cancer and Capricorn.

Thursday, December 14 (Moon in Leo) With the moon in your sign, circumstances turn in your favor. You'll know what to do and when to do it. Accept an assignment or invitation that could involve travel. You are more valuable to your employer than you think. Follow your intuition about Capricorn. You could meet your soulmate at a party tonight.

Friday, December 15 (Moon in Leo to Virgo 10:31 p.m.) Your personality shines today, attracting people who are romantically inclined. Entertain at home tonight and let the sparks fly. Show off your artistic and culinary skills to set the stage for love. You'll learn more about someone who could play a big role in your future. Your lucky number is 5.

Saturday, December 16 (Moon in Virgo) For racing luck, these selections apply to all tracks: post-position special—number 4 p.p. in the eighth race. Pick six: 1, 4,

7, 8, 3, 3. Watch for these letters in the names of potential winning horses or jockeys: H, Q, Z. Hot daily doubles: 1 and 4, 2 and 7, 8 and 8. Capricorn jockeys turn in sterling rides and will pay good prices.

Sunday, December 17 (Moon in Virgo)   You'll be musing, "Whatever else we might do, what we are doing now seems just right for Sunday!" Focus on analysis of some Bible stories, prophesies, and spiritual values. A project that was left up in the air will be completed, and you'll get proper credit. Aries is represented.

Monday, December 18 (Moon in Virgo to Libra 2:02 a.m.)   A relative helps you make a fresh start in a new direction—Libra will play a key role. Show the courage of your convictions, highlighting independence, originality, and a willingness to move with the times. Aquarius and another Leo will also play roles, and have these letters in their names—A, S, J.

Tuesday, December 19 (Moon in Libra)   The Libra moon relates to trips, visits, and the purchase of a gift that could involve music. Strive for balance, both emotional and financial. A married friend confides, "I don't want to be a homewrecker and most certainly don't want to wreck my own home, but I don't know what to do!" Offer tea and sympathy, but don't become inextricably involved!

Wednesday, December 20 (Moon in Libra to Scorpio 8:13 a.m.)   Within 24 hours, you'll know where you stand in regard to your property value, your financial interest in a building, or your marital status. The elements of timing and luck ride with you. A Sagittarian provides information enabling you to make the right choice. Lucky lottery: 3, 33, 12, 8, 10, 5.

Thursday, December 21 (Moon in Scorpio)   If you expect a peaceful Thursday, you will be disappointed. The focus is on intensity, passion, extremes, and bizarre stories. You'll be asked to uncover a mystery. You will also be given confidential information about a possible juggling of finances.

Friday, December 22 (Moon in Scorpio to Sagittarius 4:58 p.m.) Analyze information and be wary about someone of the opposite sex who acts in an irresponsible way. Don't be afraid of being regarded as a square. Gemini, Virgo, and Sagittarius play leading roles, and will have these letters in their names—E, N, W.

Saturday, December 23 (Moon in Sagittarius) Lucky lottery: 6, 12, 19, 3, 30, 1. The spotlight is on familiar ground, gardening, and communing with nature. Don't wander too far, because you are likely to be called back—at a most inappropriate time. Taurus, Scorpio, and another Leo help make major decisions, and have these letters in their names—F, O, X.

Sunday, December 24 (Moon in Sagittarius) It's Christmas Eve—the Neptune keynote symbolizes an aura of mystery, the appropriate atmosphere for a religious holiday. There will be an exchange of gifts that surprise and delight. The focus is on romance, creativity, style, and happy involvement with children. Pisces plays a role.

Monday, December 25 (Moon in Sagittarius to Capricorn 3:55 a.m.) On this Christmas Day, there is a new moon with a solar eclipse in Capricorn, bringing a summing up. The Saturn keynote accents responsibility for past obligations, including the cost of holiday preparations and gifts. The good news is that you will survive!

Tuesday, December 26 (Moon in Capricorn) This day after Christmas marks the beginning or ending of an important situation or relationship. A temporary separation may be necessary due to travel, business, or a career obligation. A loved one will return; the reunion will be hot and heavy. Aries will play an exciting role.

Wednesday, December 27 (Moon in Capricorn to Aquarius 4:27 p.m.)   Within 24 hours, questions about legal rights, partnership, and marriage will be resolved. Tonight, you gain understanding about the possibility of new love on the horizon. Imprint your style; take the initiative; highlight originality and the courage of your convictions. You'll have luck with the number 1.

Thursday, December 28 (Moon in Aquarius)   Tonight, you'll sigh, "At last I know where I stand. I now know how to handle public relations and legal affairs and I am making a decision about marriage!" You'll be invited to dine out. A Cancer extends an invitation to make this a memorable Thursday-night outing.

Friday, December 29 (Moon in Aquarius)   You'll pay attention to things that go bump in the night. Give full play to your intellectual curiosity while you have fun in laughing at your own foibles. Someone who tells tall tales will admit, "I tell some stories, but you don't do so bad yourself!" A Sagittarian is involved.

Saturday, December 30 (Moon in Aquarius to Pisces 5:29 p.m.)   For racing luck, these selections apply to all tracks: post-position special—number 4 p.p. in the fourth race. Pick six: 1, 7, 2, 4, 3, 8. Be alert for these letters in the names of potential winning horses or jockeys: D, M, V. Hot daily doubles: 1 and 7, 4 and 4, 6 and 8. Scorpio jockeys must be especially cautious to avoid injuries.

Sunday, December 31 (Moon in Pisces)   On this New Year's Eve, you'll learn more than you care to know. This involves the rough character of someone who is gentle on the surface. You also get information about the fact that someone who acts prosperous might actually be poor. Gemini, Virgo, and Sagittarius are involved and I wish all of them—and you—a Happy New Year!

Monday, January 1 (Moon in Pisces to Aries 5:13 p.m.) On this first day of the year 2001, you contemplate the past and future and realize that love will always hold a headline spot in your life. With a Pisces moon in your eighth house, you will seek guidance from unorthodox sources. Aquarius and another Leo play dominant roles.

Tuesday, January 2 (Moon in Aries) On this Tuesday, with the moon in your ninth house, a long-distance communication is received relating to travel, philosophy, or publishing. Capricorn and Cancer will play outstanding roles, and could have these letters or initials in their names: B, K, T.

Wednesday, January 3 (Moon in Aries) Lucky lottery: 3, 6, 9, 14, 12, 2. Accent diversity and versatility, check with your travel agent about the possibility of a journey overseas. The ninth house Aries moon continues to highlight a journey of the mind. Gemini and Sagittarius play important roles.

Thursday, January 4 (Moon in Aries to Taurus 1:54 a.m.) The Pluto keynote. Within 24 hours, the moon will be in Taurus; you will respond today by feeling trapped. This is only temporary. A Taurus will declare, "You are not here for a cup of coffee; you are headed for the top!" Scorpio plays a role.

Friday, January 5 (Moon in Taurus) Keep your plans flexible. You receive written notice that you are expected at a certain site—have notebooks, camera, and other necessities. You will be gone from five days to three weeks. Get familiar with the history of the countries to which you are assigned. Your lucky number is 5.

Saturday, January 6 (Moon in Taurus to Gemini 6:43 a.m.) Attention revolves around your lifestyle, where you live, music, the acquisition of an art object or luxury item. Note: Do not equate generosity with extravagance. Above all, be your gentle, charming self! Taurus, Scorpio and another Leo will play dynamic, creative roles.

Sunday, January 7 (Moon in Gemini) You will be in touch with your spiritual side. Define terms that are especially applicable to real estate. Very important: See people, places, relationships as they exist, not merely as you wish they could be. Pisces will play a dramatic role.

Monday, January 8 (Moon in Gemini to Cancer 8:07 a.m.) A very unusual Monday. There is good fortune in finance and romance. Your popularity increases; you will be musing, "I wish I knew what I did that was so right as to shower me with joy!" Focus also on promotion, production, meeting and beating a deadline—under budget!

Tuesday, January 9—Lunar Eclipse (Moon in Cancer) The full moon, lunar eclipse falls in your twelfth house. Secrets that had been under guard will be released—with a bang! Your cycle is high, so an important project will be completed. Aries and Libra will play key roles, and could have these initials in their names: I and R.

Wednesday, January 10 (Moon in Cancer to Leo 7:43 a.m.) For racing luck at all tracks: post-position special—number 7 p.p. in the third race. Pick six: 4, 2, 7, 1, 1, 3. Look for these letters or initials in the names of potential winning horses or jockeys: A, S, J. Hot daily doubles: 4 and 2, 1 and 1, 3 and 7. Leo jockeys win photo finishes. Speed horses get out in front and stay there.

Thursday, January 11 (Moon in Leo) Your intuitive intellect is honed to razor-sharpness. Follow a hunch and your heart. You meet an Aquarian whose ideas could clash with your own. Following the clash, there is a physical attraction and finally a love relationship. A Cancer is also involved.

Friday, January 12 (Moon in Leo to Virgo 7:25 a.m.) The moon in your sign coincides with your high cycle. This means take the initiative, and above all do not follow others. Fun and frivolity are featured—Gemini and Sagittarius figure prominently, and will have these letters or initials in their names: C, L, U. Your lucky number is 3.

Saturday, January 13 (Moon in Virgo) Just recently, you narrowly escaped having an automobile accident. Interpret this as a warning. Correct mechanical devices, especially in your automobile. Thank goodness you escaped, or you would not be reading these words. Taurus plays a dominant role.

Sunday, January 14 (Moon in Virgo to Libra 9:05 a.m.) On this Sunday, you gain much via the written word. The lunar position highlights your ability to locate lost articles, to increase your earning power. Information you seek is available in your own library. Gemini, Virgo, and Sagittarius figure in the exciting scenario.

Monday, January 15 (Moon in Libra) Suddenly, there is music. The sun peeks from behind the clouds. Life takes on a pleasant, Leo hue. Another Leo enters your life to teach and promote a musical score. Keep recent resolutions about exercise, diet, and nutrition. Your lucky number is 6.

Tuesday, January 16 (Moon in Libra to Scorpio 2:03 p.m.) Overcome a tendency to brood. Transform your moods into positive meditation. Forces are scattered. The moon in your third sector relates to relatives, trips, versatility, ability to return a favor to someone who helped you when most needed. Pisces and Virgo are involved.

Wednesday, January 17 (Moon in Scorpio) For racing luck at all tracks: post-position special—number 1 p.p. in the third race. Pick six: 1, 7, 1, 6, 5, 2. Watch for these letters or initials in the names of potential winning horses or jockeys: H, Q, Z. Hot daily doubles: 1 and 7, 1 and 1, 8 and 5. Favorites are in the money, a Capricorn jockey could suffer an injury.

Thursday, January 18 (Moon in Scorpio to Sagittarius 10:36 p.m.) Let go of the past; take a cold plunge into the future. Recognition previously withheld will now be awarded you. The spotlight is on where you live, the sale or purchase of property; proposals for a managerial position or marriage. Aries and Libra will play sensational roles.

Friday, January 19 (Moon in Sagittarius) Lady luck is with you today! Stick to your original selections in all areas. Refuse to be touted off potential winners. Say, thank you for the information, I am making my own choices! Aquarius and another Leo will share winnings with you.

Saturday, January 20 (Moon in Sagittarius) Don't back down from your principles. A love relationship once on fire got too hot not to cool down. Focus on independence, originality, creativity, the promotion of your unique style. The spotlight is also on marriage, home, and exotic recipes. A Cancer is involved.

Sunday, January 21 (Moon in Sagittarius to Capricorn 9:56 a.m.) On this Sunday, you will be involved in serious metaphysical discussions. It becomes obvious that you do know what you are talking about. You will serve as inspiration to those who are on the fence. Gemini and Sagittarius will become your loyal allies.

Monday, January 22 (Moon in Capricorn) You'll muse, "Everything today seems locked up!" Someone had secret access to doors or drawers. Much that was taken will be returned—don't make a federal case of it! Taurus, Scorpio, and another Leo figure in this exciting scenario. Have luck with number 4.

Tuesday, January 23 (Moon in Capricorn to Aquarius 10:42 p.m.)   You will be asking, "Is this déjà vu?" The scenario gives you the feeling that you have been here before and gone through the same experiences. A voluble Gemini helps convince that you are not the first to be here and will not be the last. Read and analyze information.

Wednesday, January 24 (Moon in Aquarius)   Lucky lottery: 2, 20, 11, 22, 13, 18. The lunar position emphasizes public appearances, cooperative efforts, a major decision relating to marriage. The conclusion is that you are going places, will grab hold of fame and fortune, and will not let go!

Thursday, January 25 (Moon in Aquarius)   The emphasis is on marital status, the battle for legal rights, making crystal clear that you will fight if the cause is right. A Pisces feels that it would be fun to trip you up. Protect yourself at close quarters. An Aquarian comes to your aid at the right moment.

Friday, January 26 (Moon in Aquarius to Pisces 11:37 a.m.)   On this Friday, you might feel as though something of value has been taken away. However, within 24 hours, what was lost or stolen will be recovered. Whatever psychic talents you have will surge forward. Capricorn and Cancer will be in the spotlight, to your advantage.

Saturday, January 27 (Moon in Pisces)   On this Saturday, you exude an aura of universal appeal. If you're not careful, you will propose without really knowing who the other person actually is. Open lines of communication. A very important person is trying to contact you. Have luck with number 9.

Sunday, January 28 (Moon in Pisces to Aries 11:33 p.m.)   Focus on originality, independence, and dealings with creative children. The emphasis is on secrets, freedom from being haunted from past actions and memories. Make a fresh start, and let others know you did not recently fall off a turnip truck. An Aquarian is in the picture.

Monday, January 29 (Moon in Aries)   You are being pulled in two directions; family members are involved. The spotlight is on proposals that include your career, business, partnership, and marriage. You will enjoy a veritable feast tonight. A Cancer puts forth your best culinary talents—seconds please!

Tuesday, January 30 (Moon in Aries)   The Aries moon relates to publishing, advertising, the overseas promotion of your product. You get a needed push from Aries. A Sagittarian promises to arrange financial backing. Stress versatility, diversity, your intellectual curiosity. Purchase a game for a dynamic youngster.

Wednesday, January 31 (Moon in Aries to Taurus 9:19 a.m.)   On this last day of January, open lines of communication, especially with those in foreign countries. Avoid getting involved in a romantic triangle. If you want to experience trouble, ignore this counsel. Taurus, Scorpio, and another Leo are in the picture.

FEBRUARY 2001

Thursday, February 1 (Moon in Taurus)   Share a special collection with a friend interested in archaeology. A Cancer-born member of the opposite sex will make a declaration of love. On this exciting first day of February, focus on partnership, cooperative efforts, and marriage. A Taurus helps you climb to the top.

Friday, February 2 (Moon in Taurus to Gemini 3:54 p.m.) On this second day, this Friday, you get funding for a fun trip that will combine business with pleasure. Gemini and Sagittarius figure in today's dynamic scenario, and will have these letters or initials in their names: C, L, U. Have luck with number 3.

Saturday, February 3 (Moon in Gemini) For racing luck at all tracks: post-position special—number 4 p.p. in the fourth race. Pick six: 4, 4, 1, 4, 3, 8. Watch for these letters or initials in the names of potential winning horses or jockeys: D, M, V. Hot daily doubles: 4 and 4, 8 and 3, 1 and 1. Favorites win, but prices are stingy.

Sunday, February 4 (Moon in Gemini to Cancer 6:59 p.m.) You could have luck with these numbers: 5, 4, 7. Read and write, disclose information that had been held secret. An attractive Gemini plays a role, which helps build your morale. Many of your fondest hopes and wishes will come true. Take notes relating to dreams.

Monday, February 5 (Moon in Cancer) The spotlight is on your home environment, beautifying your surroundings. Stress color coordination and design. People ask, "Where did you get all of this talent?" Reply, "I read it in a book!" Stubborn opposition comes from Taurus, but the two of you will eventually become bosom friends.

Tuesday, February 6 (Moon in Cancer to Leo 7:20 p.m.) At the track, racing luck: post-position special—number 1 p.p. in the second race. Pick six: 8, 1, 5, 5, 3, 7. Watch for these letters or initials in the names of potential winning horses or jockeys: G, P, Y. Hot daily doubles: 8 and 1, 4 and 6, 5 and 5. Winners come from behind, Pisces and Virgo jockeys are in photo finishes.

Wednesday, February 7 (Moon in Leo) Lucky lottery: 8, 15, 1, 5, 11, 12. Your cycle is high. The moon in your sign helps you make the right move at the crucial time. The question is, "How did you do it?" A beautiful

233

jacket could represent a token of appreciation. Capricorn and Cancer play spectacular roles.

Thursday, February 8 (Moon in Leo to Virgo 6:34 p.m.)   A project is complete. The full moon in Leo represents romance, inventiveness, style, and controversy. The Saturn keynote means people will take you seriously and purchase your product. A Cancer declares, "If anybody ever believed in luck, you should!"

Friday, February 9 (Moon in Virgo)   On this Friday, take a chance on romance. An investment tip is valid, so pay attention, follow your instincts and your heart. People comment on your creativity, originality, and pioneering spirit. Respond: "Don't praise me too much, or I'll get a big head!" An Aquarian is involved.

Saturday, February 10 (Moon in Virgo to Libra 6:45 p.m.)   Lucky lottery: 6, 50, 5, 1, 10, 13. Attention revolves around special service, decisions relating to partnership, cooperative efforts, your marital status. A lively Saturday night, but you feel something is missing. Cancer and Capricorn play outstanding roles.

Sunday, February 11 (Moon in Libra)   Puzzle pieces fall into place. The missing part is recovered. A relationship that was demolished will be restored, if the proper circumstances prevail. Gemini and Sagittarius figure prominently, and could have these initials in their names: C, L, U.

Monday, February 12 (Moon in Libra to Scorpio 9:52 p.m.)   The Libra moon relates to exploration, experimentation, making peace with a relative who, in the recent past, has been annoying. Take one step at a time regarding a new interest in your life. Special—go easy on adult beverages! The Pluto keynote may not have you thinking straight.

Tuesday, February 13 (Moon in Scorpio)   There's plenty of action behind the scenes. Unusual circumstances create aura of misunderstanding. By getting together with Scorpio and comparing notes, you revive friendship that appeared to be lost forever. Tomorrow you learn more about the value of your property.

Wednesday, February 14 (Moon in Scorpio)   Additional information helps bring the cost of management into an area of reality. The spotlight on romance, music, the spirit of Valentine's Day. The number of Valentine cards you get proves that not only are you not forgotten, but your popularity continues to grow.

Thursday, February 15 (Moon in Scorpio to Sagittarius 5:02 a.m.)   On this Thursday you'll muse, "I appreciate fun, frolic, games, but I also revere my privacy." Someone wants something for nothing, and you could be the prime target. You'll feel passion pangs—it might not be love, but it could be that you are hungry for affection.

Friday, February 16 (Moon in Sagittarius)   The Sagittarian moon stimulates fifth house activities. This includes children, challenge, change, a variety of sensations. The spotlight is on the excitement of discovery, extra responsibility. Cancer and Capricorn will play astonishing roles, and have these initials in their names: H, Q, Z.

Saturday, February 17 (Moon in Sagittarius to Capricorn 3:58 p.m.)   Lucky lottery: 9, 42, 35, 15, 3, 30. Elements of timing and luck ride with you. Reluctantly follow your inner feelings when selecting potential winners. Aries and Libra liven today's scenario. What was supposed to be a mild flirtation is going out-of-bounds.

Sunday, February 18 (Moon in Capricorn)   A dynamic, challenging Sunday. The moon in your sixth house means get things done early, a surprise has been planned for you. The emphasis is on repair work, safety measures, awareness of spiritual values. Aquarius and another Leo are featured.

Monday, February 19 (Moon in Capricorn) Don't neglect the wisdom of the heart. You owe a favor to a Cancer native—pay the debt tonight. The final result could be gourmet dining. You will conclude, "It pays to pay your debts!" Discretion is necessary; a secret meeting is held; your prestige surges upward.

Tuesday, February 20 (Moon in Capricorn to Aquarius 4:53 a.m.) You'll be asking, "Is this déjà vu?" Familiar places and faces—lessons learned in the recent past are being repeated. Attention revolves around a special diet. Your health report is good, but you will be advised that more exercise is needed, along with more attention to nutrition.

Wednesday, February 21 (Moon in Aquarius) Lucky lottery: 21, 11, 12, 13, 15, 4. It will be necessary to rewrite, review, to view products from a different angle. Taurus, Scorpio, and another Leo figure prominently, and will have these letters or initials in their names: D, M, V.

Thursday, February 22 (Moon in Aquarius to Pisces 5:44 p.m.) You will hear these resounding words, "Don't you dare toy with my feelings!" Handle this crisis with aplomb. Your own words should be soothing and promising. Don't get caught up in tall tales. Deal gingerly with Gemini. Your lucky number is 5.

Friday, February 23 (Moon in Pisces) For racing luck at all tracks: post-position special—number 2 p.p. in the fourth race. Pick six: 1, 7, 8, 2, 5, 3. Be alert for these letters or initials in the names of potential winning horses or jockeys: F, O, X. Hot daily doubles: 1 and 7, 6 and 3, 4 and 2. Hometown jockeys will be in the money.

Saturday, February 24 (Moon in Pisces)   On this Saturday night, you'll be told in whispered tones: "You are very mysterious, and also very attractive. I only wish I knew your secret!" The Neptune keynote blends with your sun rulership. People are drawn to you, as if you were a giant magnet and all others iron filings.

Sunday, February 25 (Moon in Pisces to Aries 5:19 a.m.)   You get your second emotional wind. Mistakes are corrected. A psychic adventure takes place and you say to yourself, "There are more mysteries in this world than I at first imagined." Capricorn and Cancer play leading roles, and have these initials in their names: H, Q, Z.

Monday, February 26 (Moon in Aries)   An old invoice will be paid. You will say, "This must be a lucky sign; maybe people will send in what they owe, and then I'll be able to pay my debts." A long-distance communication could be the precursor to a journey overseas. Aries will play a dominant role.

Tuesday, February 27 (Moon in Aries to Taurus 3:04 p.m.)   Everything points to a new start, pioneering spirit, getting in on the beginning on what will be a pioneering adventure. Love light shines bright. People comment, "You are dressing differently, so something must be going on. Yet you say nothing!" Another Leo is involved.

Wednesday, February 28 (Moon in Taurus)   On this last day of February, with the moon in Taurus, you will spend and earn money. There also looms large the possibility of inheritance. Cancer and Capricorn figure prominently, and have these initials in their names: B, K, T. Have luck with number 2.

Thursday, March 1 (Moon in Taurus to Gemini 10:34 p.m.) You'll be celebrating this first day of March. Gemini and Sagittarius will play fascinating roles, and could have these letters or initials in their names: C, L, U. A stubborn Taurus in a quixotic mood states, "Well, what did you expect from me?"

Friday, March 2 (Moon in Taurus to Gemini 10:34 p.m.) The moon is leaving stubborn Taurus, so you'll have more freedom of thought and action. It's time to rebuild, reorganize, and to improve safety measures. Be aware of property value, sales, and purchases. Some people will insist, "I want it in writing!"

Saturday, March 3 (Moon in Gemini) A lively Saturday night. The moon position highlights your ability to win friends and influence people. The Mercury keynote emphasizes reading, writing, and distributing information. A flirtation admittedly is fun, but please know when to say, "Enough is enough!" Your lucky number is 5.

Sunday, March 4 (Moon in Gemini to Cancer 3:23 a.m.) On this Sunday you sense an aura of victory. Your popularity is on the rise. People ask you to solve problems, some of them intimate. Focus on entertainment programs involving charity or politics. You'll be complimented on your body image, and your straightforward approach to questions.

Monday, March 5 (Moon in Cancer) Delay, play the waiting game, and refuse to be intimidated into moving. Pisces and Virgo figure prominently, and will have these letters or initials in their names: G, P, Y. You'll be especially concerned with institutions, hospitals, buildings, and theater.

Tuesday, March 6 (Moon in Cancer to Leo 5:29 a.m.) The Cancer moon relates to secrets, confidential information. The need to be discreet. You could be involved in heavy bidding for an art object or luxury item. The spotlight is on payments, collections, and invoices that have yet to be mailed.

Wednesday, March 7 (Moon in Leo)   This is one Wednesday you won't soon forget! The moon in Leo brings your high cycle and, in turn, this means you will make a fresh start in a different direction. The romantic side of your nature surges forth—Aries and Libra play significant roles.

Thursday, March 8 (Moon in Leo to Virgo 5:43 a.m.)   New challenges are featured. Money, payments, collections, and investments dominate. You'll be told by a Cancer, "With you, all things are possible!" Express your most original, controversial concepts. Another Leo is in the picture.

Friday, March 9 (Moon in Virgo)   The full moon in Virgo equates to your ability to locate lost articles, to win contests, and to display skill in sports. You'll ponder, "This is what I studied and practiced for, and I'm glad I worked as hard as I did." Cancer and Capricorn figure prominently.

Saturday, March 10 (Moon in Virgo to Libra 5:46 a.m.) Lucky lottery: 3, 33, 12, 8, 40, 17. Your sense of perception is heightened to the degree of having extrasensory perception. Attention revolves around your body image, a comedy routine, arrangements for a long journey, perhaps overseas. A Sagittarian plays a key role.

Sunday, March 11 (Moon in Libra)   Revise, review, and rebuild. Get your second emotional wind. Test the durability of those you work and play with. What at first seems impossible will be like putty in your hands. The Libra moon equates to trips, visits, relatives, and to people who tend to lose things.

Monday, March 12 (Moon in Libra to Scorpio 7:42 a.m.)
What a Monday! Today's scenario highlights flirtation, challenge, gain via the written word. A trip out of town is featured, voluntarily or otherwise. Communication from a relative in a distant city causes a change of plans. The sale or purchase of a musical instrument is part of this scenario.

Tuesday, March 13 (Moon in Scorpio) Attention revolves around your home, security, income potential, the receipt of gift symbolizing, "I love you!" Focus on luxury items, art objects, the settling of financial differences with a family member. Remember: To get a smile, you must give a smile!

Wednesday, March 14 (Moon in Scorpio to Sagittarius 1:17 p.m.) The Scorpio moon relates to problems at home. Start with the plumbing; be sure your washing machine is in order. A change of batteries is required in some areas. A domineering Scorpio attempts to take over—be kind, but not foolish. Have luck with number 7.

Thursday, March 15 (Moon in Sagittarius) For racing luck at all tracks: post-position special—number 2 p.p. in the seventh race. Pick six: 5, 3, 8, 6, 2, 1. Watch for these letters or initials in the names of potential winning horses or jockeys: H, Q, Z. Hot daily doubles: 5 and 3, 2 and 7, 3 and 8. Favorites are in the money. Capricorn and Cancer jockeys will be in the winner's circle.

Friday, March 16 (Moon in Sagittarius to Capricorn 11:02 p.m.) All indications point to travel, philosophy, publishing, and advertising. Meet with a fascinating member of the opposite sex who makes you think twice. You exude personal magnetism, an aura of sensuality and sex appeal. Also part of the scenario will be children, challenge, a variety of sensations.

Saturday, March 17 (Moon in Capricorn)   On this St. Patrick's Day, the lunar indications point to a change of work routine. Celebrate, be jovial, accent moderation in connection with adult beverages. Aquarius and another Leo play fascinating roles. Lucky lottery: 1, 12, 2, 7, 6, 5.

Sunday, March 18 (Moon in Capricorn)   The focus is on health reports, basic issues, a friendship that could get close, closer, and lead to a change of marital status. Official duties will be clearly outlined. You will be invited to air objections, if any. A Cancer will dominate today's action.

Monday, March 19 (Moon in Capricorn to Aquarius 11:35 a.m.)   Highlight versatility, diversity, and intellectual curiosity. Your superior on the job will pay an unusual compliment. Take notes regarding moods, dreams, feelings, and illusions. A dream tonight that could prove prophetic relates to an upcoming social affair. Your lucky number is 3.

Tuesday, March 20 (Moon in Aquarius)   The Aquarian moon spells direct action. The spotlight is on partnership, marriage, public relations, and overcoming legal objections. Prove skeptics wrong by doing the impossible. Taurus, Scorpio, and another Leo play major roles.

Wednesday, March 21 (Moon in Aquarius)   For racing luck at all tracks: post-position special—number 5 p.p. in the fifth race. Pick six: 3, 5, 2, 1, 5, 3. Watch for these letters or initials in the names of potential winning horses or jockeys: E, N, W. Hot daily doubles: 3 and 5, 1 and 1, 4 and 5. Horses that come out in front will be in the winner's circle. Gemini jockeys have racing luck.

Thursday, March 22 (Moon in Aquarius to Pisces 12:27 a.m.)   Be diplomatic, without being weak. Toss aside your false pride in order to make an intelligent concession. Taurus, Scorpio, and another Leo play dramatic roles, and could have these letters in their names: F, O, X. Wear shades of blue.

Friday, March 23 (Moon in Pisces)   You'll be dealing with people who see things at night. The spotlight is on psychic impressions, ability to locate lost articles, glamour and intrigue, a desire to do things and learning how to get started. Someone you trust makes a confession, "It was minor, but still it was a bad thing I did!"

Saturday, March 24 (Moon in Pisces to Aries 11:42 a.m.) Lucky lottery: 8, 12, 20, 21, 33, 15. Someone close to you, perhaps your spouse or business partner, lays it on the line about investments, profits, and losses. You learn more about money and how it gets that way. Capricorn will play a leading role.

Sunday, March 25 (Moon in Aries)   The new moon in Aries relates to eighth house matters. This includes the occult, locating missing valuables. Let go of a losing proposition. Shake off a tendency to remain where your usefulness is no longer appreciated. Aries and Libra make 'em shake, rattle, and roll.

Monday, March 26 (Moon in Aries to Taurus 8:49 p.m.)   You awaken bright-eyed and bushy-tailed. Focus on initiative, ambition, the return of vitality. You will make a fresh start. You speak from the heart, and people respond in a positive way. Aquarius and another Leo help you get started in a new enterprise.

Tuesday, March 27 (Moon in Taurus)   You'll be told, "Do what you do best, but make up your mind, because time is running out!" Within 24 hours, you will receive proof that you are appreciated and that you have been marked for a leadership role. A Cancer declares, "You win!"

Wednesday, March 28 (Moon in Taurus)   The answers to your questions will be found through meditation. A Taurus plays a paramount role, and declares, "I am with you all the way and don't hesitate to call on me for anything extra!" The element of luck is on your side; you could win a major contest. Your fortunate number is 3.

Thursday, March 29 (Moon in Taurus to Gemini 4:00 a.m.)   Get your facts in order. Rewrite, review, and rebuild. Puzzle pieces fall into place. A wish comes true, not exactly as you imagined, but nevertheless your wish will be fulfilled. A mechanical device "cries out for oil!" A change of batteries would not hurt, either.

Friday, March 30 (Moon in Gemini)   Today's scenario calls for action. The moon position shouts, "You need only ask, and your desire will be fulfilled!" Participate in fund-raising for a social, political, or entertainment project. Get ready for change, travel, and variety. A proposal was sincere, but time has passed. Gemini is involved.

Saturday, March 31 (Moon in Gemini to Cancer 9:21 a.m.)   On this last day of March, with the moon in Gemini, you will surpass previous performances. Ask questions, use information provided in the answers. The emphasis is on a domestic situation, decorating, remodeling, your marital status. Lucky lottery: 6, 12, 22, 18, 50, 51.

APRIL 2001

Sunday, April 1—Daylight Saving Time Begins (Moon in Cancer)   Those who attempt to fool you in the spirit of the day will soon be awakened by boomeranging thoughts. Be ready for a change of scene, look beyond the immediate, remember that a flirtation that is now cool could become too hot not to cool down again. Scorpio is involved.

Monday, April 2 (Moon in Cancer to Leo 1:52 p.m.)   Did anything happen to anyone that was unusual yesterday? Gemini and Sagittarius respond: "Lean back and hear some stories, some of them admittedly tall tales." Focus on unique study, reading and writing, imprinting style in your own way. Your lucky number is 5.

Tuesday, April 3 (Moon in Leo)   A reconciliation with your family produces positive results. Someone asks, "Are you serious about music and voice lessons?" Depending on your mood, you could respond, "What business is it of yours?" A written message is received from a Taurus, which gives you a good, warm feeling.

Wednesday, April 4 (Moon in Leo to Virgo 3:45 p.m.)   Some will dub you the comeback kid. Neptune is involved here and this warns of a possible deception. It's your high cycle, when you are on the winning team. Know it, and act accordingly. What seems too good to be true probably is. Remember the boxing term, "Don't lead with your right!"

Thursday, April 5 (Moon in Virgo)   The moon moves into Virgo, your second house, and that is the section of your horoscope concerning the recovery of lost objects, payments, and income potential. The key is to be discriminating. Take nothing for granted, especially in connection with payments, collections, and royalties.

Friday, April 6 (Moon in Virgo to Libra 4:46 p.m.)   As the weekend gets underway, reach beyond previous expectations. Keep abreast of foreign money rates; don't overlook the possibility of a coup. Aries and Libra play outstanding roles, and will have these letters or initials in their names: I and R. Your lucky number is 9.

244

Saturday, April 7 (Moon in Libra)   You could meet creative, exciting people who show a sincere interest in what you are doing and why. Be yourself, maintain your independent stance. Somehow or other, weave gold into a clothing pattern. Participate in a daring, pioneering project. Your lucky number is 1.

Sunday, April 8 (Moon in Libra to Scorpio 7:01 p.m.)   It is Sunday, with the full moon in Libra. Questions about legal rights, public affairs, and marriage persist. Accent showmanship, design, architecture, and color coordination. You'll be asked to talk and write about how to make your home more beautiful.

Monday, April 9 (Moon in Scorpio)   The moon in Scorpio is in your fourth house. Disputes could arise over leaving home for outside entertainment. Ultimately, your decision will be to remain comfortable, to relax, to view a movie concerning drama, glamour, and sex. A Sagittarian exerts influence.

Tuesday, April 10 (Moon in Scorpio to Sagittarius 11:47 p.m.)   Take time to make repairs, to proofread copy. A hidden ally is on the job—likely to be a Taurus or Scorpio. You are doing the right thing, despite complications, and there are pangs of conscience. A telegram arrives concerning a contest.

Wednesday, April 11 (Moon in Sagittarius)   Within 24 hours, your creative juices stir. This relates to children, change, travel, and romance. Focus on style, panache, getting major points across via the written word. Some people claim you work too hard. Your response: "Hard writing makes easy reading!" Your lucky number is 5.

Thursday, April 12 (Moon in Sagittarius)   For racing luck at all tracks: post-position special—number 6 p.p. in the second race. Pick six: 1, 6, 4, 4, 1, 2. Watch for these letters or initials in the names of potential winning horses or jockeys: F, O, X. Hot daily doubles: 1 and 6, 2 and 8,

5 and 5. Favorites tend to come in third. Taurus and Libra jockeys win.

Friday, April 13 (Moon in Sagittarius to Capricorn 8:20 a.m.)   Be on the alert for fake letters or faxes. Pisces could be involved in a Friday the Thirteenth prank. This is not April Fool, but some people never leave their adolescence. They want you to feel you are going to lose because of this special day.

Saturday, April 14 (Moon in Capricorn)   Lucky lottery: 8, 10, 12, 22, 18, 14. Work conditions improve; you meet people who share your interests, including literature and astrology. A plum assignment comes your way, almost accidentally. A Cancer wants to be with you.

Sunday, April 15 (Moon in Capricorn to Aquarius 8:10 p.m.)   You'll be invited to speak before a group associated with the occult or metaphysical world. Modesty is one thing, but hiding to avert criticism is something else. Emerge from any emotional shell. An international organization will thank you for past efforts.

Monday, April 16 (Moon in Aquarius)   Within 24 hours, you'll know where you stand in these areas—legal and marriage. Tonight, read between the lines. Display your skill as a palm reader. A young, vigorous member of the opposite sex will admit, "I am terribly attracted to you!" Aquarius is involved.

Tuesday, April 17 (Moon in Aquarius)   The emphasis is on your public image, legal rights and permissions, settling of a controversy relating to marriage. Focus on direction, motivation, and selecting dinner from a fabulous menu. Someone comments, "You really do know how to live!"

Wednesday, April 18 (Moon in Aquarius to Pisces 8:59 a.m.)   Avoid scattering your forces. Do not be under the illusion that you can please everyone—it can't be done! Share interests in a variety of subjects, including how to be a good host or hostess. An unorthodox Aquarian cites you as a creative, dynamic person. Have luck with number 3.

Thursday, April 19 (Moon in Pisces)   The Pisces moon in your eighth house emphasizes interest in subjects forbidden in some quarters. Dilemma: You are attracted to someone who is also drawn to you, but you cannot seem to get along without emotional fireworks. One or both should get out of town, but not together!

Friday, April 20 (Moon in Pisces to Aries 8:16 p.m.)   For racing luck at all tracks: post-position special—number 3 p.p. in the seventh race. Pick six: 3, 5, 7, 2, 8, 1. Watch for these letters or initials in the names of potential winning horses or jockeys: E, N, W. Hot daily doubles: 3 and 5, 7 and 7, 4 and 6. Sagittarius and Virgo must take special care to avoid injuries.

Saturday, April 21 (Moon in Aries)   A love relationship warms up, but could get too hot not to cool down. Focus on a possible change of residence or marital status. Do not be too harsh when offering constructive criticism, especially where art is concerned. Lucky lottery: 48, 8, 19, 30, 40, 9.

Sunday, April 22 (Moon in Aries)   Go slow, define terms, help someone who is sorting out a domestic mess. You'll be dealing with an independent, stubborn, creative, or controversial person. Check times of departures in connection with travel. False information is being corrected. Don't be too early or too late!

Monday, April 23 (Moon in Aries to Taurus 4:55 a.m.)   The new moon falls in the section of your horoscope associated with leadership, business, and career. Important money changes hands. Continue to be aware of foreign exchange rates. Your judgment and intuition are on target. Older persons prove they are loyal.

Tuesday, April 24 (Moon in Taurus)   A financial burden is lifted, you will be granted more independence and financial reward. What begins as defeat will conclude in a rousing victory. Aries and Libra play leading roles, and could have these letters or initials in their names: I and R.

Wednesday, April 25 (Moon in Taurus to Gemini 11:10 a.m.)   Within 24 hours, some of your most important desires will be fulfilled. Elements of timing and luck are restored. Vital juices flow, and vitality makes a dramatic comeback. You'll be musing, "What a Wednesday; it's a day I won't soon forget!" Your lucky number is 1.

Thursday, April 26 (Moon in Gemini)   The Gemini moon relates to good fortune in finance and romance. Humor is involved in the exposure of a coworker who blames errors on you. A Cancer is in the picture. Adversity will be transformed into a blessing where you could meet a future soul mate.

Friday, April 27 (Moon in Gemini to Cancer 3:48 p.m.)   What a Friday! The moon in your eleventh house, a Jupiter keynote, elements of timing and good fortune are all in your corner, awaiting your command. Emphasize coordination, reliability, an entertainment program with the proceeds going to a political or charitable campaign.

Saturday, April 28 (Moon in Cancer)   Lucky lottery: 5, 50, 12, 9, 22, 32. A secret is revealed, much to your advantage. You get credit for previous accomplishments. It's a bit late, but better late than never. Taurus, Scorpio, and another Leo figure in this scenario.

Sunday, April 29 (Moon in Cancer to Leo 7:24 p.m.)   An excellent day to develop your spiritual values. Be in touch with your mother or a mother figure. Show gratitude, without being obsequious. Winning numbers in a contest will appear almost magically. An excellent day to absorb information as result of reading. Try writing yourself!

Monday, April 30 (Moon in Leo)   On this last day of April, with the moon in your sign and Venus keynote, entertain and be entertained at home. Music is involved. There's a chance to dance to best-liked tunes. People respond almost immediately to your suggestions and criticisms. Libra and Aries could play astounding roles.

MAY 2001

Tuesday, May 1 (Moon in Leo to Virgo 10:15 p.m.)   On this Tuesday, you'll be saying, "Life can be beautiful!" The moon is in your sign, Mercury significator. Bright ideas crowd their way into your consciousness. A dream last night included writing, recognition, fame, and fortune. That dream was not too far from the truth.

Wednesday, May 2 (Moon in Virgo)   The moon leaves your sign, which coincides with the probability of hitting the jackpot. Maintain optimism and use your sense of discrimination. This means choose only the best; don't substitute for quality. A question relating to your marital status will be answered by circumstances, security, or property value.

Thursday, May 3 (Moon in Virgo)   For a time, you might be wondering, "Is this the real world or am I dreaming?" Illusion commingles with reality. You will muse, "Whatever the world is, I am glad to be here and alive and kicking!" Pisces and Virgo will play memorable roles.

Friday, May 4 (Moon in Virgo to Libra 12:49 a.m.)   A cash investment pays dividends. The spotlight is on money, collections, and high finance. A Capricorn becomes your staunch ally, helps you overcome fear, doubts, and apprehension. A Cancer also plays a role, and helps you know more about sales and purchases relating to property or home.

Saturday, May 5 (Moon in Libra)   What a Saturday night! A Libra takes you by your hand and says in a low whisper, "You do things to me just holding your hand!" Highlight your humor and versatility. Explore, investigate, and say to yourself, "I'm really glad to know you!"

Sunday, May 6 (Moon in Libra to Scorpio 4:00 a.m.) Make a fresh start in a new direction. Ask questions. Receive answers graciously. Relatives are in the picture, following a short trip based on a very warm flirtation. You decide to live your own life including separating yourself from relatives and continuing flirtation. Your lucky number is 1.

Monday, May 7 (Moon in Scorpio)   The full moon in Scorpio represents your fourth house: property, marriage, paying off an old debt. A clash of ideas involves Taurus and Scorpio. Turn on your charm; make an intelligent concession; realize that it is a matter of two-to-one and you are the "one." Your lucky number is 2.

Tuesday, May 8 (Moon in Scorpio to Sagittarius 9:05 a.m.)   What a lively Tuesday! Like a suppressed volcano, you come to life. Others realize "we must get out of the way or suffer burns." You are up-to-date on fashion; many people follow your style. And remember—to get a smile, give a smile! A Sagittarian is involved.

Wednesday, May 9 (Moon in Sagittarius)   Count your change, untie the knot that restricts and chokes. It seems like you have gone through this before, yet you will be asking, "Is this déjà vu?" Today's scenario features familiar faces and places. Scorpio is back in the picture, seems determined to settle, whether you are a friend or enemy.

Thursday, May 10 (Moon in Sagittarius to Capricorn 5:09 p.m.) You become more sensitive to trends and cycles. Gemini, Virgo, and Sagittarius play outstanding roles, and are likely to have these letters or initials in their names: E, N, W. It is not your role in the sun to be modest. Speak up, Leo, write your opinions. You will receive a love letter by tonight.

Friday, May 11 (Moon in Capricorn) Things get done. People who rely on you are being taught to rely upon themselves! Venus and the sun are keynotes for you today. Properly interpreted, this means you'll be involved in a hot love affair. This blends with your creative force. You will speak out and possibly win national recognition.

Saturday, May 12 (Moon in Capricorn) Confusion is the keyword for you on this Saturday night. You are drawn between someone who has plenty of common sense and one who is glamorous, intriguing, and who oozes sex appeal. Maintain your aura of mystery. An alluring member of the opposite sex declares, "We should take this show on the road!"

Sunday, May 13 (Moon in Capricorn to Aquarius 4:19 a.m.) Within 24 hours, your life takes a strange, exciting turn. The moon will be in Aquarius, your seventh house, depicting a unique partnership and feeling, "I am madly in love!" You'll get proposals that involve your career or marriage. A Cancer provides encouragement, says, "All of us trust you, go ahead!"

Monday, May 14 (Moon in Aquarius) Lay your cards on the table—face up! This display of daring and honesty will win friends and influence people. The Mars keynote blends with your sun, which means action, a variety of experiences. It also means the end of love frustration. You learn where you stand and what to do about it.

Tuesday, May 15 (Moon in Aquarius to Pisces 5:00 p.m.) You have been waiting for this day! People who opposed you will begin to like you. This will not be mild, but very intense. Remember, the grass always appears greener across the way. People want something from you, so be sure you are ready to give it up. Your lucky number is 1.

Wednesday, May 16 (Moon in Pisces) Lucky lottery: 2, 3, 12, 7, 5, 4. People accuse you of playing in the ballpark of the occult. That is foolish. Let critics know that you are aware they are being foolish and superstitious. The spotlight is on direction, motivation, major decisions relating to your property and marriage.

Thursday, May 17 (Moon in Pisces) Look beyond the immediate. Tap your well of reason, talent, and intuitive intellect. The stage is set for you to win a contest. Don't lose confidence just because you might not win tonight or tomorrow—within three weeks, you could be wealthy! Your lucky number is 3.

Friday, May 18 (Moon in Pisces to Aries 4:40 a.m.) Get ready for exciting changes, possibly moving from one residence to another, or the breakup of one relationship, the renewal of another. Taurus, Scorpio, and another Leo figure prominently, and could have these letters or initials in their names: D, M, V. Thank your lucky stars!

Saturday, May 19 (Moon in Aries) Before this Saturday is finished, you will have experienced traditional descriptions of love, variety, challenge, and the excitement of exploration. The Aries moon relates to travel, philosophy, and unique studies. Keep resolutions about the protection of your eyes. Your eyesight could be at stake. Your lucky number is 5.

Sunday, May 20 (Moon in Aries to Taurus 1:27 p.m.) Attention revolves around your home, security, music, and travel. The ninth house influence relates to spirituality, curiosity about how others live in various climates and nations, and how they express love. Taurus, Libra, and Scorpio play outstanding roles, and have these letters in their names: F, O, X.

Monday, May 21 (Moon in Taurus)   Tradition goes by the wayside—create your own tradition. Don't follow others; let them follow you, if they prefer. Pisces and Virgo play major roles and could have these letters or initials in their names: G, P, Y. Have luck with number 7.

Tuesday, May 22 (Moon in Taurus to Gemini 7:11 p.m.)   The emphasis is on how far you want to climb; those at the top are preparing a welcome for you. Taurus is very much involved, and heads your cheering section, Food, nourishment, and adult beverages await. You are doing the right thing, so don't quit now! Capricorn plays a role.

Wednesday, May 23 (Moon in Gemini)   For racing luck at all tracks: post-position special—number 8 p.p. in the eighth race. Pick six: 2, 4, 5, 6, 9, 8. Watch for these letters or initials in the names of potential winning horses or jockeys: I and R. Hot daily doubles: 2 and 4, 8 and 9, 7 and 6. Aries jockeys will be in the money, paying a good price.

Thursday, May 24 (Moon in Gemini to Cancer 10:41 p.m.)   Luck stays with you. You win friends and influence people. You will have good fortune today in matters of finance and romance. The Gemini moon in your eleventh house equates to obtaining funding for a favorite project. If there is a legal difficulty in any area, today you should call on Gemini—you can't lose with Gemini.

Friday, May 25 (Moon in Cancer)   The moon is leaving your eleventh house. As it progresses to your sign (Leo) there will be a volume of letters, applications, and perhaps awards. You'll hear these comments, "You must have been living right, or else there is something to your karma!" Lucky stars!

Saturday, May 26 (Moon in Cancer)   The moon moves rapidly from Cancer to Leo. Once again, luck changes and once again it changes in your favor. Don't be afraid to pay a hefty price for quality goods. Before you know it, you will be consulted on what is good, bad, or indifferent. Sagittarian in the picture.

Sunday, May 27 (Moon in Cancer to Leo 1:11 a.m.)   You'll be dealing with creative people who are ultra-temperamental. This includes Taurus, Scorpio, and another Leo. Be considerate, but don't back down from your principles. Someone behind the scenes appears determined to make trouble. Be patient to a point, then let go!

Monday, May 28 (Moon in Leo)   Your cycle is high, so circumstances move in your favor. You'll be complimented on your charm, intelligence, and sense of timing. Someone with an inquisitive mind asks, "Could I spend a little time with you?" Ask this person in a provocative tone, "I would love to spend time with you; what would it cost me?"

Tuesday, May 29 (Moon in Leo to Virgo 3:37 a.m.)   The moon continues in Leo, your house of personality. You exude an aura of personal magnetism, sensuality, and sex appeal. Laughter seals at least two or three friendships. In some ways, Leo, you are irresistible! A change of residence or marital status could be featured.

Wednesday, May 30 (Moon in Virgo)   For racing luck at all tracks: post-position special—number 4 p.p. in the third race. Pick six: 1, 2, 4, 7, 8, 6. Watch for these letters or initials in the names of potential winning horses or jockeys: G, P, Y. Hot daily doubles: 1 and 2, 3 and 7, 5 and 8. Favorites fall flat; a Pisces jockey is in danger of injury.

Thursday, May 31 (Moon in Virgo to Libra 6:40 a.m.) On this last day of May, the pressure is on, and you are up to it. Focus on money, payments, collections, the ability to be lucky in games of chance. A dark-haired Capricorn seeks to tout you off winners. Say, "Thank you, but no thanks!" Ride with the tide!

JUNE 2001

Friday, June 1 (Moon in Libra) You'll surprise those who were not aware that you are part of an inner circle. You are in the running, people become aware of it, so be selective in choosing a special offer. Focus on beauty, flowers, music, and art objects. A domestic adjustment involves where you live and questions about marriage.

Saturday, June 2 (Moon in Libra to Scorpio 10:56 a.m.) On this Saturday, put forth charm, élan, sophistication. People are drawn to you tonight, and seek an answer to, "What is the secret of your charm?" Give that Leo smile, pretend you didn't hear in the first place. Then get to work sweeping everyone off their feet. Your lucky number is 7.

Sunday, June 3 (Moon in Scorpio) The closed-in feeling is only temporary. You have mail to answer and questions to answer about an ongoing relationship. Capricorn and Cancer play outstanding roles, and could have these letters or initials in their names: H, Q, Z. A telephone call from another city reminds, "You owe us at least three pages of fresh copy!"

Monday, June 4 (Moon in Scorpio to Sagittarius 4:57 p.m.) New experiences are coming, sooner than you think. Revise, review, rebuild, and let it be known, "I adore people who know the real meaning of love!" Aries and Libra figure prominently, and will have these letters or initials in their names: I and R. Your lucky number is 9.

Tuesday, June 5 (Moon in Sagittarius)   Is it possible that this will be your first circus! A most unusual day, featuring entertainment, and finding you fascinated by a trapeze artist. Youthful sensations surface, such as running away with the circus! An Aquarius and another Leo play sensational roles, and have these initials in their names: A, S, J.

Wednesday, June 6 (Moon in Sagittarius)   The full moon in Sagittarius represents your fifth house. The spotlight is on creativity, style, an intensified relationship. You finally are getting over a situation that haunted you all month. The emphasis is on partnership, your marital status, a delicious dinner prepared by a Cancer.

Thursday, June 7 (Moon in Sagittarius to Capricorn 1:23 a.m.)   Focus on mystery, intrigue, questions persisting, "How do you do it?" A restless Gemini introduces you to a debonair Pisces. Give yourself time to sift things out. The spotlight falls on social affairs, catering, and preparing entertainment. A Sagittarian says, "You can do it, so get started!"

Friday, June 8 (Moon in Capricorn)   A knotty problem will dissolve, if you so desire. Taurus, Scorpio, and another Leo play instrumental roles, and will have these letters or initials in their names: D, M, V. A personal friend smilingly asks, "How do you get in and out of these situations?" Stand tall, face the music, and above all, do not quit!

Saturday, June 9 (Moon in Capricorn to Aquarius 12:19 p.m.)   Get ready for change, travel, and variety. A health checkup is a source of good news. The emphasis is on employment, work methods, the possibility of meeting your future soul mate. Take special care of your household pets. Owing to recent confusion you have ignored your loyal pet friends. Your lucky number is 5.

Sunday, June 10 (Moon in Aquarius)   Attention revolves around where you live, the purchase of furniture, receiving gifts that help beautify your surroundings. The spotlight is on your marital status, earning power, receiving a compliment that is strong enough to relate to love. Taurus, Libra, and Scorpio will play sensational roles.

Monday, June 11 (Moon in Aquarius)   Focus on mystery, intrigue, glamour, fashion, ability to entertain and mystify. Some people insist, "You must have been active in the playground of the occult!" When looking up the word *occult,* your tormentors will find it merely means hidden or out-of-the-way. Pisces plays a role.

Tuesday, June 12 (Moon in Aquarius to Pisces 12:52 a.m.)   Within 24 hours, the moon will be in Pisces, your eighth house. You could discover the bank book of your spouse—it might add up to hidden wealth. Capricorn and Cancer figure in this dynamic scenario, and could have these letters or initials in their names: H, Q, Z. Have luck with number 8.

Wednesday, June 13 (Moon in Pisces)   During this cycle, you have a taste for spearmint. You also participate in humanitarian or political projects. Refuse to be dissuaded by those who lack faith and insight. If attending the racetrack, stick with number 1 post position in the eighth race. You meet aggressive, creative, and attractive people who appreciate these qualities in you.

Thursday, June 14 (Moon in Pisces to Aries 1:01 p.m.)   The moon in Pisces represents Neptune, which blends with your sun ruler, enabling you to see through schemes, fraud, and tricks aimed at getting something for nothing. Aquarius and another Leo will win their way. You personally are knocking on the doors of fame and fortune. Your lucky number is 1.

Friday, June 15 (Moon in Aries)   For racing luck at all tracks: post-position special—number 6 p.p. in the fifth race. Pick six: 2, 4, 1, 3, 6, 8. Watch for these letters or initials in the names of potential winning horses or jockeys: B, K, T. Hot daily doubles: 2 and 4, 5 and 8, 6 and 6. Favorites run out of money; Cancer jockeys must protect themselves from injuries.

Saturday, June 16 (Moon in Aries to Taurus 10:37 p.m.)   Lucky lottery: 5, 50, 3, 7, 22, 18. An excellent time for entertaining, writing, an advertising campaign, and publishing. This will be a pleasant Saturday Night Live. You'll meet a vibrant Sagittarian who shows interest in your work. A Gemini assures, "I can bring you luck!"

Sunday, June 17 (Moon in Taurus)   The pace slows; events continue to build to an exciting climax. Gain additional information about a speculative venture. Taurus, Scorpio, and another Leo play intriguing roles, and will have these letters or initials in their names: E, N, W. A literary agency in the picture.

Monday, June 18 (Moon in Taurus)   You'll be sighing, "Well, I survived another weekend!" Reconcile with a family member who admits, "I insulted you, but I did not mean a word of it. I'm sorry!" Be analytical, without being overly critical. A flirtation is nice but it is necessary to declare, "Enough is enough!"

Tuesday, June 19 (Moon in Taurus to Gemini 4:41 a.m.)   Pay special attention to household pets. It could be a minor digestive problem, but it should not be ignored. Focus on a domestic adjustment, especially cleaning and beautifying your surroundings. Libra, Gemini will play featured roles. Your lucky number is 6.

Wednesday, June 20 (Moon in Gemini)   Suddenly, events transpire to bring you closer to your ultimate goal. Answers are likely to be found via meditation. Your popularity increases; you will be dubbed a glamorous, mysterious figure. You'll be told, "You most certainly are out of the ordinary!" Pisces is involved.

Thursday, June 21—Solar Eclipse (Moon in Gemini to Cancer 7:39 a.m.)   The new moon, solar eclipse in Gemini activates that section of your horoscope which relates directly to winning friends and influencing people. Highlight versatility, the ability to adapt yourself to situations or conditions subject to dramatic transformations. Capricorn is involved.

Friday, June 22 (Moon in Cancer)   The key word is *separation*. Release yourself from the bondage of being taken for granted by an arrogant person. Love and the lack of it figure prominently. Let it be known, "From now on I am going to be creatively selfish!" Aries and Libra are destined to figure prominently in your life.

Saturday, June 23 (Moon in Cancer to Leo 8:54 p.m.)   You will be confronted with this question: "Do you believe in fate or free will?" Blend your answer with humor, something like this—"At times, I am captain of my fate. At other times, I feel as if I go where the winds take me!" Your lucky number is 1.

Sunday, June 24 (Moon in Leo)   A family get-together is featured. Your cycle is high; you will bring enlightenment that will go far in settling arguments. Focus on drama, showmanship, initiative, daring, and originality. Entertain guests by sharing a provocative television show. A Cancer is involved.

Monday, June 25 (Moon in Leo to Virgo 9:57 a.m.)   What begins as a dull day will be transformed into an exciting revelation. Your confidence is restored, so go places, do things, and express your romantic feelings. Keep recent resolutions about fashion, body image, diet, and adult beverages. You will soon be saying, "What a Monday!"

Tuesday, June 26 (Moon in Virgo)   The moon is in your second house—you locate a valuable missing article. Finances improve, which coincides with an exercise in restraint. Revise a project. Review different possibilities. Tear down for the ultimate purpose of rebuilding on a more solid structure. Taurus and Scorpio are represented.

Wednesday, June 27 (Moon in Virgo to Libra 12:10 p.m.)   You will be encouraged as result of an advanced payment. Royalties are involved. Your cycle continues high, so make it crystal clear, "I am willing to take a chance on romance!" Before the moon takes over for the sun, you'll be musing, "No doubt about it, I am sitting pretty!" Your lucky number is 5.

Thursday, June 28 (Moon in Libra)   Go slow, speak softly, and overcome a tendency to suddenly be shy. What seemed out-of-reach will become available. Today's scenario also features trips, a surprise visit by a relative who says, "I wanted to drop this off for you!" It turns out to be a present, something you want and need. Express gratitude.

Friday, June 29 (Moon in Libra to Scorpio 4:28 p.m.)   You'll hear music! The sound will be of an ethereal kind. You'll hear this comment about it, "That sound is out of this world!" Play the waiting game—the offers will be forthcoming. Wait for and choose the best! People near and around you express interest in psychic phenomena, and are willing to make a game of it.

Saturday, June 30 (Moon in Scorpio)   On this last day of June, features will involve mystery, intrigue and lovemaking. Highlight versatility, diversity, and give full play to your intellectual curiosity. Authorities might consider you an upstart, but who cares? Correct mechanical defects, and be aware of weather conditions. Your lucky number is 8.

Sunday, July 1 (Moon in Scorpio to Sagittarius 11:13 p.m.) On this first day of July, spiritual values surface. It is a matter of Neptune and your sun significator. You see through what is artificial, and that includes yourself. Be realistic, view people and places as they are, not as you wish they might be. Avoid self-deception!

Monday, July 2 (Moon in Sagittarius) What appeared to be a loss regains momentum and comes back to you. Work gets done, almost as if by magic. People marvel at your strength and determination. However, you know that you did not accomplish it alone. Capricorn and Cancer will play fascinating, creative, exciting roles.

Tuesday, July 3 (Moon in Sagittarius) On this Tuesday, your view will be universal. Open lines of communication. People from other countries attempt to communicate, and by listening, you learn much. Aries and Libra have key roles and will have these letters or initials in their names: I and R. Your lucky number is 9.

Wednesday, July 4 (Moon in Sagittarius to Capricorn 8:21 a.m.) On this holiday, let's play lucky lottery: 7, 11, 4, 40, 13, 10. The moon in Sagittarius represents your fifth house, that section which equates to creativity, sensuality, and sex appeal. A young person announces, "I would like to be just like you!" Another Leo plays a creative role.

Thursday, July 5—Lunar Eclipse (Moon in Capricorn) The full moon, lunar eclipse in Capricorn equates to your sixth house. This means be prepared for a job change, get a physical examination, and renew a relationship with someone you can trust. In matters of speculation, stick with number 2. Focus on food and a variety of relationships. Capricorn is in this picture.

261

Friday, July 6 (Moon in Capricorn to Aquarius 7:32 p.m.) You'll be asking, "Is this déjà vu?" Capricorn and Libra play unusual roles. Broken promises could be mended. Highlight diversity, humor, versatility, and keep up with fashion trends. Someone who makes an exciting proposal should be politely asked, "Would you please put that in writing?"

Saturday, July 7 (Moon in Aquarius) Brooding about the past is negative. Transform a tendency to brood into a positive meditation. The moon in Aquarius represents legal affairs, public relations, partnership and marriage. A situation or arrangement will be highly unorthodox. Your interest in astrology, mysticism, theology will be fanned.

Sunday, July 8 (Moon in Aquarius) On this Sunday, with the moon in your seventh house, get ready for stunning changes. Keep your plans flexible, and display awareness during a unique meeting. What previously you regarded as nonsense could now be high on your agenda of achievement. Someone who is a writer encourages you to try it, too!

Monday, July 9 (Moon in Aquarius to Pisces 8:04 a.m.) Today starts out as ordinary. However, as the day picks up steam, you'll be involved with dynamic, fascinating, sensual, creative people. An alluring person whispers, "I can hardly keep my hands off you!" A domestic adjustment is featured, and relates to where you live, your marital status.

Tuesday, July 10 (Moon in Pisces) Focus on mystery and intrigue. The moon in Pisces represents your eighth house, that section of your horoscope which relates to the occult, the hidden, revelations. You will be apprehensive about contacting someone who once confided interest in you. Pisces is involved.

Wednesday, July 11 (Moon in Pisces to Aries 8:34 p.m.)   For racing luck at all tracks: post-position special—number 8 p.p. in the second race. Pick six: 2, 8, 5, 3, 7, 4. Be alert for these letters or initials in the names of potential winning horses or jockeys: G, P, Y. Hot daily doubles: 2 and 8, 4 and 7, 3 and 5. Favorites win. Capricorn and Cancer jockeys will be in the winner's circle.

Thursday, July 12 (Moon in Aries)   The moon was apparently in a hurry to get out of Pisces. Now, it is in your house of travel. Complete a project, look beyond the immediate, and deal with someone in a foreign country. Aries and Libra will figure prominently, and will have these initials in their names: I and R.

Friday, July 13 (Moon in Aries)   This could be your lucky day. Focus on philosophy, religions of the world, travel, doing business overseas. Aquarius and another Leo play sensational roles, and could have these letters or initials in their names: A, S, J. A love relationship is sparked. An attraction that first brought you together does it again!

Saturday, July 14 (Moon in Aries to Taurus 7:12 a.m.)   You'll sigh, "Well, I got by that Friday the Thirteenth jinx!" Now start again, make a fresh beginning, stress independence, originality, the courage of your convictions. Focus on steps that you take, but be careful not to trip. Be alert, alive, and strive for emotional equilibrium. Your lucky number is 2.

Sunday, July 15 (Moon in Taurus)   On this Sunday there are a variety of experiences and temptations. The Taurus moon relates to that section of your chart associated with your career, success, ambition, obtaining funding. The Jupiter keynote with your sun significator spells Lady Luck. Very likely, this could be the precursor to a winning streak.

Monday, July 16 (Moon in Taurus to Gemini 2:23 p.m.)   The moon in Taurus tells of stubbornly holding on to your beliefs and principles. Opposition that begins as mild could become serious—being forewarned is being forearmed. Keep resolutions about diet, nutrition, and exercise. Wear bright colors that include yellow and gold.

Tuesday, July 17 (Moon in Gemini)   For you, this Tuesday means reading and writing, teaching and learning. A flirtation with Gemini and Virgo could sap your energy. Know when to say, "Enough is enough." The Gemini moon relates to your ability to make your wishes become realities. Overcome stage fright!

Wednesday, July 18 (Moon in Gemini to Cancer 5:55 p.m.)   For racing luck at all tracks: post-position special—number 2 p.p. in the fourth race. Pick six: 1, 5, 4, 2, 3, 6. Watch for these letters or initials in the names of potential winning horses or jockeys: F, O, X. Hot daily doubles: 1 and 5, 6 and 6, 3 and 7. A long shot comes in third, Libra jockeys win photo finishes.

Thursday, July 19 (Moon in Cancer)   On this Thursday, it could be a time for brooding, unless you transform it into a period of meditation. You gain insights; where they come from, you might not know. Pisces and Virgo play instrumental roles, and will have these letters or initials in their names: G, P, Y.

Friday, July 20 (Moon in Cancer to Leo 6:42 p.m.)   The new moon in Cancer is the time for you to make up for lost time. Secrets are revealed; you learn more about yourself than if you had consulted a leading psychiatrist. Capricorn and Cancer will play outstanding roles, and will have these initials in their names: H, Q, Z.

Saturday, July 21 (Moon in Leo)   Lucky lottery: 9, 5, 14, 3, 12, 18. Your ambitions are fulfilled. Be careful of what you ask for, because that wish could be granted. Your influence spreads; doors that had been shut will open almost as if by magic. A promise made months ago will be fulfilled in an astounding way. Aries plays the top role.

Sunday, July 22 (Moon in Leo to Virgo 6:28 p.m.) In matters of speculation, stick with number 1. Your vitality makes a dramatic comeback. You emit an aura of personal magnetism, sensuality, and sex appeal—and this has nothing to do with your chronological age. It is a Sunday you won't soon forget! Another Leo becomes your ally.

Monday, July 23 (Moon in Virgo)   You are raring to go! A family member expresses confidence, and will share a magnificent dinner. Your sense of direction and motivation returns. You'll be confident, dynamic, and a winner! Cancer and Capricorn figure prominently, and have these initials in their names: B, K, T.

Tuesday, July 24 (Moon in Virgo to Libra 7:07 p.m.)   The moon in your money house almost guarantees that losses will be recovered and, if single, you could meet your future soul mate. Married or single, you will instinctively know in which direction to proceed. A Sagittarian plays a top role, and will have these letters in their name: C, L, U. Your lucky number is 3.

Wednesday, July 25 (Moon in Libra)   For racing luck at all tracks: post-position special—number 4 p.p. in the eighth race. Pick six: 8, 5, 3, 4, 1, 1. Look for these letters or initials in the names of potential winning horses or jockeys: D, M, V. Hot daily doubles: 8 and 5, 4 and 4, 1 and 1. Favorites lag behind; Scorpio and Taurus jockeys will be in the money.

Thursday, July 26 (Moon in Libra to Scorpio 10:17 p.m.)   Keep your plans flexible. A close relative talks about moving, taking risks. Be courteous, but make it crystal clear, "I do not feel this would be the right time to take unnecessary chances." Focus on the written word.

Get your thoughts on paper. Gemini plays an important role.

Friday, July 27 (Moon in Scorpio)   The questions you put forth recently concerned real estate, the sale or purchase of property. A Scorpio holds the key, seeks consultation. Protect yourself in close quarters—do not reveal too much. News is received about where you live and what to do about it. Libra is involved.

Saturday, July 28 (Moon in Scorpio to Sagittarius 4:44 a.m.)   Lucky lottery: 28, 1, 2, 8, 5, 27. A fascinating Saturday. You come to terms with someone who is close to you. Make it clear, "I no longer want to be taken for granted!" Separate fact from fiction, see people and places in a realistic way. Taurus will play a role.

Sunday, July 29 (Moon in Sagittarius)   A meaningful Sunday. You must repeat to yourself, "Character and integrity mean doing the right thing when no one is looking." A powerful relative flashes the green light, "Go right ahead!" The spotlight is on career, ambition, the ability to achieve a goal. A Cancer will play a role.

Monday, July 30 (Moon in Sagittarius)   The fickle finger of fate points to you. Through a series of coincidences, you might achieve fame and fortune. Keep things under control, so as not to attract notoriety. Finish what you start, and strive for universal appeal. Give thought and study to a foreign language. You might soon go there!

Tuesday, July 31 (Moon in Sagittarius to Capricorn 2:16 p.m.)   It's crunch time! Perhaps you made an impulsive promise three weeks ago—now face the music. New love is on the horizon, so be ready. You are about to enter a different kind of adventure. Aquarius and another Leo figure prominently, and will have these letters or initials in their names: A, S, J. Your lucky number is 1.

Wednesday, August 1 (Moon in Capricorn) What
was taken away will be returned, with a flourish. Your
inner strength remains; vitality makes a comeback. It
turns out that you really didn't lose anything. Capricorn
and Cancer play outstanding roles, and have these letters
in their names: H, Q, Z. Lucky lottery: 8, 14, 26, 33,
22, 17.

Thursday, August 2 (Moon in Capricorn) Highlight
universal appeal; overcome distance and language barriers. You will feel as if you are elevated from common,
everyday affairs. People close to you comment, "You are
a game character!" Aries and Libra play meaningful
roles, and could have these letters or initials in their
names: I and R.

***Friday, August 3 (Moon in Capricorn to Aquarius 1:52
a.m.)*** You might be going too fast for your own
good. Slow down enough to contemplate and meditate.
The saving grace here is a sense of humor. Laugh at your
own foibles. Aquarius and another Leo play fascinating
roles, and could have these initials in their names: A, S,
J. Your lucky number is 1.

Saturday, August 4 (Moon in Aquarius) For racing
luck at all tracks: post-position special—number 2 p.p. in
the second race. Pick six: 2, 2, 7, 1, 3, 5. Watch for these
letters or initials in the names of potential winning horses
or jockeys: B, K, T. Hot daily doubles: 2 and 2, 3 and 5,
4 and 6. People who favor certain horses could be in
for disappointments. Cancer jockeys must take special
precautions to prevent injuries.

***Sunday, August 5 (Moon in Aquarius to Pisces 2:29
p.m.)*** Leave details for another time. Instead of focusing on the little things, look at the big picture. Spiritual messages will be welcome. People realize there is
much more to know, and they are eager to learn. Forces

tend to be scattered, so too much of a good thing would not be good at all.

Monday, August 6 (Moon in Pisces)   Be willing to review, rewrite, and to rebuild on a more solid base. You might be musing, "This business of counseling for everyday represents a real challenge." How many of your recent resolutions have you kept? Taurus, Scorpio, and another Leo figure prominently, and have these letters in their names: D, M, V.

Tuesday, August 7 (Moon in Pisces)   This will be an exciting day that challenges your creativity. In matters of speculation, stick with number 5. Gemini, Virgo, and Sagittarius play outstanding roles, and could have these letters or initials in their names: E, N, W. Finish that manuscript!

Wednesday, August 8 (Moon in Pisces to Aries 3:03 a.m.) Lucky lottery: 12, 11, 23, 40, 6, 7. Within 24 hours, with the moon in Aries, you will be notified that the trip is on after all. Focus on a variety of experiences and sensations. A young person attempts to show off as a lover and you could be the victim. Taurus and Libra are involved.

Thursday, August 9 (Moon in Aries)   This could be one of your most intriguing Thursdays. Aries could appear as an uninvited guest. Be kind and courteous. Put manners before morals, but make it crystal clear that you don't expect this to happen again! See people and places as they are, not merely as you wish they might be.

Friday, August 10 (Moon in Aries to Taurus 2:21 p.m.)   On this Friday, you'll be saying, "I will go anywhere to track down a mystery and to solve it and explain it in an intelligent, creative way." You'll muse, "Another Friday night, and this time I intend to have fun." Capricorn and Cancer play fascinating roles, and have these initials in their names: H, Q, Z.

Saturday, August 11 (Moon in Taurus)   Someone who once blocked your way will now give you a rousing welcome. You'll deal with stubborn, creative people. An attractive member of the opposite sex declares, "I'm not letting you get away this time!" Highlight universal appeal. Find a safe place to keep your money. Your lucky number is 9.

Sunday, August 12 (Moon in Taurus to Gemini 10:56 p.m.)   The answer to your question is affirmative. Make a fresh start in a new direction, with the possibility of a new love. These words cross your mind: "I'll take a chance on romance!" Your popularity moves up, and you'll be musing, "I don't know what I did that was right, but it sure worked!" Another Leo is in the picture.

Monday, August 13 (Moon in Gemini)   Within 24 hours, the moon will be in your eleventh house, that section of your horoscope related to friends, hopes, wishes, and good fortune in finance and romance. Focus on direction, motivation, savings accounts, partnership, and marriage. Review your diet; do what is best for you, despite obstacles.

Tuesday, August 14 (Moon in Gemini)   What a Tuesday! You exude an aura of goodwill. People seek your counsel about money, payments, collections, and relationships. You might be sighing, "After all, life can be beautiful if you give it a chance to be." Gemini and Sagittarius play outstanding roles, and have these letters in their names: C, L, U.

Wednesday, August 15 (Moon in Gemini to Cancer 3:53 a.m.)   Lucky lottery: 4, 40, 24, 13, 18, 5. Be willing to tear down in order to rebuild. Keep this aphorism in mind, "Hard writing makes easy reading!" Taurus, Scorpio, and another Leo will play meaningful roles and have these letters or initials in their names: D, M, V. A message is received: read carefully!

Thursday, August 16 (Moon in Cancer) Get ready for a change of scene; keep your plans flexible. Someone is following you, but represents no danger. You might stop and ask, "Can I do anything for you?" After an embarrassing pause, the other person speaks up, declaring, "I apologize. I did not mean to upset you!" Gemini is involved.

Friday, August 17 (Moon in Cancer to Leo 5:24 a.m.) Attention revolves around luxury items, recreation, art, music, and design. A domestic adjustment is featured; make intelligent concessions. Ultimately, you will get your way! Avoid anticipating what has yet to occur. The common saying is, "Don't cross that bridge until you get to it!"

Saturday, August 18 (Moon in Leo) There's disappointment at first, but success on the second try. Material received at first proves to be flimsy, and is practically falling apart. The second chance means you insist on quality and testing before you pay for it. Pisces and Virgo play outstanding roles, and have these initials in their names: G, P, Y.

Sunday, August 19 (Moon in Leo to Virgo 4:52 a.m.) The new moon in your sign portends different kinds of experiences, possibly new love. People are drawn to you; display your sense of showmanship. Let it be known, "I believe everybody is equal in the eyes of God—but here on earth I am the best!" Capricorn is represented.

Monday, August 20 (Moon in Virgo) You will be paid handsomely for your contributions to a project. A lost article is located, presented to you in a ceremonious way. Your cycle continues high. Designate where the action will be. The spotlight is on distant countries, overcoming distance and language obstacles. Your lucky number is 9.

Tuesday, August 21 (Moon in Virgo to Libra 4:18 a.m.)   For racing luck at all tracks: post-position special—number 3 p.p. in the fifth race. Pick six: 1, 4, 5, 4, 3, 1. Watch for these letters or initials in the names of potential winning horses or jockeys: A, S, J. Hot daily doubles: 1 and 4, 5 and 5, 3 and 1. There will be upsets today, especially among younger horses in the first and second races. Leo jockeys will shine.

Wednesday, August 22 (Moon in Libra)   People weigh their options. You, specifically, make decisions about where you live and with whom. You emanate sound, music, vibrations, and all of this adds up to creativity and sex appeal. Parental authority is tossed aside, together with preconceived notions. Have luck with number 2.

Thursday, August 23 (Moon in Libra to Scorpio 5:49 a.m.)   Fun and frolic are featured; pressure is relieved. A Libra relative declares, "I want to see you having fun; I insist on it!" Highlight diversity, versatility, exploration, and intellectual curiosity. Be up-to-date about fashion. Add to your wardrobe. A Sagittarian is involved.

Friday, August 24 (Moon in Scorpio)   You'll be dealing in real estate, the sale or purchase of property. A Scorpio member of the opposite sex intrigues, challenges, and all other things being equal, does love you. Taurus and another Leo also play outstanding roles, and could have these letters or initials in their names: D, M, V.

Saturday, August 25 (Moon in Scorpio to Sagittarius 10:59 a.m.)   You will be a guest at dinner, at the other person's favorite restaurant. Everything goes along smoothly until your host insists you try the speciality of the house, which is liver and onions. Go ahead, try it— it won't kill you! Romance could be budding, so eat your liver and onions and smile. Your lucky number is 5.

Sunday, August 26 (Moon in Sagittarius)   What a Sunday night! Extricate yourself from an obligation you should not have carried in the first place. Venus, love, and music are involved. Your home has a different appearance. It is cleaner, there are fewer obstacles to trip over, and it's really beautiful! A Libra figures prominently.

Monday, August 27 (Moon in Sagittarius to Capricorn 8:01 p.m.)   With the Sagittarian moon, you will be dynamic, creative, and challenging. Keep an aura of mystery; don't tell all. Do not reveal a possible infidelity. It is not necessary to share guilt. Make crystal clear terms that exist and that you will adhere to them. Pisces plays a top role.

Tuesday, August 28 (Moon in Capricorn)   Colors are darker. A love relationship is more perilous. You have the power and authority, yet you want more and that is natural. Focus on children, challenge, change, a variety of sensations, experiences. You'll be relied upon to meet and beat a deadline. You will do so with amazing ease.

Wednesday, August 29 (Moon in Capricorn)   The moon is in Capricorn, your sixth house, which relates to work associates, jobs to be done, a possible physical examination. This examination could be preparatory to visit to another country. Participate in a political or charitable campaign. Lucky lottery: 4, 14, 44, 9, 8, 19.

Thursday, August 30 (Moon in Capricorn to Aquarius 7:47 a.m.)   Let go of preconceived notions. Remember that Napoleon decreed that *impossible* was a word used by fools. You are going to win; you will do the impossible. Stress independence, originality, and welcome a different kind of romance. Another Leo is in the picture.

Friday, August 31 (Moon in Aquarius)   For racing luck at all tracks: post-position special—number 4 p.p. in the ninth race. Pick six: 1, 8, 5, 3, 3, 6. Watch for these letters or initials in the names of potential winning horses or jockeys: B, K, T. Hot daily doubles: 1 and 8, 8 and 5, 3 and 7. Favorites win in photo finishes. Cancer jockeys will be in the winner's circle!

SEPTEMBER 2001

Saturday, September 1 (Moon in Aquarius to Pisces 8:31 p.m.) Lucky lottery: 1, 11, 5, 50, 2, 12. Open lines of communication. Someone in a foreign country wants to talk to you. Focus on legal agreements, partnership, and marriage. Aries will play an outstanding role, and will have these letters or initials in their name: I and R. Pay attention to fire prevention.

Sunday, September 2 (Moon in Pisces) The full moon relates to accounting procedures, the need to understand what's going on. Another Leo is in the picture; if you don't know, ask—remember that pride goeth before a fall. Be original, stress independence, and do not follow others. Avoid heavy lifting. Your lucky number is 1.

Monday, September 3 (Moon in Pisces) Focus on direction, motivation, the cost of participating in an unusual project. Verify estimates; make sure you have a partner, not an opponent. During the evening hours you could meet your future soul mate. Don't eat too much. A Cancer says, "It is a miracle that you haven't succumbed to some fatal illness!"

Tuesday, September 4 (Moon in Pisces to Aries 8:57 a.m.) Within 24 hours, travel plans can be completed. Focus on spiritual values, theology, the promotion of a favorite subject. Someone previously indifferent will now imply, "I would follow you anywhere!" Give full play to your intellectual curiosity. Advertise, promote, and publish.

Wednesday, September 5 (Moon in Aries) For racing luck at all tracks: post-position special—number 4 p.p. in the sixth race. Pick six: 2, 5, 4, 7, 3, 4. Watch for these letters or initials in the names of potential winning horses or jockeys: D, M, V. Hot daily doubles: 2 and 5, 3 and 7, 4 and 4. Favorites come in, photo finishes, jockeys suffer injuries.

Thursday, September 6 (Moon in Aries to Taurus 8:16 p.m.) The Aries moon relates to physical attraction, the necessity for communicating desires, the possibility of encountering your future spouse. Spiritual values surface; you might be musing, "Whatever it is, it is mystical. I sure don't know the answers!" Written material contains the answers you seek.

Friday, September 7 (Moon in Taurus) Attention revolves around the basics, including income, shelter, a decision relating to marriage. Give and receive gifts. Take special care when unwrapping delicate objects. Take the lead in offering the hand of friendship to a former enemy. Scorpio plays a top role.

Saturday, September 8 (Moon in Taurus) For racing luck at all tracks: post-position special—number 1 p.p. in the sixth race. Pick six: 3, 4, 1, 5, 2, 1. Watch for these letters or initials in the names of potential winning horses or jockeys: G, P, Y. Hot daily doubles: 3 and 4, 6 and 2, 3 and 1. Favorites run out of the money. Pisces jockeys win photo finishes.

Sunday, September 9 (Moon in Taurus to Gemini 5:40 a.m.) Pressure is relieved. A Taurus teams up with Capricorn. Apparently, they intend no good for you. Protect yourself in close quarters; let it be known you will fight if the cause is right. You will be asked to meet and beat a deadline. A distant relative will communicate.

Monday, September 10 (Moon in Gemini) Most people regard Monday as the start of an off day. Not for you, not this Monday. The astrological and numerical aspects coincide with numerous contacts, some overseas. Aries and Libra play outstanding roles, and could have these letters or initials in their names: I and R. Your lucky number is 9.

Tuesday, September 11 (Moon in Gemini to Cancer 12:07 p.m.) You get a second wind. The Gemini moon favors you all the way, with good fortune in finance and romance. Your contacts pay off. Your ability to fund a project surges forth. You win friends today; you influence people; you make a fresh start in a new direction. A new and different kind of love is on the horizon.

Wednesday, September 12 (Moon in Cancer) Lucky lottery: 12, 20, 2, 5, 6, 16. If single, this could be a day when you make a decision leading to marriage. If married, you rediscover your mate. The discovery excites mental, emotional, and physical aspects of the relationship. A Cancer is in the picture.

Thursday, September 13 (Moon in Cancer to Leo 3:14 p.m.) Plenty of surprises, all favorable! What was hidden will be revealed to your advantage. Your cycle moves up; so within 24 hours, you can name your price. The spotlight is on versatility, international travel, fun and games, a night of love and laughter. A Sagittarian plays a role.

Friday, September 14 (Moon in Leo) Check the details; be sure bills are paid; be willing to revise, review, rewrite, and to tear down in order to rebuild. Taurus, Scorpio, and another Leo figure prominently, could have these letters or initials in their names: D, M, V. You'll change your wardrobe; you might be a new person.

Saturday, September 15 (Moon in Leo to Virgo 3:38 p.m.) Lucky lottery: 5, 10, 19, 30, 50, 51. The spotlight is on the written word, a torrid relationship that might get too hot not to cool down. You are going places, possibly a trip out of town. Gemini, Virgo, and Sagittarius figure in this exciting scenario, and have these initials in their names: E, N, W.

Sunday, September 16 (Moon in Virgo) Attention revolves around affairs connected with a possible change of residence and marital status. It's important to maintain your emotional equilibrium. People who ask, "How can you remain so calm?" should be told, "It is because I live a good and wholesome life." Libra plays a role.

Monday, September 17 (Moon in Virgo to Libra 2:59 p.m.) The new moon in your money house symbolizes opportunities previously kept hidden. Define terms, play the waiting game, avoid self-deception. Neptune is involved; you'll be dealing with people, no matter what age, who are persuasive, alluring and sexy. Pisces and Virgo dominate this scenario.

Tuesday, September 18 (Moon in Libra) For racing luck at all tracks: post-position special—number 8 p.p. in the ninth race. Pick six: 4, 4, 1, 7, 1, 1. Be alert for these letters or initials in the names of potential winning horses or jockeys: H, Q, Z. Hot daily doubles: 4 and 4, 2 and 6, 1 and 7. Cancer and Capricorn jockeys will be up on horses in winner's circle.

Wednesday, September 19 (Moon in Libra to Scorpio 3:27 p.m.) Lucky lottery: 7, 19, 26, 34, 12, 22. A relationship is on tenterhooks. Be pliable, not weak. Let it be known, "I will make intelligent concessions, but never will I abandon principles!" You'll be dealing with aggressive people who attempt to bully you. An Aries figures prominently.

Thursday, September 20 (Moon in Scorpio) Make a fresh start; shed light over areas previously dark. Avoid heavy lifting, imprint your style, and do not follow others. Your living quarters command attention, so spruce

up things. An Aquarian makes a declaration of loyalty—
and love. Have luck with number 1.

*Friday, September 21 (Moon in Scorpio to Sagittarius
7:02 p.m.)* Many experiences are repeated, so much
so that you are tempted to feel you are experiencing déjà
vu. The spotlight is on a relationship relating to a business partnership, career, your marital status. A Cancer
invites you to dinner. Accept. The main course could be
broiled lobster.

Saturday, September 22 (Moon in Sagittarius) For
racing luck at all tracks: post-position special—number 5
p.p. in the seventh race. Pick six: 1, 3, 4, 2, 6, 8. Watch
for these letters or initials in the names of potential winning horses or jockeys: C, L, U. Hot daily doubles: 1 and
3, 2 and 4, 6 and 7. Favorites act in eccentric manner,
Gemini and Sagittarius jockeys will be in the winner's
circle.

Sunday, September 23 (Moon in Sagittarius) This
will be a memorable Sunday! Your creative juices stir,
you meet someone who finds you delightful and sexy—
and says so. Taurus, Scorpio, and another Leo will play
outstanding roles, and have these letters or initials in
their names: D, M, V. The gift of wine is received.

*Monday, September 24 (Moon in Sagittarius to Cap-
ricorn 2:48 a.m.)* Get your thoughts on paper; record
your dreams. Last night's dream, if properly interpreted,
could prove to be a doorway to the future. Tonight's
dream will involve words with special meanings. Gemini,
Virgo, and Sagittarius will play major roles, and will have
these initials in their names: E, N, W.

Tuesday, September 25 (Moon in Capricorn) The
pace slows. Someone in a position of authority makes an
unusual offer. Take a conservative view; don't expect too
much, too soon. Capricorn will play a memorable role
as will a Taurus and a Libra. Attention revolves around

your home, family, decorating, remodeling, and beautifying your surroundings.

Wednesday, September 26 (Moon in Capricorn to Aquarius 2:04 p.m.)   Lucky lottery: 15, 50, 1, 7, 22, 18. Be quiet within; don't brood over situations if you can't do something about them. Neptune is involved; serves as a warning against seeing people and relationships only as you wish they might be, instead of how they actually are.

Thursday, September 27 (Moon in Aquarius)   A relationship intensifies. You are asked to make a decision about cooperative efforts, partnership, or marriage. A series of coincidences places you in a corner. Let it be known that you are more than mildly interested. Capricorn and Cancer will play stunning roles. Your lucky number is 8.

Friday, September 28 (Moon in Aquarius)   Be diplomatic today. This means pay special attention to the language, the habits, the foods, and the cultures of people you are dealing with in foreign countries. Finish what you start; look beyond the immediate; predict the future and make it come true! Aries and Libra are involved.

Saturday, September 29 (Moon in Aquarius to Pisces 2:49 a.m.)   What a Saturday! New experiences are featured. The moon is leaving Aquarius to enter Pisces. For you, this relates to hidden resources, the mantic arts and sciences, including astrology. Avoid heavy lifting; imprint your style. Do not follow others; let them follow you. Your lucky number is 1.

Sunday, September 30 (Moon in Pisces)   On this last day of September, you learn more about the financial status of someone who would be your partner, or of hidden assets belonging to a spouse. Questions about marriage or partnership continue to loom large. Close out

September with a fabulous meal. Invite a Cancer to be your guest.

OCTOBER 2001

Monday, October 1 (Moon in Pisces to Aries 3:06 p.m.) On this first day of October, vitality makes a comeback. Confidence is restored; you make a fresh start in a different direction. People admire your courage and they don't hesitate to say so. Leo and Aquarius figure prominently, and could have these letters or initials in their names: A, S, J.

Tuesday, October 2 (Moon in Aries) The full moon in your ninth house coincides with a new attitude toward people who live in foreign countries. You could be traveling to one of those countries. The emphasis is on where you go and what to do. A Cancer declares, "I will always be with you!"

Wednesday, October 3 (Moon in Aries) Lucky lottery: 3, 30, 1, 10, 19, 46. Out of the blue, it will seem that allies appear, including some who originally were against you. This is one Wednesday you won't soon forget! Gemini and Sagittarius play amazing roles in your life today, and are likely to have these initials in their names: C, L, U.

Thursday, October 4 (Moon in Aries to Taurus 1:59 a.m.) For racing luck at all tracks: post-position special—number 4 p.p. in the fourth race. Pick six: 1, 3, 2, 4, 5, 8. Watch for these letters or initials in the names of potential winning horses or jockeys: D, M, V. Hot daily doubles: 1 and 3, 2 and 4, 6 and 6. Favorites disappoint, despite excellent rides by Taurus, Leo, and Scorpio jockeys.

Friday, October 5 (Moon in Taurus) A boost in your career is featured. Taurus will play instrumental role.

You overcome difficulties through persistence. Emphasize the courage of your convictions. Obtain written permission to pioneer a project. What seemed impossible one week ago will fall into place and you will get proper credit.

Saturday, October 6 (Moon in Taurus to Gemini 11:10 a.m.) Attention revolves around your home, art, music, decoration and a reunion with a loved one. You will muse, "Life can be beautiful, and it is beautiful for me today!" Color coordination is important; display advertising is featured. Taurus, Libra, and Scorpio will play astonishing roles. Your lucky number is 6.

Sunday, October 7 (Moon in Gemini) This is a very good Sunday! Many of your hopes, wishes, and desires are fulfilled in a dramatic way. People are drawn to you; at first you find this annoying but finally you are pleased. Following a temporary delay, you win friends and admirers by displaying your skills in character analysis and in predicting the future.

Monday, October 8 (Moon in Gemini to Cancer 6:18 p.m.) This certainly will not be a dull Monday! In matters of speculation, stick with these numbers: 1, 2, 11, 14. Focus on a relationship that is getting too hot not to cool down. You undergo tests; and you amaze people by your excellent condition. Capricorn plays a top role.

Tuesday, October 9 (Moon in Cancer) Strive for universal appeal; refuse to be limited; find a representative for your talent or product overseas. A Cancer works behind the scenes, and takes Aries as a partner. Both are dedicated to your cause. Red tape is tossed aside, so work fast and utilize various subtle tricks of advertising. Your lucky number is 9.

Wednesday, October 10 (Moon in Cancer to Leo 10:52 p.m.) Lucky lottery: 1, 45, 18, 22, 6, 12. Make a fresh start; be original and up-to-date with fashion. People who advise you will comment, "It should be you advising us!" Trim down the size of your head if you intend to fit in any doors! Aquarius and another Leo play meaningful roles, and have these letters in their names: A, S, J.

Thursday, October 11 (Moon in Leo)   Your intuitive intellect is honed to razor-sharpness. Even as I speak, the moon is leaving its own sign, Cancer, and getting ready to position itself in Leo. A Cancer will provide valuable information if only you will listen and learn. Drive with care; a near accident!

Friday, October 12 (Moon in Leo)   Your cycle jumped up! This means designate where the action will be and it will be. Focus on your personal magnetism, personality, sensuality, creativity, and sex appeal. Wear bright colors, make personal appearances, exercise color coordination and drama. Gemini and Sagittarius will play astounding roles, and have these initials in their names: C, L, U.

Saturday, October 13 (Moon in Leo to Virgo 12:56 a.m.)   For racing luck at all tracks: post-position special—number 4 p.p. in the fifth race. Pick six: 8, 5, 1, 4, 4, 2. Watch for these letters or initials in the names of potential winning horses or jockeys: D, M, V. Hot daily doubles: 8 and 5, 3 and 4, 1 and 1. Prestige that had fallen will rise again. Speed horses get out in front and win.

Sunday, October 14 (Moon in Virgo)   On this Sunday, it will be proven once again that truly the pen is mightier than the sword. Evaluate and define words. It's an excellent day for playing word games. Display your skill at solving crossword puzzles. Gemini, Virgo, and Sagittarius play fascinating roles, and have these letters in their names: E, N, W.

Monday, October 15 (Moon in Virgo to Libra 1:25 a.m.)   Attention revolves around family members, home life, serious discussions about a change of residence, and marital status. Be diplomatic; accept suggestions relating to decorating and remodeling. Money counts! Strive to obtain the best price. A Libra will prove to be your valuable ally.

Tuesday, October 16 (Moon in Libra)   The new moon in Libra represents a section of your solar horoscope associated with trips and visits, relatives who seem intent on telling you their troubles. Don't hesitate to let it be known that you are not a human crying towel! Strive to transform a tragedy into humor. It can be done, has been done; you will do it tonight.

Wednesday, October 17 (Moon in Libra to Scorpio 2:02 a.m.)   You get down to serious business. Interpret messages. Be sure you understand what people are saying and actually meaning. Give full play to your intellectual curiosity. Examine, explore, and report. Someone who wears dark colors will present you with current duties or assignments. Your lucky number is 8.

Thursday, October 18 (Moon in Scorpio)   Finish what you start. Overcome obstacles relating to language and distance. Idealism in love will be featured. Make personal appearances; wear shades of red. A dynamic member of the opposite sex intrigues, and helps you fulfill an ambition. Aries and Libra play top roles.

Friday, October 19 (Moon in Scorpio to Sagittarius 4:46 a.m.)   Turn over a new leaf! Let go of preconceived notions. Imprint your style, and do not follow others. Let it be known, "I am here as a new person, so get used to my way." Then continue, "There are two ways to do things, the right way and my way!" Another Leo plays a dramatic role.

Saturday, October 20 (Moon in Sagittarius)   The Sagittarian moon relates to physical attraction, children, challenge, change, and variety. Focus on theology, spirituality, starting a program that reaches overseas. The spotlight is on direction, motivation, a decision relating to marriage. Capricorn is involved. Lucky lottery: 8, 5, 50, 1, 10, 11.

Sunday, October 21 (Moon in Sagittarius to Capricorn 11:12 a.m.)   Today's cycle highlights fun, frolic, experimentation, and exploration. Someone who advises you about weight, diet, nutrition, and exercise really does care, so try to be patient and understanding. The Jupiter keynote means that luck rides with you. Be and feel lucky without overdoing it!

Monday, October 22 (Moon in Capricorn)   You are one or two steps away from reaching your ultimate goal. Be aware of it; push forward; reject an offer of compromise. You are gaining allies, even as we speak. Someone who said it could not be done is drawing back, ready to join you. Scorpio plays an important role.

Tuesday, October 23 (Moon in Capricorn to Aquarius 9:26 p.m.)   You won't soon forget this Tuesday! Read and write notes, record dreams. Last night's dream episode was exciting and revealing. Tonight, your dream is likely to feature steel and iron structures or revelatory material. Gemini will play an immensely important role.

Wednesday, October 24 (Moon in Aquarius)   Life takes many strange turns, including what will happen within 24 hours. The spotlight is on partnership, cooperative efforts, public appearances, and marriage. Taurus, Libra, and Scorpio play dramatic roles, and will have these letters or initials in their names: F, O, X.

Thursday, October 25 (Moon in Aquarius)   A dream world blends with reality. You know you are here and now, but you also realize there might be a parallel world. The Aquarian moon heightens prospects for overcoming legal red tape. Maintain unorthodox procedures. Pisces and Virgo will play unusual roles.

Friday, October 26 (Moon in Aquarius to Pisces 9:54 a.m.)   Nothing is trivial; almost everything is serious today. The spotlight revolves around business agreements, career, and marriage. Someone who once had the reputation of being a playgirl or playboy enters into this scenario, so be careful! You will find way of hitting the financial jackpot. Your lucky number is 8.

Saturday, October 27 (Moon in Pisces)   The moon in Pisces relates to accounting methods, the earning ability of your partner or mate. Reject superficial explanations. Look to the future and demand honesty. If you feel you are entangled, then you are! A physical attraction exists; it is difficult, and represents a mixture of joy and pain. Aries is represented.

Sunday, October 28—Standard Time Begins (Moon in Pisces to Aries 9:13 p.m.)   You'll be among people who do not mix—sort of like fire and water. Maintain your equilibrium, stress originality, and let people know you are capable of defending yourself. You are capable now also of bringing peace to those who ordinarily would be fighting tooth-and-nail.

Monday, October 29 (Moon in Aries)   As you read these lines, the moon is leaving Pisces and getting ready to enter Aries. Conditions change. You might be traveling, publishing, or promoting various concepts. The scenario highlights proposals, business, career, and marriage. A Cancer plays a top role.

Tuesday, October 30 (Moon in Aries)   The Aries moon relates to philosophy, theology, writing, advertising, and publishing. You will enjoy being famous. Gemini and Sagittarius play outstanding roles, and could have these letters or initials in their names: C, L, U. Participate in a social group that promotes charitable-political campaigns. Your lucky number is 3.

Wednesday, October 31 (Moon in Aries to Taurus 7:46 a.m.)   Do not frighten or hurt black cats! If you do, you will be casting an evil spell over yourself for the next year. A mechanical apparatus is in need of repair—take care of it. Check electrical outlets in your home and automobile. Taurus, Leo, and Scorpio play important roles, and have these initials in their names: D, M, V. Have a happy, safe Halloween!

NOVEMBER 2001

Thursday, November 1 (Moon in Taurus)   The full moon is in your career house. Cancer and Capricorn will play outstanding roles, and could have these letters or initials in their names: B, K, T. The question of marriage looms large; remember that you do owe a gift to a Cancer. In taking public transportation for the purpose of a visit, don't jostle others. And speak up if *you* are jostled.

Friday, November 2 (Moon in Taurus to Gemini 4:11 p.m.)   You'll enjoy a discussion by a psychologist on subjects of partnership and marriage. Someone from your past makes an appearance and you are right, this deserves a celebration. A fine dinner is in store tonight, featuring seafood. Concentrate on questions you want to ask; this will be a learning experience. Your lucky number is 3.

Saturday, November 3 (Moon in Gemini)   What a Saturday! The Gemini moon relates to gaining popularity, winning friends, and influencing people. Give a smile to get a smile. A psychological consultation could set you straight on problems relating to marriage. Check apparatus relating to electricity or automobile. Scorpio is involved.

Sunday, November 4 (Moon in Gemini to Cancer 10:42 p.m.)   Emphasize versatility, humor, and experimentation. Exploration will be a major part of today's scenario. Keep resolutions about diet, exercise, and nutrition. Gemini, Virgo, and Sagittarius figure in today's exciting scenario. The written word carries power. You have more skill as a writer than you think.

Monday, November 5 (Moon in Cancer)   Focus on sound, vibrations, learning new dance steps. Some people observe, "You seem different when you hear music and dance." A domestic adjustment is featured. A Cancer openly states, "I am interested in you!" Maintain equilibrium, express interest in music, and accept an invitation to practice.

Tuesday, November 6 (Moon in Cancer)   A family member decides to pursue the study of psychic phenomena. Your counsel is sought. Your response: "Just so long as you maintain mental balance, it is okay to go ahead. It is a thrilling, learning experience!" Pisces and Virgo will play dynamic, exciting roles.

Wednesday, November 7 (Moon in Cancer to Leo 3:32 a.m.)   What had been nebulous will take form. A Capricorn states, "I always feel safer and more productive when I am with you!" Something inside you draws you to a Cancer who does have your best interests at heart. A business or stock market venture will prove encouraging. Your lucky number is 8.

Thursday, November 8 (Moon in Leo)   A foreign currency exchange is part of today's scenario. This could prove a reason for travel, mixing business with pleasure. Stress universal appeal, highlight color coordination, showmanship, and derring-do with romance. Aries, Libra, another Leo will play dramatic roles.

Friday, November 9 (Moon in Leo to Virgo 6:48 a.m.) People admire your ability to make a comeback following a failure. Show the courage of your convictions. Let it be known, "I have not yet begun to fight!" This could be the precursor to a winning streak. In matters of speculation, stick with number 1. Keep up-to-date with fashion; wear bright colors.

Saturday, November 10 (Moon in Virgo)   You become suddenly aware of costs, savings, or lack of them. During the entire month of November, you estimate costs of travel, participating in a new enterprise. That is part of this cycle. Make a fresh start in new direction, with independence of thought and action. Lucky lottery: 1, 11, 2, 12, 22, 18.

Sunday, November 11 (Moon in Virgo to Libra 8:52 a.m.)   On this Sunday, you might find yourself confused, very ambitious, but not knowing exactly how and when to start. Cancer and Aquarius figure prominently. Give full play to your intellectual curiosity. Show that you are capable of laughing at yourself.

Monday, November 12 (Moon in Libra)   It starts out as sluggish Monday. The moon in Libra in your third house equates to experimentation, exploration, and a new kind of entertainment. Taurus, Scorpio, and another Leo figure in a change of pace. Check on repairs, especially furniture that could collapse from the weight of someone sitting on it.

Tuesday, November 13 (Moon in Libra to Scorpio 10:44 a.m.)   A Mercury keynote. You will be on the move; you will not be satisfied with the status quo. Pay more attention to family members and to a lover. A very good day for writing a love letter. Read, send messages, and open lines of communication. A flirtation is getting very warm!

Wednesday, November 14 (Moon in Scorpio)   For racing luck at all tracks: post-position special—number 2 p.p. in the fourth race. Pick six: 1, 7, 8, 2, 5, 6. Watch for these letters or initials in the names of potential winning horses or jockeys: F, O, X. Hot daily doubles: 1 and 7, 2 and 2, 5 and 6. Favorites will be in the money, but are not likely to win first place. Cancer jockeys win photo finishes.

Thursday, November 15 (Moon in Scorpio to Sagittarius 1:51 p.m.)   The new moon in Scorpio equates to property value, the need to check plumbing. Consult an expert who is also a friend. Follow your hunch, dig deep; you may find that pipes are not really suitable for plumbing purposes. Pisces and Virgo play outstanding roles, and have these initials in their names: G, P, Y.

Friday, November 16 (Moon in Sagittarius)   It would not be a bad idea to get a shopping list ready. Christmas is just around the corner and you remember how hectic it was last year. Capricorn and Cancer people insert themselves in your personal scenario. Someone you wanted to forget is back once again.

Saturday, November 17 (Moon in Sagittarius to Capricorn 7:39 p.m.)   Your intuitive intellect works overtime. In matters of speculation, stick with number 9. Attention revolves around metaphysics, number divination, the cabala, and astrology. As a result, some persons, speaking out of ignorance, will dub you an "odd bird." Aries is involved.

Sunday, November 18 (Moon in Capricorn)   On this Sunday, you meet fascinating people who can speak and debate on theology without becoming fanatical. Avoid heavy lifting; make personal appearances; wear shades of bright yellow and blue. Aquarius and another Leo in this exciting scenario. Your lucky number is 1.

Monday, November 19 (Moon in Capricorn)   Take stock of stock. For a time, you were overloaded, but now supplies are diminishing. Your partner or mate assumes the role of critic and accountant. It is necessary to get tedious work over with. It would be worth considering an advertising campaign. Capricorn is in this picture.

Tuesday, November 20 (Moon in Capricorn to Aquarius 4:54 a.m.)   Make inquiries to various manufacturers. Legitimate bargains are available, so take advantage of them. Your sales ability is heightened. Focus on intellectual curiosity, explore and experiment. Gemini and Sagittarius will play fantastic roles. You'll be rewarded for your dedication.

Wednesday, November 21 (Moon in Aquarius)   Suddenly, life takes a strange turn. The spotlight will be on proposals that include business, career, and marriage. People who said it could not be done will now express an eagerness to climb aboard. This is an excellent experience, which will reveal that you must follow your dreams and not rely on others.

Thursday, November 22 (Moon in Aquarius to Pisces 4:51 p.m.)   You will have much to be thankful for. The Aquarian moon highlights the unorthodox, being with people whose ideas are stimulating. Much talk revolves around food, the state of the nation, and around a relative about to take a step into matrimony. Happy Thanksgiving!

Friday, November 23 (Moon in Pisces)   Memories linger, and it is hoped that only memories are present and not reminders that "I ate too much!" Attention revolves around where you live, luxury items, a serious decision associated with partnership and marriage. Taurus, Libra, and Scorpio prove to be delightful companions.

Saturday, November 24 (Moon in Pisces)   Lucky lottery: 1, 12, 18, 7, 40, 13. Keep an aura of mystery—don't tell all. Discretion is the better part of valor. You will be engaged in a clash of ideas with someone who knows nothing and talks too much. Separation from a loved one is only temporary. Know it, and fight a tendency to brood.

Sunday, November 25 (Moon in Pisces to Aries 5:20 a.m.) Transform the abstract into recognizable material. Married or single, members of the opposite sex will be drawn to you. Some declare, "You are a perfect blend of the physical, emotional, mental.". On this Sunday, you'll realize that, indeed, you are powerful and special. Capricorn is involved.

Monday, November 26 (Moon in Aries) The realization hits home: "I do have universal appeal and might very well succeed in beginning a new enterprise overseas." Your creative juices stir; you will muse: "This is one of the most inspiring Mondays I have ever experienced!" The emphasis is on travel, participating in an exciting project that is not without risks.

Tuesday, November 27 (Moon in Aries to Taurus 4:04 p.m.) You might feel like the travel bug has bit you. You might be yearning for new places, faces. Highlight originality, your pioneering spirit, the determination to create an unusual situation or project. What you once took for granted takes on the aspect of a different kind of challenge. Your lucky number is 1.

Wednesday, November 28 (Moon in Taurus) Lucky lottery: 2, 12, 22, 6, 11, 4. The spotlight is on your career; an investment that will pay dividends. Cancer and Capricorn play outstanding roles, and could have these letters or initials in their names: B, K, T. Highlight experimentation, exploration, and learning through the process of teaching others.

Thursday, November 29 (Moon in Taurus) You will be told, "You are fascinating; it is fun to be with you!" A Gemini declares, "It is a pleasure to be with you because I feel alive and I learn!" A Sagittarian is part of this scenario, is physically attractive, and has a marvelous sense of humor. Have luck with number 3.

Friday, November 30 (Moon in Taurus to Gemini 12:02 a.m.)   On this last day of November with the moon leaving Taurus, you are right in anticipating a significant tomorrow. A burden is lifted. Some of your most important hopes and wishes will be fulfilled within 24 hours. Today, stay on familiar ground. Repair mechanical defects. A Scorpio dominates this scenario.

DECEMBER 2001

Saturday, December 1 (Moon in Gemini)   On this Saturday, the first day of December, there will be much confusion, but nothing fatal. A Gemini becomes your staunch ally, and has the gift of making you laugh, even though you might be sad. Experiment, advertise, publish, read, and write. Lucky lottery: 12, 1, 8, 18, 9, 45.

Sunday, December 2 (Moon in Gemini to Cancer 5:29 a.m.)   On this Sunday, two relatives will visit—one a Gemini, the other a Sagittarius. Be willing to revise, rewrite, review, and to stop putting off the necessity for proofreading. The Gemini moon in your eleventh house equates to your ability to win friends and influence people and to have dreams come true.

Monday, December 3 (Moon in Cancer)   The moon in its own sign, Cancer, equates for you to revelation, secrets, the necessity for visiting someone close to you temporarily confined to home or hospital. Gemini, Virgo, and Sagittarius will help you participate in a writing project. A flirtation is featured that might get too hot not to cool down.

Tuesday, December 4 (Moon in Cancer to Leo 9:14 a.m.)   You will have something important to celebrate. The Cancer moon helps you solve money problems. You have a product to sell, relating to beauty or vitality. Keep valuables under lock and key. Taurus,

Libra, and Scorpio figure prominently, and could have these letters or initials in their names: F, O, X.

Wednesday, December 5 (Moon in Leo)   For racing luck at all tracks: post-position special—number 1 p.p. in the fourth race. Pick six: 1, 3, 2, 1, 7, 3. Watch for these letters or initials in the names of potential winning horses or jockeys: G, P, Y. Hot daily doubles: 1 and 3, 2 and 4, 5 and 8. A muddy track relates to slow times and possible injuries.

Thursday, December 6 (Moon in Leo to Virgo 12:10 p.m.)   Your cycle is high, so what appeared impossible not only becomes possible, but marks you as a genius. Participate in a power play. Focus on merchandise, supplies, the ability to cope with an emergency. Capricorn and Cancer will play fascinating roles, and have these initials in their names: H, Q, Z.

Friday, December 7 (Moon in Virgo)   A remarkable day! People talk and write about World War II. Focus on explosives, anecdotes associated with Pearl Harbor. Dig deep into your memory bank. Share experiences with a member of the opposite sex who is mystifying and exciting. Aries and Libra will be featured.

Saturday, December 8 (Moon in Virgo to Libra 2:56 p.m.)   Turn down an offer to change places. Emphasize what is new, exciting, dominating, and be receptive to a different kind of romance. Make personal appearances; test original material; wear bright colors. Don't lift heavy objects. Be in an area where plenty of sun shines. Your lucky number is 1.

Sunday, December 9 (Moon in Libra)   You are being pulled in two directions—at the same time! The emphasis will be on the need to be selective. Where you live, the value of your property, marital status figure prominently. A relative announces the intention of becoming a musician. Don't object. The more you object, the more determination your relative exhibits.

Monday, December 10 (Moon in Libra to Scorpio 6:08 p.m.)   Enjoy entertainment, but go easy on adult beverages. Someone who appeared happy on the outside might be miserable emotionally. Your advice will be sought. Be cooperative, but make it crystal clear that, to get well, you must want to be free of the alcoholic scourge.

Tuesday, December 11 (Moon in Scorpio)   The Scorpio moon relates to home, property, future marriage prospects. A battle of wits involves Taurus. A mechanical problem creates danger; repair work is necessary, pronto! Details pile up. What begins as routine could be transformed into an exciting experiment.

Wednesday, December 12 (Moon in Scorpio to Sagittarius 10:29 p.m.)   Free your mind of the tendency to brood, because everything will turn out okay. Find outlets for creative expression, especially writing. A flirtation is exciting, but it is necessary to know when to say, "Enough is enough!" Today's scenario features sensuality, sex appeal, adding to your wardrobe, and having luck with number 5.

Thursday, December 13 (Moon in Sagittarius)   As the moon leaves Scorpio, you will be saying, "Good luck to you; have a happy life and please don't come back too soon!" That closed-in feeling will evaporate—although the experience was horrific, you would not want to change places with anyone. Libra is represented.

Friday, December 14—Solar Eclipse (Moon in Sagittarius)   The new moon, solar eclipse is in Sagittarius, your house of romance. Your emotions act like a whirling dervish. A young person confides, "My life is confusing, and I don't know where to go next!" Steer clear of self-deception. See people, places, and relationships in a realistic light.

Saturday, December 15 (Moon in Sagittarius to Capricorn 4:47 a.m.)   For racing luck at all tracks: postposition special—number 5 p.p. in the third race. Pick six: 1, 3, 5, 6, 3, 2. Watch for these letters or initials in the names of potential winning horses or jockeys: H, Q, Z. Hot daily doubles: 1 and 3, 4 and 6, 5 and 5. Veteran jockeys will be in the winner's circle, paying excellent prices.

Sunday, December 16 (Moon in Capricorn)   On this Sunday, you get in touch with your spiritual nature. Look beyond the immediate; fulfill dreams of the future. You are destined to be special, unique, and evidence of this will surface tonight. Aries and Libra will play sensational roles, and could have these letters in their names: I and R.

Monday, December 17 (Moon in Capricorn to Aquarius 1:43 p.m.)   Your vitality makes a comeback, enabling you to create a situation that taps your creative resources. You might be humming these words, "I'm in love again . . . !" People approach you with these words, "Please tell my fortune!" Aquarius and another Leo play dynamic and fascinating roles.

Tuesday, December 18 (Moon in Aquarius)   If single, the emphasis will be on partnership, cooperative efforts, and marriage. Stress independence, originality, and inventiveness. You'll muse, "I've got it going again!" A Cancer insists, "Tell me all about it: love, romance, marriage!" Plan ahead for Christmas. New Year's Eve, too!

Wednesday, December 19 (Moon in Aquarius)   The Aquarian moon in your seventh house relates to a clash of ideas, legal nuances, partnership, and marriage. The Jupiter keynote highlights social affairs, ability to be an excellent fundraiser. Elements of timing and luck ride with you, despite obstacles. Lucky lottery: 40, 50, 3, 30, 14, 1.

Thursday, December 20 (Moon in Aquarius to Pisces 1:09 a.m.)   On this Thursday, much will be accomplished in a quiet way. Check your accounting procedures. Take a critical look at your bank balance. Proofreading may be necessary if facts are to be verified. Taurus, Scorpio, and another Leo figure in this dynamic scenario. Stick with number 4.

Friday, December 21 (Moon in Pisces)   The spotlight is on written material, unusual or borderline subjects, fulfilling a desire to investigate psychic phenomena. You'll have more freedom of thought and action. A member of the opposite sex admires you and makes no secret of it. Gemini and Virgo could dominate this scenario.

Saturday, December 22 (Moon in Pisces to Aries 1:44 a.m.)   The spotlight is on your family. A recalcitrant Sagittarian insists, "I know what is best for me, I don't care what the rest of you do!" Make an effort to regain your emotional equilibrium. Some people are making a game of it. Will you do it, or will you fall back into a form of psychological dependence on others? Taurus is involved.

Sunday, December 23 (Moon in Aries)   Try doing what comes naturally. You achieve your objective by being your unique self. An Aries becomes one who is easy to remember, so hard to forget. Your intuition is strong, so pay heed! Pisces and Virgo figure in this dynamic, dramatic scenario.

Monday, December 24 (Moon in Aries)   On this Christmas Eve, you will be together with people who have been residing in foreign countries. The Aries moon in your ninth house enables you to spell out spiritual values. The use of symbolism tonight will be featured.

Cancer and Capricorn play leading roles. A guest will recite the Christmas story.

Tuesday, December 25 (Moon in Aries to Taurus 1:10 a.m.)   A pleasant, productive Christmas Day. Your self-esteem is elevated; you are well aware that you can control your destiny. Some associates are cynics—bypass them; you have the ability to predict the future and make it come true. Gifts received are just what you need. This includes books on astrology!

Wednesday, December 26 (Moon in Taurus)   Turn over a new leaf; vow to pay more attention to money management. A Taurus becomes your strong ally, in career and financial matters. Make a fresh start. Stress independence of thought and action. Refuse to be thwarted by those who lack imagination and talent. Your lucky number is 1.

Thursday, December 27 (Moon in Taurus to Gemini 9:37 a.m.)   The emphasis is on associations with the high and the mighty. Make certain that others realize that you have not forgotten your roots. Walk the fine line between being a good person and becoming so accessible that you no longer command respect. A Cancer provides a good example.

Friday, December 28 (Moon in Gemini)   The emphasis is on diversionary tactics, the ability to achieve your objective, even though you might lack the proper papers. Gemini and Sagittarius figure in this seductive scenario. People verify how attractive you are, admire your sense of humor and high intelligence. This serves as a signal not to underrate yourself. Have luck with number 3.

Saturday, December 29 (Moon in Gemini to Cancer 1:38 p.m.)   Practical matters grab the spotlight. Projects require solid foundations. The emphasis is on architecture, structure, design, and safety measures. Some of your fondest hopes and wishes are being fulfilled, even as you read these lines. Take a chance on romance. Let it be known you are available for a lucrative assignment.

Sunday, December 30—Lunar Eclipse (Moon in Cancer) The full Moon, lunar eclipse falls in your twelfth house. Interpreting astrological lingo, this means you will be responsible for a building program, for the sale or purchase of property. Someone previously lively could suffer a foot ailment, including gout. A flirtation could be more serious than you thought.

Monday, December 31 (Moon in Cancer to Leo 5:08 p.m.) If celebrating outside your home, check the invitation list and reservations. If you have your choice, campaign for being close to home. Strange things are happening in the world, so it would be best for to you to remain on familiar ground. Have fun on this New Year's Eve, but accent moderation with adult beverages.

HAPPY NEW YEAR!

ABOUT THE AUTHOR

Born on August 5, 1926, in Philadelphia, Omarr was the only person ever given full-time duty in the U.S. Army as an astrologer. He also is regarded as the most erudite astrologer of our time and the best known, through his syndicated column (300 newspapers) and his radio and television programs (he is Merv Griffin's "resident astrologer"). Omarr has been called the most "knowledgeable astrologer since Evangeline Adams." His forecasts of Nixon's downfall, the end of World War II in mid-August of 1945, the assassination of John F. Kennedy, Roosevelt's election to the fourth term and his death in office . . . these and many others are on the record and quoted enough to be considered "legendary."

ABOUT THIS SERIES

This is one of a series of twelve
Day-by-Day Astrological Guides
for the signs of 2001
by Sydney Omarr